Books are to be returned or renewed
before the last date below

12 MAR 2014		

South Leicestershire College Library.
To renew, telephone:
0116 264 3527

Hodder Arnold

A MEMBER OF THE HODDER HEADLINE GROUP

To my son, Tom Jennings,
with love and affection.

Photographs by John Walmsley, Education Photos.

Orders: please contact Bookpoint Ltd, 130 Milton Park, Abingdon, Oxon OX14 4SB.
Telephone: (44) 01235 827720. Fax: (44) 01235 400454. Lines are open from 9.00–5.00, Monday to
Saturday, with a 24 hour message answering service. You can also order through our website
www.hoddereducation.co.uk

British Library Cataloguing in Publication Data
A catalogue record for this title is available from the British Library

ISBN-10: 0 340 811234
ISBN-13: 978 0 340 81123 8

First Published 2003
Impression number   10 9 8
Year   2010 2009 2008 2007

Typeset by Phoenix Photosetting, Chatham, Kent
Printed in Great Britain for Hodder Arnold, an imprint of Hodder Education, a member of the
Hodder Headline Group, 338 Euston Road, London NW1 3BH by CPI Bath

Contents

Introduction

This book aims to provide a comprehensive and practical guide to supporting pupils' development and assisting their learning across the curriculum.

The book covers practical considerations such as:

o Maintaining pupils' safety and security
o Preparing and maintaining classroom resources
o Record keeping
o Behaviour management
o Using ICT to support learning.

The book clearly links practice and theory by exploring different **theoretical** aspects of children's development:

o Social and emotional
o Sensory and intellectual
o Language and communication skills.

It demonstrates how these relate to providing practical support for pupils' learning in the classroom. The book explains complex theoretical issues in ways which can be easily understood, but is sufficiently challenging to assist students in developing a sound knowledge-base to complement their practical skills.

There is particular emphasis on the role of the teaching assistant in supporting learning activities including detailed information on helping pupils to develop literacy and numeracy skills as well as supporting pupils with special educational needs.

This book is for students (and their tutors/assessors) on teaching assistant courses and provides the background knowledge relevant to the requirements of supporting the learning of pupils aged 3 to 16 years in primary, secondary and special schools.

How to use this book

This book contains the knowledge evidence requirements for a range of topics related to supporting pupils' development and learning. The book includes practical ideas for linking knowledge evidence with performance criteria, and is suitable for students on the following courses:

o NVQ/SVQ Levels 2 & 3 for Teaching/Classroom Assistants
o CACHE Levels 2 & 3 Certificates for Teaching Assistants (CTA2 & CTA3)
o OCR Level 2 Certificate in Supporting Teaching and Learning.

Students on the CACHE Specialist Teacher Assistant award (STA), the OCR Certificate for Literacy and Numeracy Support Assistants or the City & Guilds Learner Support 7321 course may find many sections of the book useful.

The book may also be of interest to experienced teaching assistants who are updating their current practice as part of their Continuing Professional Development.

The headings in each section are related to NVQ Levels 2 & 3 for ease of reference. Read the relevant chapter for the topic you are currently studying and do the exercises/activities as specified. The **key tasks** can be done in any order, as appropriate to your college and/or school requirements, and can contribute to your formal assessment e.g. as part of your portfolio of evidence. However, it is suggested that you read Chapter 5: **Planning Learning Activities** before you start planning and implementing your own activities for pupils. Do remember to follow your school/college guidelines.

The chart at the back of the book will help you to keep a record of the key tasks as you complete them.

Acknowledgements

Many thanks to the pupils and staff at Rood End and Withymoor Primary Schools where I gained much of my experience of working with children.

Thanks also to the students and staff at Birmingham College of Food, Tourism & Creative Studies and Sandwell College of Further & Higher Education where I developed my skills of designing and implementing learning/assessment materials for students on early years care and education courses; special thanks to Pam Steer (for some ideas about child observations especially the courtroom analogy on pages 110–111) and Florence Awunor (for some ideas on planning learning activities).

Special thanks to Chris Helm and Phil Adams for technical (and emotional!) support.

The Learning Environment

1

Key points:

- The supporting role of the teaching assistant
- Children's needs
- Special educational needs
- The responsibilities of the teaching assistant
- Effective communication with pupils
- Learning styles
- Group dynamics
- Preparation and organisation of the learning environment
- Record keeping

The supporting role of the teaching assistant

Adults who work in classrooms alongside teachers have various job titles including:

o learning support assistant
o classroom assistant
o special needs assistant
o non-teaching assistant.

Teaching assistant is now the preferred term for adults (in paid employment) whose main role is to assist the teacher in a primary, secondary or special school.

To function effectively you need to be clear about your role as a teaching assistant. Your role will depend on the school and your experience/ qualifications. There may be different requirements between teaching assistants even within the same school. A teaching assistant may have a *general* role working with different classes in a year group/Key Stage or *specific* responsibilities for a pupil, subject area or age group.

Exercise:
Make a list of the things expected from you as part of your role in supporting an individual pupil or group of pupils.

Effectively managed, skilled teaching assistants make a valuable contribution to pupil achievement within the learning environment. Teaching assistants may be needed to attend to a pupil's care needs; or they may have a more educational role working with a pupil or group of pupils under the guidance of the class or subject teacher; or they may be involved in implementing a programme devised by a specialist, such as a speech and language therapist. The term 'teaching assistant' indicates their central role of supporting the teacher. Teachers are responsible for planning and directing pupils' learning.

Teaching assistants give *support* to class or subject teachers by *assisting* with the teaching of pupils in whole-class, small groups or with individuals, but *always* under a teacher's direction.

In order to provide effective support, teaching assistants need to know:

○ teacher and school expectations for pupils' progress
○ learning objectives for pupils
○ behaviour expectations
○ inclusion of pupils with special educational needs.

Teaching assistants working with specific pupils need information regarding their special educational needs and provision including details of any statement of special educational needs, Individual Education Plans (IEPs) and/or Behaviour Support Plans.

Teaching assistants supporting children

Supporting the pupil

Teaching assistants support the individual pupil by:

o understanding the pupil's learning support needs
o listening to the pupil
o enabling the pupil to access the curriculum
o respecting and valuing the pupil
o gaining the pupil's trust and confidence
o responding appropriately to the pupil's physical needs
o encouraging independence
o promoting acceptance by the rest of the class
o using plenty of praise and rewards.

(See Chapter 6: Supporting Learning Activities)

Supporting the teacher

Teaching assistants support the class or subject teacher by:

o working in partnership to prepare and maintain the learning environment
o helping to monitor and evaluate pupil progress
o providing feedback about pupils' learning and behaviour
o helping with classroom resources and pupil records.

(See Chapter 10: Professional Practice)

Supporting the school

Teaching assistants support the school by:

o working with other members of staff as part of a team
o attending staff meetings
o working in partnership with parents
o making contributions to assessments and reviews
o knowing and following relevant school policies and procedures
o recognising and using personal strengths and abilities
o developing skills through in-service training and other courses.

(See Chapter 10: Professional Practice)

Supporting the curriculum

Teaching assistants also provide support for the curriculum under the direction and guidance of the class or subject teacher. This involves an awareness and understanding of:

o theories concerning how pupils think and learn
o the sequences of expected development
o factors affecting pupils' learning progress in learning difficulties

○ National Curriculum documents
○ the National Literacy Strategy
○ the National Numeracy Strategy
○ the planning process.

(See Chapter 4: Thinking and learning)

Children's needs

All children have the following essential needs:

☆ **P hysical care**: regular, nutritious meals; warmth; rest and sleep
☆ **R outines**: a regular pattern to their day; with any changes explained
☆ **I ndependence**: encouraged to do things for themselves and make choices
☆ **C ommunication**: encouragement to talk and interact with others
☆ **E ncouragement and praise**: for trying as well as achieving
☆ **L ove**: from parents/carers which is unconditional e.g. expecting nothing back
☆ **E ducation**: appropriate to their ages and levels of development
☆ **S incerity and respect**: honest and courteous treatment
☆ **S timulation**: opportunities to explore their environment and tackle new challenges

All children are special and unique – *all* children have individual needs because they perceive the world differently and interact with others in different ways. *All* children (including identical twins) have different life experiences that affect their view of the world. Children experience different social and environmental factors, which along with their genetic differences, shape their personalities, knowledge and skills. Children may be individuals, but they exist as part of various social groups, such as family, local community, school and wider society. Adults working with children in schools must appreciate the uniqueness of every pupil while ensuring that the needs of both the individual and the group are met (Brennan, 1987). How children react to learning in school depends on their individual needs and life experiences. Some children may find school challenging or even exciting and are well motivated to learn. Others may find the school environment daunting and may experience learning difficulties. Still others may find this type of learning environment uninviting or boring and may demonstrate signs of difficult behaviour.

All children have individual educational needs that require:

○ opportunities to explore their environment
○ adult assistance to aid their knowledge and understanding
○ activities which are appropriate to their abilities and development.

All children also have *social and emotional* needs that should be met by the school:

O assistance in adjusting to new learning environments
O help in relating comfortably with other children and adults
O opportunities to interact/play with other children
O opportunities to find out about people and the world they live in.

Some children have *special or additional needs* that mean they may require:

O special equipment or resources
O modified surroundings (wheelchair access, ramps)
O extra learning support to access the National Curriculum
O a special or modified curriculum.

These children have **special educational needs** arising from:

O physical disability
O learning difficulty
O emotional or behavioural problem.

Special Educational Needs

The Warnock Report on Special Educational Needs (**1978**) was concerned with the difficulties that affect pupils' educational progress either temporarily or permanently. The report concluded that up to 1 in 5 (20 per cent) pupils required some form of special education at some point during their school career. Warnock viewed this 20 per cent of pupils as being part of a **continuum** of special needs. This continuum is related to the child's **individual need** for support to participate in educational activities and *not* on their particular learning difficulty or disability. Some pupils with serious disabilities need substantial support for learning while at the other end of the continuum are pupils with moderate learning difficulties or behavioural problems who need less support. Some pupils may have '*only a temporary learning difficulty … Others, however, require special help and support throughout their school lives …*'(DES, 1978a, p. 47). Even if a pupil's disability is permanent, their individual learning needs may change, for example they may require more or less physical assistance as they grow older. Environmental changes may also affect the pupil's learning needs, for example an increase or reduction in appropriate resources including support staff; transition from primary to secondary school.

The 1981 Education Act put into effect many of the recommendations of the Warnock Report. The Act established that *a child has special educational needs if he or she has a learning difficulty which requires special educational provision to meet these needs.* The term **learning difficulty** includes not only physical and mental disabilities or sensory impairment but any kind of learning difficulty experienced by a child provided it is significantly greater than that of the majority of children of the same age. The Act also established the principle of **integration**: all children with special educational needs are to be educated in 'ordinary' (mainstream) schools where reasonably practicable and should participate in school activities with other children. A small percentage of children with severe or complex disabilities and/or learning difficulties still need to attend special schools.

The Special Educational Needs Code of Practice 2001 replaces *The 1994 Code of Practice on the Identification and Assessment of Special Educational Needs* and gives practical advice to Local Education Authorities, maintained schools and others concerning their statutory duties to identify, assess and provide for children's special educational needs. The new code came into effect on 1 January 2002. This code retains a great deal of the guidance from the first Code of Practice, but also includes developments in education since 1994 and utilises the experiences of schools and LEAs. The central aim of the government's special needs policy is to enable *all* children to have the opportunities available through inclusive education. The new code re-enforces the right for children with SEN to receive education within a mainstream setting and advocates that schools and LEAs implement a graduated method for the organisation of SEN. The code provides a school-based model of intervention for children with special educational needs. The five stages of the 1994 code have been replaced with:

- **Early Years Action or School Action** (old Stages 1 & 2)
- **Early Years Action Plus or School Action Plus** (old Stage 3)
- **The Statementing process.** (old Stages 4 & 5).

The code also includes new chapters on:

- Parent partnership and disagreement resolution
- Pupil participation including *The UN Convention on the Rights of the Child*
- Early years including extra information
- The *Connexions Service* for young people aged 13–19 years.

Accompanying the new code is the **Special Educational Needs Toolkit**, which expands on the guidance contained in the code. This Toolkit is not law, but does provide examples of good practice that LEAs and schools can follow.

As 20 per cent of pupils have special educational needs and the majority of these are pupils within mainstream education, there is a need for *learning support* to enable them to access the curriculum. A teaching assistant can provide more intensive support for an individual or small groups of pupils, which allows the teacher to concentrate on teaching the rest of the class. This ensures that the needs of *all* pupils can be met in an *inclusive* way. Many teaching assistants work as part of the special educational needs team and their role involves supporting pupils identified as having *special educational needs* including those with Individual Education Plans (IEPs), Behaviour Support Plans (BSPs) and/or Statements of special educational needs.

Teaching assistants can offer individual support

Equal opportunities

It is important to show sensitivity to the needs of all children. All pupils need to feel valued and accepted by others especially if they might feel different from the rest of the class due to a disability/learning difficulty or because of their race/culture. Teaching assistants can help by *'maximising each child's motivation by encouraging her or his sense of being included, personally, racially and culturally, in all aspects of the learning experience'* (Commission for racial equality, 1989; p. 21).

Teaching assistants must have a positive attitude and be able to learn how to maximise all pupils' individual potential. Pupils' special educational needs should be considered within the context of their overall development –

7

learning difficulties as part of their intellectual development. Pupils with special needs still need opportunities to learn through play as part of their intellectual development and IEPs should take account of this, particularly in Key Stage 1. (There is more information on equality of opportunity and anti-discriminatory practice in Chapter 10.)

Exercise:
1. Find out about your school's policies for inclusion including:
   - disability awareness
   - equal opportunities.
2. What are the school's policies and procedures for ensuring non-discriminatory behaviour and valuing cultural diversity?
3. What is *your* role in promoting inclusion?

The responsibilities of the teaching assistant

You need to understand clearly what your responsibilities are as a teaching assistant. Your responsibilities should be set out in your job description if you are already employed as a teaching assistant. (As a student you should have guidelines from your college.) The head teacher is responsible for all the pupils in the school while each class or subject teacher is responsible for all the pupils in their own class. The teacher is responsible for the learning of all pupils including those with special educational needs and IEPs.

Exercise:
Find out what your responsibilities are.

When you know what your responsibilities are, you will be clear about what is required from you. You should not be required to perform duties or activities that you are not qualified or not allowed to do, for example give first-aid or administer medicines. However, do not refuse to do a task just because it is not in your job description – sometimes it may be necessary for everyone to help out. (There is more on understanding your responsibilities and those of others in Chapter 10: Professional Practice.)

General tasks

Here are some of the general tasks you may be expected to do as a teaching assistant:

- set out or put away equipment
- help younger pupils, or older pupils who have physical disabilities get ready for a PE lesson
- check pupils work
- encourage pupils to correct their own mistakes
- supervise practical work activities
- keep an individual pupil and/or group on task
- assist the pupil(s) to catch up on any missed work
- check equipment for safety.

Specific tasks

Teaching assistants also have specific tasks that the class or subject teacher asks them to do. For example, supporting pupils' learning during a lesson or activity by:

- repeating instructions given by the teacher
- taking notes for a pupil while the teacher is talking
- transcribing a pupil's dictation
- clarifying meaning and/or ideas
- explaining difficult words to a pupil
- promoting the use of dictionaries
- reading and clarifying textbook/worksheet activities for a pupil
- reading a story to an individual pupil or small group
- listening to pupils read
- playing a game with an individual pupil or small group
- directing computer-assisted learning programmes
- assisting pupils with special equipment (e.g. hearing aid or a Dictaphone)
- making worksheets and other resources as directed by the teacher
- observing/recording pupil progress during an activity
- providing any other appropriate assistance during an activity
- reporting problems and successes to the teacher
- contributing to planning and review meetings about pupils.

Exercise:
List examples of your own general and specific tasks.

The care and support of pupils

Effective communication with pupils

The first step towards effective communication with children (and adults, too, of course) is being able to listen attentively to what they have to say.

Nearly all breakdowns in communication are due to people not listening to each other. Effective communication requires good inter-personal skills such as:

○ **availability** – make time to listen to pupils
○ **attentive listening** – concentrate on what pupils are saying
○ **appropriate use of non-verbal skills** – facing the pupil, leaning slightly towards them, smiling, nodding, open-handed gestures not clenched fists
○ **follow the rules of turn-taking** in language exchanges; every person needs to have their say while others listen
○ **politeness and courtesy** – no shouting, no talking over other people, avoiding sarcasm (especially with younger pupils, who do not understand it and can be frightened by your strange tone of voice)
○ **being relaxed, confident and articulate**
○ **using appropriate vocabulary for your listener(s)**
○ **encouraging others to talk** by asking 'open' questions
○ **responding positively** to what is said
○ **being receptive** to new ideas
○ **being sympathetic** to other viewpoints (even if you totally disagree with them!)
○ **providing opportunities** for meaningful communication to take place.

Active listening

Communication is a two-way process that depends on the sender (talker) and on the receiver (listener). Research has shown that adults tend to be poor listeners. Adults working in schools do too much talking and not enough listening to pupils' talk. While most primary schools appreciate the benefit of 'listening time', many secondary schools do not (Hutchcroft, 1981). Active listening depends on:

○ listening carefully to pupils' talk
○ considering the mood of the participants
○ minimising distractions in the immediate surroundings.

Asking and answering questions

You need to develop your skills at being able to initiate and sustain pupils' talk by providing questions, prompts and cues, which encourage and support the pupils' language and learning without doing the thinking for them. Some questions require only limited responses or answers from pupils. These 'closed' questions usually receive one-word answers such as 'yes' or 'no' or the name of a person/object. These types of questions do not help pupils to develop their own language and communication skills. 'Open' questions, on the other hand, are a positive way to encourage a variety of responses allowing more detailed answers, descriptions and accounts of pupils' personal experiences, feelings and ideas. For example: the question 'Did you ride your bike?' can only be answered by 'yes' or 'no'. Instead you could ask 'Where did you go on your bike?' and then use questions like 'What happened next?' to prompt further responses.

As well as asking questions, you need to be able to *answer* pupils' questions. Encouraging pupils to ask questions helps them to explore their environment more fully, to look for reasons/possible answers and to reach their own conclusions as to why and how things happen. Always treat their questions seriously. Try to answer them truthfully and accurately. If you honestly do not know the answer, then say so and suggest an alternative way for the pupil to obtain an answer. For example, 'I don't know where that animal comes from, let's look in the encyclopaedia or on the Internet to find out.' Or 'I'm not sure what that word means exactly; go and look in your dictionary to see if it's in there.' You should encourage pupils to find their own answers as appropriate to their age and level of development. Give them information in an appropriate form, which will increase their vocabulary and add to their knowledge/understanding of their world. Your answers should use words that are appropriate to the pupil. For example, if a younger pupil asks: 'Why does it rain?' you need to give a simple reply such as 'Clouds are full of water which falls back to the ground as drops of rain' while an older pupil can be given a more technical description of cloud formation and rainfall.

 KEY TASK

1. Listen to adults talking with children in a variety of situations, both within and outside your school (e.g. on buses, in shops, in the street, in the playground). Pay particular attention to the questions asked by the adults *and* the children, and *how* they are answered.
2. Consider these points:
   - Which inter-personal skills were used?
   - How effective was the communication?
   - Did the adult use active listening skills?
   - What did the children learn about language, the activity and/or the environment?

NVQ Links: Level 2: 2–2.1; Level 3: 3–2. 1, 3–2. 2

The language of learning

Effective communication also involves pupils being able to understand and use *the language of learning*. That is, the language needed to:

o understand concepts
o participate in problem-solving
o develop ideas and opinions.

You need to be able to utilise language effectively yourself in order to encourage and extend pupils' learning. A sound knowledge of child development plus the realistic organisation of the school, classroom, activities and time are essential components for effective communication with pupils.

The importance of feedback and encouragement

Praise and encouragement are essential components when supporting pupils' learning and development. All pupils need immediate and positive affirmations or rewards to show that their learning is progressing in accordance with expectations. You should emphasise the **positive** aspects of each pupil's attempts at developing knowledge and skills. Pupils must be praised and/or rewarded for *effort* not just achievement. Pupils gain confidence and increased positive self-esteem when they receive praise and encouragement for their efforts and achievements. There are four main methods used to praise and encourage pupils:

1 **Verbal** – 'Well done, Tom! This is a lovely story! Tell me what happened next.'; 'praise' assemblies, news time, 'circle' time, tutorials.

2 **Non-verbal** – body language: leaning forward or turning towards a pupil to show interest in what the pupil is communicating; facial expressions: smiling; using sign language: 'good boy/girl!'

3 **Symbolic** – 'smiley faces' for carefully done drawing/writing; stickers for being a good listener or for reading well; stars or merit points for attempting/completing tasks.

4 **Written** – comments written (or stamped) on pupil's work such as 'Well done!'; merit certificates; comments in head teacher's book; newsletter recording achievements.

(The importance of praise and rewards is explained in more detail in Chapter 2: Behaviour Management and information on developing pupils' positive self-esteem is in Chapter 3: PSHE.)

Exercise:
1. What methods do *you* use to provide positive feedback and encouragement for pupils' efforts and achievements in your school?
2. Give examples from your own experiences of supporting pupils' learning.

Learning styles

Children and adults have different ways of processing information. People use the skills of looking, listening or touching in varying amounts depending on their individual **learning style**. For example, some pupils require visual stimulation, some respond well to verbal instructions while others need more 'hands-on' experiences. In addition, different times of the day affect individual levels of concentration; some pupils work better in the morning, others in the afternoon. You need to be aware of the individual learning styles of the pupils you work with in order to plan and provide appropriate learning opportunities. Recognising learning styles will help you to understand the ways pupils learn and to assist them achieving educational success. (For more information see Chapter 4: Thinking and Learning.)

Working with groups of pupils

As a teaching assistant, you need to be aware of the stages in the development of groups and how these affect group dynamics. Research suggests that groups grow and develop through a four-stage cycle.

The forming stage: a group starts by learning about others in the group. First impressions are important and adults should assist pupils in this early stage by providing appropriate introductions and 'ice-breaking' activities. The adult acts as the leader of the group to ensure participation by all pupils.

The storming stage: group members establish their positions within the group and decide on group functions. There may be arguments and personality clashes between certain members of the group. The adult can assist by providing opportunities for group discussions that tackle these matters in an open and positive manner; helping pupils to sort out minor disagreements between themselves (as appropriate to their age/level of development) and acting as an impartial referee if necessary. This can be a difficult stage, but is essential to the healthy development of the group – more serious conflicts may emerge later on if the group does not work through this stage.

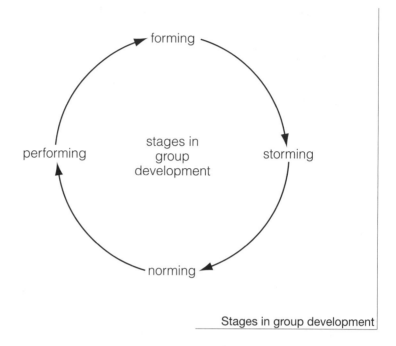

Stages in group development

The norming stage: group members reach agreement on how to work together including establishing group rules and individual responsibilities. Teaching assistants may help with the formation of group rules in line with the school/class rules as directed by the teacher. Adults also plan and organise the groups working practices including the timetable/provision of activities/subjects and the rota for routine classroom tasks such as tidying up, collecting the register, etc.

The performing stage: group trust is established and the group works well together. At this stage the group is usually positive, enthusiastic, co-operative and energetic with group members supporting each other. Adults can assist by providing opportunities for the group to work together in ways which foster a spirit of co-operation rather than competition. Adults need to use praise and encouragement to help maintain positive group interactions. (Houghton and McColgan, 1995).

You need to be aware of the possible problems that can arise within groups and how to identify any signs of tension. These include:

○ frequent arguments about differing views and ideas
○ uncertainty concerning group purpose or activity
○ confusion over roles and responsibilities within the group
○ lack of participation by some group members
○ poor concentration among group members.

Remember that pupils will need to work through the group stages again when changes arise, for example a pupil leaves or joins the group.

Group dynamics

You also need to understand how **group dynamics** affect the various stages of group development – that is, pupil interaction and their behaviour within social groups. As well as coping with the demands of the curriculum, pupils are dealing with their peers and the social world of other pupils. Friendship and membership of a peer group seem especially important. Each individual has different personal characteristics that affect their ability to communicate effectively and work comfortably alongside others. From your experiences of working with pupils you may have identified their differing characteristics, which influence their willingness or reluctance to interact within a group.

Exercise:
1. Think about the personal characteristics of the pupil or pupils you work with.
2. How do they interact in group situations?
   - Do they take turns at speaking and listening?
   - Do they work co-operatively?
   - Do they try to impose their own ideas on the group?

Group interaction plays an essential role in a child's development

Where the group size is appropriate to the task and the group dynamics are right, the contribution levels from pupils will be fairly even. Pupils usually know when it is their turn to speak and are aware if anyone has not had an opportunity to contribute and will try to involve that member of the group. Most pupils understand that to effectively work together it is important to utilise the offerings of all the group – even when this means considering different viewpoints and conflicting ideas. To achieve this level of positive social interaction and effective learning experience, the composition of any group is very important. Pupils may not work well with certain others; they may ask to work with pupils they know well in order to make better progress.

Opportunities for learning should be flexible and available in a variety of groupings:

○ one-to-one
○ pairs/small groups
○ large groups
○ whole class.

This allows for individual differences within the class and gives every pupil opportunities to develop many different learning skills in a variety of meaningful ways.

Group work allows pupils to:

○ Identify and solve problems
○ Select relevant information
○ Collaborate socially to increase own knowledge
○ Structure effective discussions
○ Evaluate conflicting ideas
○ Develop communication skills.

(Prisk in Pollard, 1987; p. 97)

Dealing with conflict between pupils and anti-social behaviour

When working with pupils it is inevitable that situations will arise involving arguments and fights between pupils or anti-social behaviour. You need to be aware of the school policy for dealing with these and be clear about your own responsibilities, for example when and how to intervene – remembering pupils' and your own safety, procedures for reporting incidents and use of sanctions. (See Chapter 2: Behaviour management and Chapter 3: PSHE.)

Exercise:
Find out what your school's policies and procedures are for dealing with conflict situations and anti-social behaviour. What are *your* responsibilities?

Caring for pupils who are upset or unwell

Teaching assistants need to know how to provide immediate care and support for pupils who become upset or unwell and how to deal with minor accidents or ailments. You need to know the procedures for reporting any serious problems to the relevant person, such as the class teacher, designated First-Aider and/or a member of the senior management team as appropriate to the situation. (See Chapter 3: PSHE.)

Preparation and maintenance of the learning environment

Preparing the learning environment

Central to creating an appropriate learning environment for all pupils in school is providing space, time and resources relevant to the needs of the pupils and the requirements of the National Curriculum. As well as provision for the National Curriculum subjects, there should be regular times for routines such as playtimes/breaks, lunchtime, etc. A daily routine provides stability and security for pupils. The class timetable should be clearly displayed in a manner appropriate to the ages of the pupils; older pupils should have their own copy of their weekly timetable. Flexibility is also important to allow for special events such as educational visits, swimming lessons or visitors to the school. In addition to knowing the timetable for the pupil and/or class you work with, you should have your own timetable showing where, what and with whom you are working throughout the school day.

Exercise:
1. Outline the daily/weekly routine for the pupil and/or class whose learning you support.
2. Provide a copy of your own personal timetable.

Organising the learning environment

The head teacher and senior management team are responsible for creating and maintaining the learning environment of the school as a whole. The class or subject teacher is responsible for establishing and maintaining the learning environment within their classroom and/or subject area. Working as part of a team, the teacher decides how best to use the resources allocated to their class, which includes adult resources such as nursery nurses, teaching assistants and parent helpers as well as equipment and materials. The teacher should ensure that these adults are used to their full potential in order to respond to the needs of all pupils. As a teaching assistant you must help prepare and organise the learning environment as directed by the teacher.

As part of your role you may have responsibility for:

○ **A pupil with special educational needs** and be involved in ensuring they have the necessary materials to participate in the lesson including any specialist equipment.

○ **A group of pupils** and be involved in setting out materials or helping the pupils to access them, explaining a task, maintaining their concentration and interest, asking/answering questions, helping pupils to clear away afterwards before moving on to supporting them with their next activity.

○ **An activity** with different groups of pupils throughout the day/week (e.g. supporting literacy, numeracy, science or ICT).

An example of a good learning
environment

Here are some general guidelines about organising room space:

○ Fire exits must not be obstructed, locked or hidden from view.
○ Chairs and tables need to be the correct size and height for the age/level of development of the pupils.
○ Books, jigsaws, art/design materials and computers need to be used in areas with a good source of light, if possible near a natural source of light.
○ Water, sand, art or design technology activities need to be provided in an area with an appropriate floor surface with washing facilities nearby.
○ Any large or heavy equipment that has to be moved for use should be close to where it is stored.

The learning environment should be welcoming and user-friendly. This includes taking account of cultural differences by providing displays and notices that reflect the cultural diversity of the school and local community. The classroom layout should be free from clutter and easily accessible to all pupils including those with physical disabilities or sensory impairment.

Some health and safety issues

You must know and understand the school's health and safety policy including who is responsible for health and safety as well as the procedures for reporting any concerns or problems to the appropriate person. You need to know the location of safety equipment in different learning environments. You must be clear about the safety arrangements for the areas and pupils you work with including: the position of fire exits, extinguishers, blanket, first-aid boxes; your role during fire drill; what to do in case of fire or other emergency especially the procedures for pupils with physical or sensory disabilities, escape routes and alternatives if blocked by fire, etc. You should also know the local and national requirements regarding health, hygiene, safety and supervision in the school, including: access to premises; storerooms and storage areas; the health and safety requirements for the materials and equipment being used. You must follow the school's procedures for gaining access to school premises, for example entry systems, identity tags for visitors in school.

Storage areas should be kept tidy with sufficient space for the materials/ equipment being stored there. They should be easily accessible and lockable; any potentially hazardous materials must be stored away from pupils and locked away. Storage space should be organised so that heavy equipment is stored at a low level. Light-weight equipment may be stored above head-level if space is limited.

One of your responsibilities may be to ensure that all equipment and surfaces are safe, hygienic and usable. If working with pupils who have been using messy materials such as glue or paint, you will need to wipe tables or easels clean after they have finished and clean any brushes so that they are ready for the next time. Any major cleaning tasks, which are not part of your duties, should be referred to the class or subject teacher for attention.

It is also important to ensure hygiene and maintain equipment. For example, using fresh ingredients when doing cooking activities and ensuring pupils wash their hands before and after, or following the correct procedures during science experiments. (There is more information on health and safety in Chapters 3: PSHE and 10: Professional Practice.)

 KEY TASK

1. Draw a plan of the classroom or areas you work in the most. Include the following:
   - age range of pupils
   - heating and lighting
   - ventilation including windows
   - layout of furniture/equipment
   - fire doors/safety equipment
   - storage areas
   - other significant features.
2. Highlight any specific features of the classroom/work areas that make the learning environment suitable for *all* pupils including those with special educational needs or from different cultural backgrounds. If there are none, show how this room/area could be modified for pupils with special needs, such as physical disability/sensory impairment or different cultures/religions.

NVQ Links: Level 2: 2–1.1; Level 3: 3–5.1

Materials and equipment

All equipment should be safe and approved for safety, (e.g. BSI Kitemark, European standards markings, BEAB mark of safety). You should know the operating procedures and safety requirements of your school BEFORE using any equipment. Operating instructions should be available and in many cases an experienced/knowledgeable member of staff may show you how to use the equipment beforehand. If not, it is essential to ask especially when dealing with electrical equipment because of safety or damaging expensive equipment – you do not want to cause hundreds or even thousands of pounds worth of damage to a computer or photocopier! Follow any instructions carefully.

Allow yourself plenty of time to do this thoroughly. Five minutes before you need to show the group/class a video, is not the time to start learning how to use the school's video player for the first time! It is unprofessional. As for any activity you need to plan ahead. Make sure you understand the specific requirements for equipment used by you and/or the pupils in subjects such as:

o P.E.
o Science
o Cooking/home economics
o ICT
o Art and design technology.

It is always a good idea to check equipment which is used regularly to ensure that it is in good working order – plan ahead, check the television, video or computer is in working order before you need it so that you can sort out any problems in advance. If there is a fault and the equipment is not functioning properly or not at all you need to know the procedures for dealing with faults – which can be dealt with yourself, which require reporting to the appropriate person. It is also important to check equipment and materials regularly for damage and to report any damage to the appropriate person. Serious damage will have to be repaired by a professional (technician or school caretaker) or the item will have to be replaced.

As part of your daily or weekly routine you should make sure that you are not running out of any materials or equipment. There will be a school procedure for doing this. There will be an inventory or stock list that is checked on a regular basis. Clearing away and storing equipment and materials provides you with a good opportunity to check whether, or not, supplies are running low.

 KEY TASK

1. List the equipment you use in your setting.
2. How did you find out how to use each piece of equipment?
3. What are the school's safety arrangements regarding the use of such equipment?
4. What are the school's procedures for reporting equipment breakdown or damage and any shortages of materials/ equipment?

NVQ Links: Level 2: 2–1.1, Level 3: 3–5.2, 3–5.3

Encouraging pupils to help maintain their learning environment

The routine of getting out and putting away equipment can seem like a chore, but it is part of the learning experience for pupils. Most pupils like being involved in sorting and putting things away. As well as helping to develop mathematical concepts such as sorting and matching sets of objects and judging space, capacity and volume, pupils develop a sense of responsibility for caring for their learning environment. Pupils can also gain confidence and independence if they are involved in setting out and clearing away learning materials as appropriate to their age/level of development and safety requirements. Store and display materials and equipment in ways which will enable pupils to choose, use and return them easily. Ensure that pupils help in ways that are in line with the school's health and safety policies. Pupils must never have access to dangerous materials such as bleach or use very hot water for cleaning and they should not carry large, heavy or awkward objects due to the potential risks of serious injury.

Record keeping

The role of the teaching assistant in maintaining and updating pupil records

As a teaching assistant, most of your work will be planned by others (e.g. the class or subject teacher, SENCO or specialists). They will need regular information about your work, such as updates about a particular pupil's progress. Some of this information may be given orally, for example outlining a pupil's progress on a particular activity or commenting on pupil's behaviour. Even spoken information needs to be given in a professional manner – to the appropriate person (teacher or SENCO), in the right place (not in a corridor where confidential information could be overheard) and at the right time (urgent matters need to be discussed with the class or subject teacher immediately while others may wait until a team meeting). Some information will be in the form of written records or reports. For example:

o Reading records	
o Maths records	
o Tick charts/lists	Formative
o Observation sheets	Assessments
o Daily target records for pupils with IEPS	
o Behaviour cards for pupils with BSPs.	
o SATs results	
o Class teacher assessments	Summative
o Reviews of pupils with SEN	Assessments
o Pupils' annual school reports.	

The types of records you will need to keep will depend on the planning and assessment requirements of the school, the class/subject teacher, SENCO and any other professionals involved in meeting the pupils' educational needs. Where, when and how to record information should be as directed by the teacher. For example, if using time or event sampling, you will need to agree on specific dates and times on which observations will take place.

Using simple, attractive record keeping systems and involving pupils in the monitoring process helps their motivation and increases the potential for success. (For more information see Chapter 5: Planning Learning Activities.) Requests for records or reports should be dealt with professionally and handed in on time. This is particularly important if the information is needed for a meeting or review as any delay may stop others from performing their responsibilities effectively. Remember to maintain confidentiality as appropriate to your school's requirements. (See Chapter 10: Professional Practice.)

The importance of record keeping

It is essential to keep records for the following reasons:

o To monitor pupil progress
o To provide accurate and detailed information regarding learning/behaviour
o To determine the effectiveness of an activity or target
o To determine the effectiveness of adult support or intervention
o To give constructive feedback to the pupil
o To share information with the teacher, other professionals and parents
o To identify and plan for new learning objectives/behaviour targets.

It is important to update records on a regular basis; the frequency of updating depends on the different types of records that you make a contribution towards. Records which may indicate potential problems with individual pupils should be shown to the class teacher (observations of unacceptable behaviour; daily records that show poor performance, etc.).

You should be aware of any legal requirements with regard to record keeping in your school. These include:

o Data Protection Act 1998
o Children Act 1989
o The Education Act 2002
o Race Relations Act 1976
o SEN Code of Practice 2001.

KEY TASK

1. Outline the record keeping systems and procedures used within your school.
2. What is the school policy for the storage and security of pupil records, including confidentiality requirements?
3. Give examples of the types of pupil records used for the pupils with whom you work.
4. List the roles and responsibilities within the school for maintaining pupil records and the record keeping systems.
5. What are your responsibilities concerning record keeping?

NVQ Links: Level 2: 2–1.2; Level 3: 3–6.1, 3–6.2

 Further reading...

Burton, G. and Dimbleby, R. (1995) *Between ourselves: an introduction to interpersonal communication.* Revised edition. Arnold.

Dare, A. and O'Donovan, M. (1997) *Good Practice in caring for children with special needs.* Stanley Thornes.

DfES (2001) *The Special Educational Needs Code of Practice 2001.* HMSO.

Houghton, D. and McColgan, M. (1995) *Working with children.* Collins Educational.

Johnstone, D. (2001) *An Introduction to Disability Studies.* David Fulton Publishers.

Petrie, P. (1989) *Communicating with children and adults: interpersonal skills for those working with babies and children.* Edward Arnold.

Steiner, B. *et al* (1993) *Profiling, recording and observing – a resource pack for the early years.* Routledge.

Tilstone, C. *et al* (1998) *Promoting Inclusive Practice.* RoutledgeFalmer.

Tobias, C. (1996) *The Way They Learn.* Focus on the Family Publishing.

Behaviour Management 2

> Key points:
>
> - Influences on pupil behaviour
> - Strategies for positive behaviour management
> - The effective use of rewards and sanctions
> - Preventing or reducing disruptive behaviour
> - Key indicators of unwanted behaviour
> - Contributing factors to unwanted behaviour
> - Pupils with Attention Deficit Hyperactivity Disorder (ADHD)
> - Approaches to persistent unwanted behaviour
> - Sharing concerns with parents, colleagues and other professionals
> - Dealing with bullying

Defining pupil behaviour

Pupil behaviour can be defined as a pupil's actions and reactions or a pupil's treatment of others. Behaviour involves children *learning to conform* to parental expectations for behaviour, school expectations for behaviour and society's expectations for behaviour.

Children who are not prepared (or are unable) to conform have to accept the consequences, such as sanctions or punishments for unacceptable behaviour. Learning about behaviour (as with all learning) always takes place within a social context. Certain types of behaviour may be acceptable in one context but not in another (e.g. families may make allowances for their child's behaviour), however different rules apply in school because adults must consider the needs of *all* pupils. What is acceptable in one situation may not be acceptable in another, even within the same school, for example loud, boisterous behaviour *is* acceptable in the playground but *not* in the classroom. Conforming brings limitations to pupils' behaviour, for example following school rules and participating in all National Curriculum areas even those they do not like.

Exercise:
What are *your* expectations regarding what is acceptable behaviour for yourself, for the pupils in your school, for the individual in society?

Parental expectations of behaviour

Many parents may have idealised or unrealistic expectations concerning their children's behaviour because:

1 Some child care/education books and the media promote unrealistic age-related expectations; many children do not 'measure up' to what the experts say.

2 Parents compare their children to other children (of relatives, friends, neighbours) not realising that all children are individuals and develop at their own rate.

3 Parents of children with special needs may be unsure of what to expect from their children in terms of behaviour; they may over compensate for their child's special needs by being over protective or by letting the child get away with behaviour that would not be acceptable in a child of similar age/level of development.

4 Parents often have expectations for behaviour based on perceptions of their own childhood and *their* parents' attitudes to behaviour.

Smaller families (often with few or no relatives nearby) mean many parents lack first-hand experience of caring for young children *before* they have their own children and may feel less confident about their parenting skills.

Parents have social/cultural expectations relating to their children's behaviour based on:

o cultural or religious beliefs
o individual variations in child-rearing practices
o adherence to traditional child-rearing practices.

Traditionally children did not dare challenge parental authority for fear of physical punishment. Today some parents still feel that if they were brought up this way, then this is what they expect from their children. In the 21st century, society recognises the rights of the child and has the expectation that all parents should be more caring and responsive to their children's needs by using positive methods such as praise, encouragement, negotiation and rewards to achieve socially acceptable behaviour. The UN Convention on the Rights of the Child states that '*children have the right to be protected from all forms of physical and mental violence and deliberate humiliation*'. Where parental expectations concerning punishment conflict with those of the school, staff should point out to parents the school's **legal** requirements under the Children Act 1989, that is *no* physical punishment. (See page 37.)

Children learn what their parents consider to be acceptable behaviour and will bring these expectations to school. Children also observe their parents' behaviour, which may be:

○ **Assertive:** sensitive to their own *and* other people's needs
○ **Passive:** too sensitive to other people's needs so *ignores own needs*
○ **Aggressive:** obsessed with own needs so *ignores other people's needs.*

(See also information on socialisation in Chapter 3: PSHE.)

Teaching assistants also need to be aware of negative or traumatic family incidents (such as bereavement, serious illness or abuse) which may be experienced by the pupils with whom they work and the impact these might have on their cognitive and physical abilities, behaviour and emotional responsiveness.

Other influences on children's behaviour

We live in a very competitive society as demonstrated in sport, business and politics. Schools also actively encourage **competition** through sports and merit/house points. Pupils may also be aware of being assessed and compare their achievements with others. Most pupils want to be part of a group and are willing to co-operate with others, but they can also be very competitive on behalf of themselves and their group/class or team. This type of competition may be seen as 'team spirit' or demonstrating loyalty to the group. Competition can be used to promote positive behaviour, for example:

○ winning merit/house points for self, class or team;
○ sharing common interests and activities within the school such as clubs, sports or hobbies;
○ belonging to clubs in the local community.

Peer pressure may have a negative influence on pupils' behaviour as they may be:

○ persuaded by others to participate in dangerous activities including 'dares'
○ pressured into socially unacceptable behaviour such as lying, stealing or bullying
○ excluded from or threatened by a group unless they conform which puts pressure on pupils to behave like the rest of the group
○ encouraged to behave in ways they never would as an individual ('mob rule').

Adults can use peer pressure to encourage positive behaviour by highlighting the positive benefits of certain behaviour for the group, class or whole school.

The **media** (television, magazines, comics, Internet and computer games) can have positive or negative influences on pupil behaviour, depending on what pupils see and how they are affected by it. Pupils exposed to violent images may see aggressive behaviour as an acceptable way to deal with others. Pupils who observe more assertive behaviour (with its emphasis on negotiation and compromise) are likely to demonstrate similar positive behaviour. Television programmes, characters and personalities provide powerful role models for pupils. Consider the effectiveness of advertising! (See also group dynamics in Chapter 1 and information on ADHD below.)

What is positive behaviour?

Tolerance is often the key factor as to what is considered to be positive or acceptable behaviour. Each person has different levels of tolerance for different kinds of behaviour depending on:

o how that person feels at the time
o the expected behaviour in relation to age/level of development
o the social context.

Examples of positive and negative behaviour

POSITIVE BEHAVIOUR	NEGATIVE BEHAVIOUR
sharing resources and adult's attention	not sharing; attention-seeking; jealousy
taking turns	taking things; stealing
working co-operatively	fighting or arguing; disrupting activities
helping/comforting others	hurting others
being friendly	being aggressive/abusive inc. bullying
remaining on task	easily frustrated or distracted
concentrating on activities	not concentrating on activities
complying with adult requests	refusing reasonable requests; defiant
contributing creative ideas	overriding/ridiculing other people's ideas
expressing self effectively	emotional outbursts; whining; nagging
being aware of danger	no sense of danger; too compulsive
being polite	rude, cheeky; interrupting others
being responsible for own actions	blaming others, lying
being independent	being easily led; too dependent on others
being flexible	resisting change; overly upset by change
being an active participant	over-active or passive

EXERCISE:
List positive and negative behaviours that you consider to be appropriate to the age/level of development of the pupils you work with in school.

POSITIVE BEHAVIOUR	NEGATIVE BEHAVIOUR	CONTEXT/ACTIVITY

The benefits of positive behaviour

Promoting positive behaviour can bring many benefits to pupils, staff and schools. These benefits include:

○ creating a positive framework with realistic expectations for pupils' behaviour
○ providing consistent care/education for pupils with clear rules and boundaries
○ the security and stability of a welcoming and structured environment
○ positive motivation through praise, encouragement and rewards
○ positive social interaction between pupils and staff
○ encouraging pupils' self-reliance, self-confidence and positive self-esteem
○ encouraging staff confidence in supporting pupils' learning
○ promoting a positive atmosphere which makes educating pupils more interesting and enjoyable
○ opportunities for more effective thinking and learning leading to improved educational achievement/test results.

There are also potential benefits for society such as:

○ more positive social interactions including friendships, clubs, etc.
○ re-development of community spirit and belief in citizenship
○ positive attitudes towards others e.g. equal opportunities, racial harmony, etc.
○ research shows that pupils who have positive early years experiences are more likely to maintain an interest in education leading to further training/qualifications and are less likely to go on to experience 'juvenile delinquency' and adult unemployment (Ball, 1994).

Managing pupil behaviour

As part of your role as a teaching assistant you will be promoting the school's policies regarding pupil behaviour by consistently and effectively implementing agreed behaviour strategies as directed by the class teacher, SENCO or other professional. You will help pupils to follow the school rules and also work towards specific **goals** and within certain **boundaries** as set by the teacher including individual, group or class targets for behaviour.

Goals are the *expectations* for behaviour; usually starting with 'Do …'

Boundaries are the *limitations* to behaviour, often starting with '**Don't** …'

Adults need to set goals and boundaries that take into account:

○ the age/level of development of the pupils
○ the pupils' individual needs and abilities in different areas of the curriculum
○ the social context (e.g. the class, activity, group size).

Setting goals and boundaries involves teaching pupils to:

○ respect other people
○ respect the possessions of others
○ develop self-control.

Setting goals and boundaries involves adults:

○ seeing things from a pupil's point of view
○ respecting pupils' needs and ideas
○ realising pupils will test boundaries from time to time
○ having realistic expectations for pupil behaviour
○ recognising the limitations of some pupils' level of understanding and memory skills.

Pupils are more likely to keep to goals and boundaries if they have some say about them. Pupils need to be active participants, not only in following rules, but in establishing them. Having a feeling of ownership makes rules more real and gives pupils a sense of control. Tutorials or 'circle time' with pupils can provide opportunities for you to support the teacher in establishing and maintaining class rules as well as encouraging pupils to work co-operatively with each other.

1 *What* **is the goal or boundary?** Focus on the behaviour staff would like to change. Encourage pupils to talk about, draw a picture or write down what *they* would like to change. Remember to be positive.

2 *Why* **is the goal necessary?** To improve behaviour, to provide happier atmosphere, to encourage co-operation or for safety reasons.

3 *Who* **does the goal or boundary apply to?** Does it apply to everyone in the school, just the group/class, or one particular individual?

4 *Where* **does the goal or boundary apply?** Does it apply everywhere in school, in a particular room/class, indoors or outdoors?

5 *When* **will the pupils start working towards the goal?** *When* **will the**

Setting goals and boundaries

boundary apply? Will it apply at all times in the classroom or school or only at certain times?

6 *How* will the goal or boundary be implemented? *How* will the pupils be encouraged to keep to the goal or boundary? Include positive incentives such as smiley faces, stickers or merit/house points.

7 *What* happens when the goal is achieved? Ask the pupils what *they* would like. Rewards might include a badge, certificate, assembly praise or a special treat.

8 Set new goal. Start with the next goal or boundary which needs changing.

EXERCISE:
1) Think about the goals and boundaries that might be appropriate to the pupil or pupils you work with in your school.
2) If possible, encourage the pupil or pupils to draw up their own list of rules that promote positive behaviour.

Supporting behaviour management strategies

While implementing agreed behaviour strategies, you need to recognise and respond promptly and appropriately to anti-social behaviour; remember to follow school policies. For example, you may need to remind pupils about the school/class rules or protect other pupils and yourself from harm when challenging behaviour is demonstrated by a pupil. You will need to report any problems in dealing with unacceptable/challenging behaviour to the class or subject teacher. You should also be able to identify and report any pupil's uncharacteristic behaviour patterns to the appropriate person, usually the class or form teacher. As part of your role in supporting the implementation of behaviour management strategies you will need to provide constructive feedback on the effectiveness of the behaviour strategies including the improvements or setbacks of pupils with Behaviour Support Plans. You may also be asked to contribute to ideas for improvements for behaviour management strategies.

Strategies for positive behaviour management

1 **Keep rules to a minimum.** Too many rules make it difficult for pupils to remember and follow them. Pupils will often accept and keep to a few rules if they have some freedom. Explain why certain rules are necessary. All pupils should learn to understand the need for rules, but they also need to develop their own self-control and to make their own decisions regarding behaviour.

2 **Be proactive.** This means preparing things in advance and taking action *before* something happens to prevent the pupil, group or class from working well. Advance planning and preparation is essential to avoid disruption. This includes having the correct materials and equipment ready for the lesson/activity. You should also be clear about the behaviour guidelines for the pupil or group you work with and what your responsibilities are for dealing with any problems that might occur.

3 **Work within a clear framework.** As directed by the teacher, organise work and give pupils clear instructions/explanations so as to minimise opportunities for disruption. Follow set routines – getting books out straight away, etc. While clear structures and routines are essential, there should be room for flexibility for example when pupils are not responding well to an activity, be prepared to adapt or postpone the activity; do a less demanding activity if the pupils are tired. Pupils often behave inappropriately when their needs or wishes conflict with adult expectations. Pupils should develop independence and have some control over their lives. Their wishes need to be considered and their

ideas respected. Give pupils some freedom to explore (within safety limits) or to select and carry out activities. Some activities and routines *have* to be done, but it may be possible to negotiate with pupils as to *when* these tasks are done or give an *incentive* for completion.

4 **Set goals for lessons/activities.** These may be for the class, a group or individual pupils as well as goals and boundaries for behaviour. Pupils need to be clear about both sets of goals. Have appropriate and realistic goals for a given set of conditions. Be prepared to negotiate some goals and boundaries with pupils.

5 **Be positive.** Once goals have been set, encourage pupils to keep them through rewards or other positive incentives. Make sure the pupil, group or class knows when they are working well. Reward positive behaviour using verbal and/or written praise, stickers or merit points for behaviour not just academic achievement. Pupils with Behaviour Support Plans may have a behaviour card – remember to record any positive behaviour no matter how small. Note that the emphasis in secondary schools tends to be on sanctions for breaking the rules, but despite this try to emphasise positive behaviour and reward 'good' behaviour. Keep smiling! A sense of humour goes a long way.

6 **Be realistic about pupils' behaviour.** Accept that pupils will be inquisitive, noisy and messy at times! Work with the teacher to organise a pupil-oriented environment and implement activities in appropriate areas, such as quiet activities in areas where pupils can concentrate without too many distractions. Organise the class or group effectively – when using visual aids, pupils need a clear and unobstructed view as they may become disruptive if they cannot see what is going on. Carefully thought out seating arrangements can also minimise the opportunities for disruption: sensible distances between pupils depending on the nature of the work; checking who sits next to who (avoid putting two 'chatterboxes' together!); keeping potentially disruptive pupils close to you.

7 **Be alert** to signs of potential bad behaviour and nip it in the bud, e.g. poor concentration, excessive chatter or fidgeting. Respond to cues that an individual pupil, group or class are not working well. Use pupil names to maintain control. Give verbal rebukes or warnings as appropriate. Apply sanctions as necessary and consistent with your role. Reactions can provide positive reinforcement of good work as well as serving to deal with disruption. Explain and help pupils who are 'stuck'. Use questions and prompts to check pupils' understanding of tasks.

8 **Ignore certain behaviour.** It may be appropriate to ignore some unwanted behaviour especially attention-seeking or behaviour that is

not dangerous or life-threatening. Sometimes it is not possible or appropriate to ignore unwanted behaviour, for example if the pupil is in danger. With younger pupils it may be more effective to distract the pupil or to divert their attention to another activity – diversionary tactics can often avoid the confrontations that can lead to emotional outbursts.

9   **Be consistent.** Once rules, goals and boundaries have been negotiated and set, stick to them. Pupils need to know where they stand; they feel very insecure if rules and boundaries keep changing for no apparent reason. Pupils need to understand that 'no' always means 'no' especially where safety is concerned.

10   **Know your pupil or pupils.** An awareness of a pupil's home background, previous behaviour in class/school and their abilities (including any special educational needs) influences the way you respond to disruptive pupils. It may be appropriate to act differently to the same offence depending on the individual pupil and/or circumstances. Use a variety of techniques; different pupils respond differently to different methods sometimes a reminder of a rule may be sufficient or a specific warning.

11   **Take account of time.** The time of day, week or year affects how pupils behave: tiredness and poor concentration at the end of the day particularly on Friday afternoons; stress and anxiety prior to SATs or GCSEs; excitement and lack of concentration before the Christmas or summer holidays.

12   **Keep calm!** Be calm, quiet, firm and in control; shouting only makes matters worse. If you feel you are losing control, count to 5 and then proceed calmly. You may need to use strategies like **time out** to give the pupil a chance to calm down, but keep it short – only a few seconds until the pupil is a little calmer.

Some pupils may not recognise or accept school rules or share the same views as to what is acceptable behaviour. Remember pupils from different social or cultural backgrounds may have different expectations regarding behaviour. Where children are given clear guidelines for behaviour at home, they are much more likely to understand and keep to rules, goals and boundaries in the school. Adults within the school also need to be good role models for behaviour. Your use of inter-personal skills with pupils and other members of staff should provide a positive role model for behaviour and effective working relationships.

The importance of praise and encouragement

Praise and encouragement promote positive behaviour in pupils by encouraging:

o emotional well-being and high self-esteem
o strong motivation for behaving in positive ways
o positive attitudes to behaviour and learning
o effective communication and social interaction.

The principles of positive reinforcement include:

o Positive expectations lead to positive behaviour.
o Rules, goals and boundaries are framed in positive and realistic terms.
o Positive feedback leads to positive behaviour.
o Effort is as important as achieving goals or desired behaviour.
o Rewards encourage or reinforce appropriate behaviour; sanctions are kept to a minimum.

Positive feedback for positive behaviour can make an enormous difference to the atmosphere of the school, and to pupils' concentration levels and learning abilities.

Praise is most effective when it:

o provides positive feedback about a specific behaviour or achievement 'Well done, Tom, you worked really well with Alex today while doing your science experiment!' rather than just 'Well done, Tom!'
o is sincere and given with maximum attention
o recognises effort not just achievement, especially with difficult tasks or goals
o encourages pupils to focus on their *own* individual behaviour or achievement
o shows the adult's positive expectations for the pupil's behaviour and learning.

Rewards can provide positive incentives for positive behaviour. Pupils can be motivated by rewards such as:

o choice of favourite activity
o special responsibility
o smiley faces, stars, stamps, stickers or badges
o merit points and certificates
o mention in praise assembly
o mention in Head teacher's praise book
o letter from head teacher to pupil's parents.

Rewards are most effective when they are:

○ immediate and clearly linked to the pupil's behaviour, effort or achievement so that the pupil connects the reward with the behaviour

○ meaningful and appropriate to the pupil's age/level of development (smiley faces and stickers are more real to young children than merit or house points)

○ related to an *individual's* behaviour, effort or achievement rather than a group; every pupil needs the chance to obtain rewards for some positive aspect of their own behaviour

○ recognised and consistently applied by *all* the staff in the school; some adults hand out rewards like confetti (making them meaningless), while others strictly ration them (making rewards virtually unobtainable); either way pupils will not be motivated.

The difficulty with some school reward systems is that pupils who find it easier to behave appropriately may do very well, but those with emotional or behavioural difficulties may not do so. Reward systems that display stars or points for the whole group can be particularly damaging to pupils' self-esteem and often they do not indicate what the reward was for. An individual chart or book for each pupil can be better as they are then clearly competing against their own past efforts or improving their own behaviour. For example, each pupil could have a small exercise book with a page a week for stickers, smiley faces or merit points, which are clearly linked to the pupil's behaviour and/or learning. The teacher can negotiate with each pupil the

Example cover

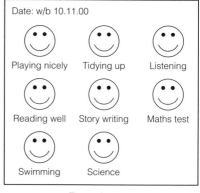

Example page

Examples of rewards from
a pupil's record book

targets they are expected to achieve that particular week. If the pupil achieves this target they receive an appropriate reward such as a certificate or choose a favourite activity. This makes it easier for pupils to see their individual efforts and achievements and can help to set future goals for behaviour and learning.

While the emphasis should be on promoting positive behaviour through encouragement, praise and rewards, there may be times when these do not work. Sometimes it is necessary to impose **sanctions** for pupils whose behaviour goes beyond acceptable boundaries or who break the rules.

Sanctions are most effective when they are:

o balanced against appropriate rewards
o reasonable and appropriate to the pupil's action so that major sanctions do not apply to minor lapses in acceptable behaviour
o applied to the pupils responsible and not the whole group/class
o aimed at discouraging unwanted/unacceptable behaviour without damaging pupils' self-esteem
o used as a last resort; every effort should be made to be positive and to encourage acceptable behaviour through positive rather than negative reinforcement.

Physical or corporal punishment is illegal in maintained schools:
'*Corporal punishment (smacking, slapping or shaking) is illegal in maintained schools and should not be used by any other parties within the scope of this guidance. It is permissible to take necessary physical action to prevent personal injury either to the child, other children or an adult or serious damage to property.*'

(The Children Act 1989 Guidance and regulations: Volume 2 Family Support, day care and educational provision for young children, Section 6.22.)

EXERCISE:
Outline your school's policy for rewards and sanctions relating to pupil behaviour.

Preventing and reducing disruptive behaviour

You can promote positive behaviour and thus prevent or reduce disruptive behaviour by:

○ learning and using pupils' names
○ using effective communication skills and encouraging these in pupils
○ identifying pupils' needs and interests to provide appropriate learning opportunities
○ helping to organise a stimulating environment to encourage learning opportunities
○ having well prepared learning materials
○ encouraging pupils to take appropriate responsibilities (e.g. tidying up)
○ helping to encourage parental involvement.

 KEY TASK

1. Working with the teacher, negotiate and set goals and/or boundaries with a pupil or group of pupils as part of a framework for positive behaviour.
2. Outline how you would implement this framework. Remember to emphasise the positive aspects of behaviour.
3. Devise a system of rewards for encouraging the pupils to demonstrate the targeted positive behaviour. If appropriate, include possible sanctions for unwanted/unacceptable behaviour.

N.V.Q. Links: Level 2:2–2.2; Level 2/3: 3–1.1, 3–1.2; Level 3: 3–15.1, 3–15.2, 3–15.3, 3–9.2, 3–2.2

The key indicators of unwanted behaviour

The adult response to a pupil's behaviour is as important as the behaviour itself. Different people have different attitudes to what is or is not acceptable behaviour. The social context also affects adult attitudes towards children's behaviour (see above). Certain types of behaviour should be considered unacceptable by all adults; these include behaviour that causes:

○ physical harm to others
○ self-harm
○ emotional/psychological harm to others
○ destruction to property.

Key indicators of unwanted behaviour include having:

o limited attention-span and concentration levels
o restricted range of communication skills
o hostile, uncaring or indifferent attitude towards others
o negative self-image and low self-esteem
o behaviour and/or learning patterns which are inconsistent with expected development.

Pupils whose unwanted behaviour is demonstrated through aggressive or disruptive behaviour are usually the ones to attract the most adult attention as they are easily identified and hard to ignore. Pupils who demonstrate unwanted behaviour in a withdrawn manner may be overlooked especially by inexperienced adults or in very busy schools or classrooms.

Contributing factors to unwanted behaviour

It is also important to be aware of the factors that can affect pupils' behaviour. Contributing factors include environmental, social or emotional factors such as: bereavement or prolonged illness; divorce or separation; family violence or child abuse; moving house; changing school; negative early years experiences in previous settings.

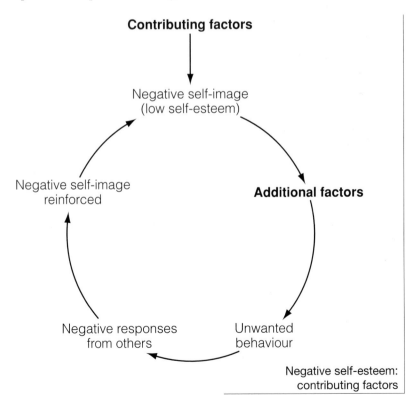

Negative self-esteem: contributing factors

Adults working in schools may have little or no control over these contributing factors but they *do* have control over additional factors such as: their response to pupils' unwanted behaviour; insensitivity or inflexibility towards individual needs; inappropriate learning opportunities; unwarranted disapproval from staff or other pupils in the school; pupils who are being bullied.

Pupils are more likely to behave in positive ways if they are:

- in a welcoming and stimulating environment
- engaged in interesting and challenging activities which are appropriate to their age and level of development
- given clear and realistic guidelines on behaviour with staff who have high/positive expectations for pupils' behaviour and learning.

Rare factors causing unwanted behaviour include:

- **Psychosis:** a serious psychological disorder characterised by mental confusion, hallucination and delusions; in younger pupils, symptoms include: regression, speech loss and extreme hyperactivity
- **Autism:** a rare and complex condition usually present from birth (although identification may not be made until 3 years +); autistic tendencies include speech loss or unusual speech patterns, isolation and withdrawal, intense dislike of environmental changes (see Chapter 7)
- **Attention Deficit Hyperactivity Disorder (ADHD):** a biological condition affecting children's behaviour and concentration (see below).

 KEY TASK

1. Observe a pupil who regularly demonstrates unwanted behaviour during group activities.
2. In your assessment include information on:
   - the pupil's behaviour during the activity
   - the pupil's communication skills
   - how the adult responds
   - how the other pupils respond to the pupil's behaviour.
3. Suggest ways to monitor the pupil's future behaviour.
4. Suggest ways to encourage the child to behave more appropriately.

N.V.Q. Links: Level 2/3: 3–1.1, 3–1.2; Level 3: 3–15.1, 3–15.2, 3–15.3, 3–9.2

Attention Deficit Hyperactivity Disorder (ADHD)

About 3 per cent of children have ADHD and it is possible that about 10 per cent of children have a milder form of the disorder. Boys are more likely to be affected than girls. ADHD is rarely diagnosed before the age of 6 years because many young children demonstrate the behaviours characteristic of this disorder as part of the usual sequence of development. From about 6 years old it is easier to assess whether the pupil's behaviour is *significantly* different from the expected norm. Most pupils with ADHD are formally identified between 5 and 9 years old. Pupils with ADHD are usually:

o **inattentive** with a short attention span; unable to concentrate on tasks, easily distracted; they forget instructions due to poor short-term memory; they may seem distant or be prone to 'day dreaming'.
o **over-active** with high levels of activity and movement; restless and fiddle with objects.
o **extremely impulsive**, which may lead to accidents as they have no sense of danger; they often speak and act without thinking.

Pupils with ADHD may also be:

o **discontent** as they are rarely satisfied with themselves or others; they generate lots of tension by interrogating, nagging or pestering others.
o **lacking in social skills** as they do not know how to behave with others; very bossy and domineering; unable to make or keep friends; they may demonstrate inappropriate behaviour or misread social cues, for example treating complete strangers as close friends.
o **lacking in co-ordination skills** and may have poor pencil control resulting in untidy written work; they may be accident-prone.
o **disorganised** and unable to structure their own time; unable to motivate themselves unless directed on a one-to-one basis; they may be very untidy.
o **changeable and unpredictable** with severe, unexplained mood swings; short-tempered with frequent emotional or extremely aggressive outbursts.

Some pupils with ADHD may also have specific learning difficulties such as dyslexia. Most pupils with ADHD have problems with handwriting but this could be due to poor hand-eye co-ordination and short attention-span.

ADHD is a hereditary, biological condition caused by a slight difference in brain function, which can be seen clearly on a brain scan. The medication Ritalin (a stimulant that enhances brain function) has been very effective in about 80 per cent of children with ADHD. Such medication helps focus the child's attention, keeps them on task and allows the child to think before they act. Once the child's concentration and behaviour improves the dose can be decreased. With or without medication, it is important to have a consistent system for managing the child's behaviour within the school and at home.

In school, staff need to provide:

o a quiet group/class with one or two adults who are firm but fair and can provide consistent care and education throughout the year
o calmness and a clear routine
o seating near a known adult away from distracting pupils
o step-by-step instructions
o constant feedback, praise and encouragement.

When working with a pupil who has ADHD you should aim to:

1 Encourage the pupil's enthusiasm for learning.

2 Improve the pupil's self-esteem.

3 Maintain harmony and peace (as far as possible) within the classroom/school.

EXERCISE:
Describe how *you* have responded to a pupil who demonstrates challenging or unwanted behaviour.

Approaches to responding to persistent unwanted behaviour

1 **Think approaches not solutions.** There are no easy answers or quick solutions to dealing with challenging or unwanted behaviour. You may need to use a variety of approaches.

2 **Consider past experiences.** Children learn about behaviour through their early relationships and experiences; the effects these have depends on individual personality (see Chapter 3). No one's behaviour is static; they can acquire new behaviour patterns and discard behaviour which is ineffective or inappropriate.

3 **Remember adult influences on children's behaviour.** Adults working in schools have major influences on pupils' behaviour. Adult responses to pupil behaviour can make things better or worse. You may need to modify your own behaviour and responses.

4 **Be patient**. Changing pupil behaviour takes time, so do not expect too much all at once – take things one step at a time. Remember that behaviour may get worse before it gets better because some pupils will resist attempts to change their behaviour (particularly if they have behaved this way for some time) and will demonstrate even more challenging behaviour especially if minor irritations are being ignored.

5 **Establish clear rules, boundaries and routines**. Pupils need to understand rules and the consequences if they do not follow the rules. Pupils need clear boundaries as to what is or is not acceptable behaviour, including frequent reminders about what these are.

6 **Be consistent**. Staff need to be consistent when responding to pupils with persistent unwanted behaviour or the pupils become confused. Adults need to discuss and agree on responses to the pupil's behaviour. Adults in schools need to work with the child's parents so the child sees that both are working together to provide a consistent framework for behaviour.

7 **Use diversionary tactics.** You can sometimes divert the pupil from an emotional or aggressive outburst or self-damaging behaviour. This does not always work, but often does. Be aware of possible triggers to unwanted behaviour and intervene or divert the pupil's attention *before* difficulties begin. Pupils can also be diverted by being offered alternative choices or being involved in decision making.

8 **Encourage positive social interaction**. Help pupils to develop their social skills so they can join in activities with other pupils. Start off with one to one, then small groups and then larger groups. Play tutoring can help e.g. using adult involvement to develop and extend social play. With older pupils encourage them to join school clubs.

9 **Help pupils find alternative ways to gain attention**. Most children want adult attention; it is the *way* they behave to gain attention that may need changing. Instead of being disruptive, pupils need to be encouraged to use more acceptable ways to get adult attention by asking or showing the adult that they have something to share.

10 **Help pupils to express their feelings.** Encourage pupils to express strong feelings such as anger, frustration or fear in positive ways – through play and communication. Older pupils need opportunities to express their grievances.

11 **Look at the environment**. Identify and, where possible, change aspects of the environment and routines within the classroom/school which may be contributing towards the pupil's unwanted behaviour.

12 **Label the behaviour not the pupil.** Make sure any response to unwanted behaviour allows the pupil to still feel valued without any loss of self-esteem e.g. 'I like you, Tom, but I don't like it when you …'

13 **Be positive.** Emphasise the positive and encourage pupils to be positive too. Phrase rules in positive ways, e.g. 'do' rather than 'don't'. Think about which unwanted behaviour must be stopped and which can simply be ignored so that pupils are not being told 'No' or 'Don't do …' all the time. Encourage pupils to focus on positive aspects of school, e.g. friends, favourite subjects, school clubs.

14 **Remember punishments rarely work.** Punishments may satisfy the people giving them, but they are often of little value in changing pupil behaviour. Pupils may become devious or blame others in order to avoid being punished. Quiet reprimands are more effective than a public 'telling off', which only causes humiliation in front of other pupils and increases the pupil's resentment towards the adult. Rewarding positive behaviour is more effective than punishing unacceptable behaviour.

15 **Use praise, encouragement and rewards.** Set realistic and achievable goals and use pupils' interests to motivate them. Use regular positive feedback to encourage pupils to behave in acceptable ways and raise their self-esteem. Praise pupils' *efforts* as well as achievements. Find out which kinds of rewards matter to the pupils and use them.

16 **Avoid confrontation if at all possible.** Use eye contact and the pupil's name to gain/hold their attention. Keep calm, sound confident and in control. If the pupil is too wound up to listen, give them a chance to calm down e.g. **'time out'**.

17 **Give individual attention and support.** This encourages pupils to share their worries or concerns with a trusted adult. **'Time in'** involves giving pupils special individual attention to reinforce positive behaviour and decreases the need for them to gain adult attention through unwanted behaviour. It involves pupils talking one to one (or in a small group) with an adult about their day including reviewing positive aspects of the day.

18 **Use behaviour modification.** Using positive reinforcement to encourage acceptable behaviour; ignoring all but harmful unwanted behaviour. Work on one aspect of behaviour at a time and reward the pupil for any progress no matter how small. The basic principles of behaviour modification are:

☆ Praise and reward acceptable behaviour
☆ Reduce the opportunities for unwanted behaviour
☆ Avoid confrontations
☆ Ignore minor unwanted behaviour
☆ Structure appropriate sanctions
☆ Establish clear rules, boundaries and routines.

Using behaviour modification techniques

1 Focus on the pupil's behaviour.

2 Target the aspect of unwanted behaviour that needs to be changed first.

3 Observe and monitor the specific behaviour; how often the behaviour occurs, when, where and in what situations.

4 Outline the usual response to this behaviour and the result.

5 Observe and record the activities/rewards that the pupil responds to positively.

6 Discuss possible strategies and decide on appropriate responses to the behaviour – adapt routines; change sanctions; reward appropriate behaviour.

7 Discussions should include the pupil, their parents as well as colleagues.

8 Implement the proposed strategies – remember to be positive.

9 Continue to observe, monitor and record the pupil's behaviour using simple, straightforward recording systems which can also involve the pupil and their parents.

10 Use regular positive feedback, praise and rewards to encourage the pupil.

11 Assess the effectiveness of the strategies. If they are working, continue to use them; if they are not, adapt them or try new ones. It may also be necessary to consult more senior colleagues or other professionals.

12 Once the agreed behaviour target has been reached, focus on the next aspect of unwanted behaviour that needs changing.

 **KEY TASK**

1. Think about the basic principles of behaviour modification.
2. Look back at your behaviour observation on page 40 and focus on one aspect of that pupil's behaviour.
3. Outline a step-by-step approach to encourage the pupil to behave in more acceptable ways. Remember to include appropriate rewards (and sanctions).

N.V.Q. Links: Level 2/3: 3–1.1, 3–1.2; Level 3: 3–15.1, 3–15.2, 3–15.3

Sharing concerns about a pupil's behaviour with their parents

It is easier to discuss concerns about a pupil's behaviour with their parents if sharing information with parents and parental involvement are established practices within the school.

○ *Be welcoming* and create an environment that provides opportunities to talk with parents. If face-to-face contact is difficult use a home-school diary to share information.
○ *Be clear* about which aspects of the pupil's behaviour are causing difficulties within the school. Ask the parents about any similar difficulties in the child's behaviour at home and how they respond to it.
○ *Be sensitive* when talking with parents; be willing to share positive information about the child's behaviour not just the negative.
○ *Be tactful* when asking the parents if they think their child may be worried or upset about anything.
○ *Be attentive* and listen carefully to the parents' views and any particular concerns *they* may have concerning their child's behaviour. Show parents that their involvement in their child's care and education is respected and valued.

Sharing concerns with colleagues and other professionals

Serious concerns about a pupil's persistent unwanted behaviour should be discussed with colleagues and sometimes with other professionals. Remember confidentiality. However, adults in schools have a legal duty to report serious concerns about a pupil's welfare (e.g. possible child abuse) – each school has guidelines about this. You may need specialist advice, guidance or support to provide the best possible approaches to responding to some pupils' behavioural and/or emotional difficulties. Colleagues may include: the pupil's class, form or subject teacher; key stage/year group co-ordinator;

special educational needs co-ordinator; deputy head teacher; head teacher. Every school has clear structures for reporting concerns about pupil behaviour to colleagues and appropriate ways to deal with these concerns. Be aware of your own role and responsibilities within this structure. Other professionals may include: health visitor; paediatrician; clinical psychologist; educational psychologist; social worker; education welfare officer; play therapist; music therapist.

Bullying

Bullying occurs in both primary and secondary schools. Research suggests that 85 per cent of 5–11 year olds have experienced bullying in some form, such as name-calling, being hit or kicked. In a recent survey of 11–16 year olds, '*36 per cent of children said they had been bullied in the last 12 months; 26 per cent had been threatened with violence and 13 per cent had been physically attacked*' (MORI/ATL, 2000). Bullying is such a serious problem that schools must now have an anti-bullying policy clearly setting out the ways in which they try to prevent bullying and deal with bullying behaviour.

Dealing with bullying behaviour

o Know the school's strategies for dealing with bullying behaviour.
o Use appropriate sanctions for such behaviour.
o Provide help for the bully so they can recognise that this behaviour is unacceptable (e.g. discussion, mediation, peer counselling).
o Work with teachers and parents to establish community awareness of bullying.
o Make sure all pupils know that bullying will not be tolerated.
o Schools may exclude pupils who demonstrate persistent bullying behaviour especially if they use physical violence towards others in school.

Recognising when a pupil is being bullied

The signs to watch out for are:
o Pupil who usually enjoys school suddenly does not want to go.
o Pupil has unexplained cuts and bruises.
o Pupil's possessions have unexplained damage or are persistently 'lost'.
o Pupil's academic performance declines for no apparent reason.
o Pupil becomes withdrawn or depressed, but will not say what is the matter.

Helping pupils who have been bullied

Ways to help pupils who have been bullied, include:
o Encourage the pupil to talk.
o Listen to the pupil's problems.

o Believe the pupil if they say they are being bullied.
o Reassure them that it is not their fault; no one deserves to be bullied.
o Discuss the matter with the pupil's teacher.
o Take appropriate action, following the school's policy on anti-bullying.

EXERCISE:
1. Outline your school's policy regarding bullying behaviour.
2. Devise an activity to encourage pupils to speak up about bullying, e.g. story/discussion, role play/drama or poster making.

Further reading...

Blandford, S. (1998) *Managing Discipline in Schools*. RoutledgeFalmer.

Green, C. and Chee, K. (1995) *Understanding ADD*. Vermilion.

Harding, J. and Meldon-Smith, L. (2000) *How to make observations and assessments*. 2nd edition. Hodder & Stoughton.

Leach, P. (1994) *Children First*. Penguin.

Lindenfield, G. (1994) *Confident Children*. Thorsons.

Lyus, V. (1998) *Management in the early years*. Hodder & Stoughton.

Reid, K. (1992) *Discipline in Schools: A Practical Handbook*. Simon & Schuster Education.

Rigby, K. (1997) *Bullying in Schools: And what to do about it*. Jessica Kingsley Publishers.

Sharp, S. and Smith, P. K. (ed) (1994) *Tackling Bullying in Your School: A Practical Handbook for Teachers*. Routledge.

Train, A. (1996) *ADHD: How to deal with very difficult children*. Souvenir Press.

Yeo, A. and Lovell, T. (1998) *Sociology for childhood studies*. Hodder & Stoughton.

Personal, Social and Health Education **3**

Key points:

- The importance of Personal, Social and Health Education (PSHE)
- Factors affecting social and emotional development
- The process of socialisation
- The sequence of social and emotional development
- Understanding social play
- Helping pupils to develop positive relationships
- Promoting pupils' self-reliance and positive self-esteem
- Recognising and dealing with emotions
- The importance of 'emotional intelligence'
- Transitions: helping pupils adjust to new settings
- Supporting pupils in maintaining health and hygiene standards

The importance of Personal, Social and Health Education

What is Personal, Social and Health Education?

Personal, Social and Health Education (PSHE) can be defined as the planned provision in schools to encourage and support the personal (emotional) and social development of all pupils. PSHE includes helping pupils to:

o develop and maintain positive self-esteem
o develop self-reliance
o take responsibility for their own actions
o have confidence in themselves and their own abilities
o make and keep meaningful and rewarding relationships
o be aware of their own feelings and those of others
o consider and respect the differences of other people
o be active participants as citizens of a democratic society
o develop and sustain healthy lifestyles
o keep safe and maintain the safety of others.

Why is Personal, Social and Health Education important?

Promoting the emotional and social development of pupils increases their self-confidence and improves their chances of educational success. It also helps pupils to face life's demands and challenges in preparation for adult life. Well-planned provision for PSHE improves the quality of the school environment and wider community by helping pupils to develop the inter-personal skills they need to engage fully and positively in school and community activities. PSHE also provides a framework for schools to support pupils dealing with negative social or environmental factors, which might hinder their learning and educational achievement. For example, developing pupils' confidence in their educational abilities and future career prospects may help reduce the numbers involved in teenage pregnancies, alcohol/drug misuse, truancy and crime.

PSHE is particularly important because it helps pupils to:

1 Deal with risk and meet new challenges.

2 Work for and achieve educational success.

3 Identify and keep personal values.

4 Understand and respect equal opportunities.

5 Develop and maintain better health and emotional well-being.

Exercise
What is your school's policy with regard to PSHE?

What is social and emotional development?

Social and emotional development can be defined as the development of **personality** and **temperament**. This involves how each person:

○ develops as a unique individual
○ sees and feels about themselves
○ *thinks* other people see them
○ expresses their individual needs, desires and feelings
○ relates to others
○ interacts with their environment.

Adults working with pupils need to understand the process of personality development in order to provide appropriate assistance and guidance.

Factors affecting social and emotional development

Genetic inheritance

In the same way as babies inherit their physical characteristics, they also inherit genetic information that contributes towards their **personality** development. Studies of very young babies show that they already have distinct temperaments or personality types: 40 per cent were easy-going; 10 per cent were 'difficult'; 15 per cent were 'slow to warm up'; 35 per cent did not fit any category! (Fontana, 1984.) *Note: Labelling* personalities is not really a good idea, as every child is a unique individual.

Environmental factors

1 *Attachments:* having at least one secure and personal relationship (with parent/carer) enables children to form other relationships.

2 *Parental care:* consistent, loving care from parent/carer who is sensitive to the child's particular needs enables children to feel secure and to develop self-worth.

3 *Role models:* observing the behaviour of parents and other significant adults (carers, teachers, support staff) affects children's own behaviour, how they deal with their own feelings and how they relate to others.

4 *Social context:* positive interactions with other people in various settings lead to positive ways of relating to others and appropriate social skills.

5 *Culture and gender:* cultural expectations and child-rearing practices vary. Different cultures within society may have differing cultural expectations relating to what is considered to be appropriate behaviour including the expected roles for boys and girls.

6 *Family size and birth order:* children in large families may find it more difficult to get their parents' attention and this may affect their social adjustment especially in group settings. Some research studies indicate that the position of children in the family may also affect their personality. Any differences in personality are probably due to the way in which adults treat the children rather than birth order.

7 *Other factors:* children's social and emotional development may also be affected by: special needs and/or difficulties at birth; family circumstances such as separation/divorce, one-parent families, step-families; death, abandonment or other permanent separation from parent or main carer; adoption, foster care or temporary/permanent residential care.

The process of socialisation

Socialisation involves the development of:

o behaviour patterns
o self-control

○ self-reliance (including self-help skills)
○ awareness of self in relation to others
○ relationships
○ understanding the needs and rights of others
○ moral concepts (e.g. understanding the difference between right and wrong; making decisions based on personal values).

Socialisation determines how children relate socially and emotionally to others. Children need to learn how to deal appropriately with a whole range of emotions including anger and frustration within a supportive environment. Socialisation occurs through:

○ observation
○ identification
○ imitation
○ assimilation
} of the behaviour of other people

Schools involve society's attempts at socialisation; as well as educating pupils by providing opportunities to gain knowledge and understanding in a wide range of subjects, schools influence children's attitudes and actions by providing a framework for socially acceptable behaviour with rules that have to be followed by all. (See Chapter 2: Behaviour Management.)

The sequence of social and emotional development

There is a recognised sequence of social and emotional development that depends on children's interaction with others and their environment. For ease of reference and to assist your understanding of pupils' social and emotional development the following sequence of development has been related to specific ages. Remember that all pupils are unique individuals who develop in their own way and at their own pace depending on their individual life experiences. Note that social and emotional development have been listed *separately* to assist your observations, assessments and understanding of these two complex aspects of psychological development but you will see that there are *overlaps* between the two.

The Sequence of Social and Emotional Development: 3–16 Years

Age 3–4 years

Social
○ enjoys the company of others; learns to play *with* other children, not just alongside them
○ uses language to communicate more and more effectively with others

---

- develops self-help skills (e.g. dressing self, going to the toilet) as becomes more competent and confident in own abilities
- wants to please and seeks approval from adults
- observes closely how others behave and imitates them
- fairly egocentric (e.g. considers own needs first) so may get angry with other children if disrupt play activity; expects adults to take *their* side in any dispute
- gradually is able to share group possessions at nursery or school

Emotional
- less reliant on parent/carer for reassurance in new situations so able to stay at nursery or school without them
- may be jealous of adult attention given to others e.g. to younger sibling or other children in group situations
- argues with other children but is quick to forgive and forget
- has limited awareness of the feelings and needs of others
- may be caring towards others who are distressed
- begins to use language to express feelings and wishes
- may have occasional emotional outbursts especially when tired, stressed or frustrated

Age 4–7 years
Social
- continues to enjoy the company of other children; may have special friend(s)
- uses language even more effectively to communicate, share ideas, engage in more complex play activities
- appears confident and competent in own abilities
- co-operates with others, takes turns and begins to follow rules in games
- still seeks adult approval; will even blame others for own mistakes to escape disapproval
- continues to observe how others behave and will imitate them; has a particular role model
- may copy unwanted behaviour e.g. swearing, biting, kicking, to gain adult attention.

Emotional
- becomes more aware of the feelings and needs of others
- tries to comfort others who are upset, hurt or unwell
- may occasionally be aggressive as still learning to deal with negative emotions
- uses language to express feelings and wishes

○ uses imaginative play to express worries and fears over past/future experiences e.g. hospital visits, family disputes/upheaval
○ has occasional emotional outbursts when tired, stressed or frustrated
○ argues with other children but may take longer to forgive and forget
○ confidence in self can be shaken by 'failure'
○ may have an 'imaginary friend'.

Age 7–11 years
Social
○ continues to enjoy the company of other children; wants to belong to a group; usually has at least one special friend
○ uses language to communicate very effectively, but may use in negative ways e.g. name-calling or telling tales, as well as positively to share ideas and participate in complex play activities often based on television characters or computer games
○ is able to play on own; appreciates own space away from others on occasion
○ becomes less concerned with adult approval and more concerned with *peer* approval
○ is able to participate in games with rules and other co-operative activities.

Emotional
○ becomes less egocentric as understands feelings, needs and rights of others
○ still wants things that belong solely to them e.g. very possessive of own toys, puts own name on everything they possess!
○ becomes more aware of own achievements in relation to others but this can lead to a sense of failure if feels does not measure up; hates to lose
○ may be very competitive; rivalry may lead to aggressive behaviour
○ argues with other children but may take even longer to forgive and forget
○ has increased awareness of the wider environment e.g. the weather, plants, animals, people in other countries.

Age 11–16 years
Social
○ continues to enjoy the company of other children/adolescents; individual friendships are still important; belonging to group or gang becomes increasingly important but can be a major source of anxiety or conflict

- o the desire for peer approval can overtake the need for adult approval and causes challenges to adult authority at home and/or at school particularly in the teenage years
- o participates in team games/sports or other group activities including clubs and hobbies; can follow complex rules and co-operate fully but may be very competitive
- o strongly influenced by a variety of role models especially those in the media e.g. sports celebrities and film/pop stars
- o is able to communicate very effectively and uses language much more to resolve any difficulties in social interactions
- o can be very supportive towards others e.g. people with special needs or those experiencing difficulties at home, school or in the wider community

Emotional

- o sensitive to own feelings and those of others with a growing understanding of the possible causes for why people feel and act as they do
- o understands issues relating to fairness and justice
- o can anticipate people's reactions and consider the consequences of own actions
- o is increasingly able to see different viewpoints in order to resolve difficulties in relationships
- o has confidence in own skills and ideas; is more able to be assertive rather than aggressive or passive
- o may have very strong opinions or beliefs, leading to arguments with adults and peers; may hold grudges and find it difficult to forgive or forget
- o has more understanding of complex issues concerning the wider environment e.g. ethics, philosophy, religion, politics

Promoting pupils' social and emotional development

Social play

Play is an essential aspect of pupils' social and emotional development as it enables them to:

- o learn and develop new social skills
- o practice and improve existing social skills
- o experiment with new social situations (e.g. anticipate what they *might* do in new situations)

○ prepare for new experiences
○ act out past experiences
○ express emotions in positive ways.

Children playing and
interacting

Children go through a recognised sequence of social play. Younger pupils
tend to engage in more solitary or parallel play activities because they are
more egocentric; while older pupils are capable of more co-operative play
activities as they can take turns, share play equipment and follow rules more
easily. There will be times when quite young children can be engaged
happily in play activities with some interaction with other children
(associative play) such as dressing-up, home corner, doing jigsaws, simple
construction or painting. There will be occasions when older children
become engrossed in solitary or parallel play activities with no interaction
with other children such as doing detailed drawings and paintings or
building intricate constructions that require complete concentration to the
exclusion of everyone else.

Supporting pupils in developing relationships with others

We have all experienced jealousy in our relationships with others. Unchecked
jealousy can become a very destructive and hurtful emotion, which prevents
children (and adults) from developing respect and care for others. Younger

pupils especially may show their jealousy by crying; being clingy; displaying attention-seeking behaviour, such as shouting or biting; or regressing to previous levels of development. Younger pupils are often unable to co-operate with other pupils in group activities. Older pupils will use language to negotiate and compromise when there are disagreements. Gradually pupils should be able to participate in more complex co-operative activities, including games with rules, as their understanding of abstract ideas increases.

Co-operative activities encourage:

- self-confidence and high self-esteem
- relating positively to others, working together and helping others
- making joint decisions
- full participation (no one is left out or eliminated)
- a sense of belonging.

Competitive sports and games have their place and can be beneficial to pupils' social and emotional development as long as they emphasise:

- co-operation and working as a team
- mutual respect
- agreeing on rules and following them
- participation and the pleasure of taking part are more important than winning
- doing our personal best.

Golden Rules for positive social interaction

1 Welcome and celebrate differences; everyone is important and should be valued as unique individuals.

2 Listen and be attentive to what others have to communicate.

3 Regard and value the needs and rights of others.

4 Recognise and respect the culture and beliefs of other people.

5 Be considerate and courteous towards others.

6 Help and care for each other as much as possible.

7 Co-operate and work together to reach the best solutions.

8 Share and take turns; remember 'compromise equals wise.'

9 Praise and encourage others to raise their self-esteem.

10 Inspire respect in others through own kindness, fairness and honesty.

 **KEY TASK**

Plan and implement an activity which encourages pupils to relate positively towards others. Evaluate the activity afterwards.

N.V.Q. Links: Level 2:2–2.2, Level 3: 3–9.1, 3–2.2

Help pupils to deal with conflict situations

All pupils will experience situations where they feel that life is not fair. They will have disagreements and disputes with other pupils. Initially children rely on adults to help resolve these disputes, but gradually they learn how to deal with these for themselves. Pupils need to learn how to use language to reach agreements so that as far as possible their needs and other people's can be met fairly. Pupils need to learn that resolving conflicts does not mean getting your own way all the time (being aggressive) or allowing others to get their own way all the time (being submissive/passive). There is a better way that allows everyone to reach a satisfactory compromise – being **assertive.**

Ways to resolve conflicts:

- **Fight/Bully** = **Aggressive** → 'I win so you lose'.
- **Submit/Retreat** = **Submissive/Passive** → 'I lose because you win'.
- **Discuss/Negotiate** = **Assertive** → 'I win and you win'.

Point out to pupils that shouting or physical violence never resolves conflicts, they usually make matters worse and only demonstrate who is the loudest or strongest or has more power. Conflicts need to be discussed in a calm manner so that a mutually agreed compromise can be reached.

Exercise
1. Describe how you have dealt with a conflict situation.
2. Look at the conflict situations listed below. Suggest how these could be resolved to achieve a 'win/win ' result.

You can use books, stories and videos that depict potential conflict situations such as:

○ sharing or borrowing toys
○ deciding on rules for a game or choosing a game
○ choosing partners or teams fairly

o knocking over models or spoiling work *accidentally*
o disrupting other children's activities *deliberately*.

Discuss with the pupils afterwards:

o what caused the conflict or disagreement?
o how they were resolved?
o what were the best solutions?
o how would they have resolved it?

Younger pupils can do this with appropriate situations and guidance from sensitive adults. Using puppets and play people can also help. Where pupils are used to doing role play or drama, adults can get them to act out how to resolve conflicts in peaceful ways.

Contributing to pupils' health and well-being

What is self-reliance?

Self-reliance involves:

o *dependence* on own capabilities and personal resources
o *autonomy* – the ability to think and act for oneself
o *competence* in looking after self
o *trust* in own judgement and actions
o *confidence* in own abilities and actions.

Pupils gain self-reliance by:

o developing self-help skills
o making choices and decisions
o taking responsibility for their own actions.

Pupils need the freedom to develop their self-reliance in ways appropriate to their overall development. Some pupils may need more encouragement than others to become increasingly more independent and less reliant on other people.

The teaching assistant has an important role in encouraging pupils to develop self-reliance.

You can encourage pupils to be self-reliant by:

1 Providing **freedom** for pupils to become more independent.

2 Being **patient** and providing **time** for pupils to do things for themselves, for example letting younger pupils dress themselves takes

longer, but is an essential self-help skill; with practice they will get faster so do not rush them. Pupils with physical disabilities may need sensitive support in this area.

3 **Praising** and **encouraging** pupils' efforts at becoming more independent.

4 Acknowledging **pupils' individual needs** for independence; every pupil is different and requires encouragement relevant to their particular level of development. Do not insist pupils be self-reliant in a particular area until they are ready.

5 Being **sensitive to pupils' changing needs** for independence. Remember a pupil who is tired, distressed or unwell may require more adult assistance than usual.

6 Offering limited **choices** to make pupils feel more in control. As pupils develop, increase the scope of choices.

7 Providing **opportunities for play** for pupils which encourage self-reliance e.g. dressing-up helps younger pupils learn to dress independently in a fun way.

8 Using **technology** to enable pupils to work more independently e.g. self-correcting computer tasks; voice-activated word processing; motorised wheelchairs.

 KEY TASK

Observe a pupil demonstrating their self-help skills such as:

o feeding self
o washing hands
o getting dressed/undressed (e.g. for PE)
o tidying up.

Assess the pupil's ability to perform the skill independently. Outline the adult's role in developing the pupil's self-reliance in this area.

NVQ Links: Level 2: 2–2.1; Level 3: 3–9.2, 3–15.3

What is self-esteem?

Self-esteem involves:

○ feelings and thoughts about oneself (positive or negative)
○ respect or regard for self (or lack of it)
○ consideration of self
○ self-worth (i.e. value of self)
○ self-image (i.e. perception of self).

How we feel about ourselves depends on a number of factors:

○ *who* we are with at the time
○ the social context – *where* we are
○ current and past *relationships*
○ past *experiences* (especially in early childhood).

A person's self-esteem is changeable; sometimes we feel more positive about ourselves than other times. Even if we have had past experiences that resulted in negative or poor self-esteem, we can overcome this and learn to feel more positive about ourselves.

We cannot *see* self-esteem, but we can assess children's (and adults') levels of self-esteem by their emotional responses, attitudes and actions. People with positive or high self-esteem are usually calm and relaxed; energetic, enthusiastic and well motivated; open and expressive; positive and optimistic; self-reliant and self-confident; assertive; reflective (e.g. aware of own strengths and weaknesses); sociable, co-operative, friendly and trusting.

People with negative or low self-esteem tend to be: anxious and tense; lacking in enthusiasm, poorly motivated and easily frustrated; secretive and/or pretentious; negative and pessimistic; over-dependent, lacking in confidence and constantly seeking the approval of others *or* over-confident, arrogant and attention seeking; aggressive *or* passive; self-destructive *or* abusive towards others; resentful and distrustful of others.

Reasons for low self-esteem

All children begin with the *potential* for *high* self-esteem, but their interactions with others contribute to whether positive self-esteem is encouraged or diminished. Experiences in early childhood have the most significant affect on children's self-esteem; sometimes these effects may not become apparent until adolescence or adulthood when serious psychological and social problems may result due to very low self-esteem. Children (and adults) are very resilient and can learn to have greater self-esteem even if their earlier experiences were detrimental to their esteem. Factors that lead to low self-esteem include: being deprived of basic needs or having these needs inadequately met; having feelings denied or ignored; being put-down, ridiculed or humiliated; participating in inappropriate activities; feeling that their ideas and opinions are unimportant; being over-protected, under-disciplined or excessively disciplined; being physically or sexually abused (Lindenfield, 1995).

Ways to promote positive self-esteem

You can help build pupils' self-esteem by:

1 Listening calmly and attentively to pupils.

2 Taking time before replying to what pupils have to say; using prompts to encourage pupils to continue talking or to answer questions.

3 Encouraging pupils to talk about and express their feelings including anger and jealousy; reassuring pupils that having strong feelings is acceptable.

4 Taking an interest in pupils' drawings, paintings, stories and other activities.

5 Praising and encouraging pupils' *attempts* at activities not just the end result.

6 Showing an interest and appreciation of pupils' personal qualities such as kindness or humour not just their academic abilities.

7 Using language that is appropriate to the pupils' level of understanding without being condescending.

8 Communicating with pupils *literally* at their level, e.g. squatting down or sitting down so that they are not intimidated.

9 Providing a pupil-centred, language-rich and stimulating learning environment.

10 Responding to each pupil's *individual* needs.

11 Providing a clear framework for behaviour and using rewards rather than punishments.

12 Encouraging pupils to value their individuality.

13 Encouraging pupils to be self-reliant by helping them to develop self-help skills and to make choices.

14 Asking pupils for their ideas and opinions and listening to these with respect and interest.

15 Being a positive adult role model; increasing your own self-esteem will help you to inspire feelings of self-worth in pupils.

 KEY TASK

Devise a reward system that encourages pupils' self-reliance and promotes positive self-esteem. Remember to avoid comparing pupils or encouraging too much competition as these can damage self-esteem. Instead focus pupil attention on their *individual* achievements/behaviour and on improving these skills to achieve their *personal* best. Individual charts or booklets might be more appropriate then a large chart for all to see.

N.V.Q Links: Level 2:2–2.1, Level 3: 3–9.2

Helping pupils recognise and deal with feelings

An essential aspect of children's social and emotional development is helping them to recognise and deal with their own feelings and those of other people.

Feelings can be defined as:

o an *awareness* of pleasure or pain
o physical and/or psychological *impressions*
o the *experience of emotions*, such as anger, joy, fear or sorrow.

There is an enormous range of emotions that are experienced by humans. We all experience a variety of **personal emotions**, which are related to our individual perceptions of, and responses to, our life experiences and ourselves. Personal emotions include: happiness, joy, pleasure, satisfaction; sadness, grief, pain, despair; enthusiasm, excitement, impulsiveness, courage; reluctance, anxiety, caution, fear. We also experience **interpersonal emotions**, which affect the way we relate to other people and how they respond to us. Interpersonal emotions include: love, affection, kindness, acceptance; hate, anger, malice, contempt; respect, compassion, patience, trust; jealousy, insensitivity, impatience, distrust.

In British society we are often encouraged to keep our feelings to ourselves. Males are discouraged from expressing sensitive emotions; females are discouraged from demonstrating aggressive emotions. Babies and very young children naturally demonstrate clearly how they feel by crying, shouting and/or rejecting objects. They openly show affection and other emotions such as jealousy or anger. Young children do not always understand that others can be physically or *emotionally* hurt by what they say or do. Gradually, children become conditioned to accept that the feelings and needs of others *do* matter. We need to ensure that children do not forget their own feelings and emotional needs by becoming too concerned with the feelings of others or trying to please others. This can be a particular problem for females in a male-dominated society. Pupils need to know that it is natural to feel a wide range of emotions and that it is acceptable to express strong feelings such as jealousy and anger openly – as long as they do so in positive and appropriate ways.

You should encourage pupils to:

○ identify and name their own feelings
○ express these feelings in positive ways
○ recognise feelings in other people
○ deal with emotional responses from other others in appropriate ways
○ deal with conflict situations.

You can help pupils by using:

○ **books, stories and poems** about feelings and common events experienced by others to help them recognise and deal with these in their own lives
○ **creative activities** to provide positive outlets for feelings, e.g. pummelling clay to express anger; painting/drawing pictures or writing stories, poems and music, which reflect their feelings about particular events/experiences
○ **physical/outdoor play and sports** that allow a positive outlet for anger or frustration
○ **Imaginative/role play or drama** to act out feelings, e.g. jealousy over new baby; worries over past experiences; fears about future events such as visit to dentist, hospital.

Pupils may become upset or distressed for a number of reasons: family/friends' accidents, illness or bereavement; family separation/parental divorce; pet illness or death; pressures at home/school; arrival of new baby/step-siblings; concerns about tests/exams; bullying; local, national or international crises; specific fears or phobias (e.g. the dark, storms, spiders). Teaching assistants need to be aware of possible signs of distress and help pupils to cope with stress or fear. Pupils who are upset may suddenly burst into tears for no apparent reason, or they may say they have a headache,

Working with clay can be a means for children to express their feelings

'tummy ache' or that they feel sick. A sudden behaviour change might indicate distress, e.g. regression to early level of development or atypical reliance on adults.

Ways you can help

1 Let pupils know they can talk to you about their worries or problems.

2 Listen sympathetically to their concerns.

3 Give practical support as appropriate (e.g. following school policy for helping pupils who experience bullying or offering tips to help with revision).

4 Be consistent – limits and boundaries help pupils feel secure especially when stressed.

5 Be honest and open about fears.

6 If a pupil begins to panic, encourage them to breathe slowly then talk about a pleasant memory you share or the pupil's particular interest or hobby.

7 Discuss your concerns about a pupil's distress/fears with their class or form tutor, especially if the pupil seems very distressed for a long time or for no obvious reason.

Dealing with pupils' emotional outbursts

Sometimes pupils, especially young children, are overwhelmed by their emotions and will act inappropriately or regress to previous patterns of behaviour. When pupils are unable to use language to express their feelings (because they lack the appropriate words, are too worked up, have behavioural/emotional difficulties or other special needs) they are more prone to demonstrate their emotional responses in physical ways, such as biting, scratching, kicking, shouting, screaming, throwing things, throwing themselves on the floor, etc. These emotional outbursts or 'temper tantrums' can be very frightening to the pupil and others in the group/class. Adults too can find pupils' emotional outbursts difficult to deal with.

It is essential that you:

○ remain calm yourself; speak quietly but confidently, shouting will only make things worse
○ ignore the emotional outburst as much as possible while maintaining pupil safety
○ avoid direct confrontations
○ give the pupil time and space to calm down
○ reassure the pupil afterwards but do not reward them
○ when the pupil has calmed down talk about what upset them in a quiet manner
○ suggest to the pupil what they could do instead if they feel this way again.

The best way to deal with emotional outbursts is to minimise the likelihood of them happening in the first place:

○ Avoid setting up situations where emotional outbursts are likely to happen, such as making unrealistic demands or doing complex activities when a pupil is tired.
○ Give advance warning – prepare the pupil for new experiences; give a five-minute warning that an activity is coming to an end and that you want them to do something else.
○ Provide reasonable choices and alternatives to give the pupil a sense of responsibility and control, e.g. choice of activity to do next, choice of materials.
○ Encourage the pupil to express their feelings in more positive ways.

 **KEY TASK**

1. Outline your setting's policy for dealing with pupils' emotional outbursts.
2. Describe how you have dealt with a pupil's emotional outburst.
3. Give examples of activities used in your school to help pupils recognise and explore feelings.

N.V.Q. Links: Level 2:2–2.1, Level 3: 3–9.3, 3–15.3

The importance of 'emotional intelligence'

Adults working in schools must remember the importance of the *all-round* development of pupils. As well as becoming literate, numerate and developing scientific/technological skills, pupils need to engage in activities that help them to:

o learn about their feelings
o understand the feelings of others
o develop their creative abilities (i.e. art, music)
o participate in physical activities, games and sport
o interact with other pupils and make friends (i.e. play).

What is emotional intelligence?

Emotional intelligence or emotional well-being involves developing:

o positive self-esteem and self-image
o emotional strength to deal with life's highs and lows
o confidence to face the world with optimism
o awareness of own feelings and those of other people.

We all need to feel valued – that who we are and where we come from is respected; that our ideas and abilities are important. We need a solid belief in our own self-worth and self-identity. On this solid emotional platform the building blocks for a stimulating and fulfilling life can be successfully constructed.

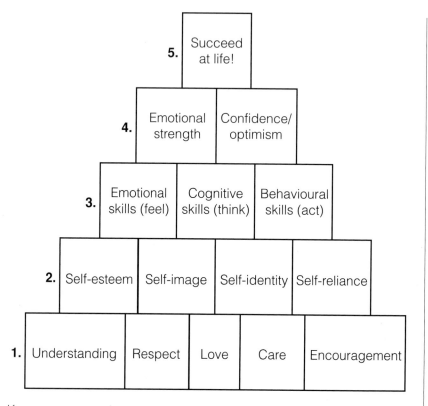

5. Succeed at life!

4. Emotional strength | Confidence/optimism

3. Emotional skills (feel) | Cognitive skills (think) | Behavioural skills (act)

2. Self-esteem | Self-image | Self-identity | Self-reliance

1. Understanding | Respect | Love | Care | Encouragement

Key:
1 These **foundation stones** are established by parents, grandparents, and carers in childhood; as adults we can regain them through partners/spouses, close friends, etc.
2 These **self-building blocks** are influenced by others including family, carers, teachers, friends, peers, colleagues, etc. throughout life.
3 These **skills** can be developed as a child and/or as an adult.
4 These **qualities** can be demonstrated as a child and/or as an adult.
5 **Individual achievements** in different areas of life as a child *and* as an adult.

Emotional building blocks

Even if the building blocks shown above are damaged by life experiences, personal difficulties, tragedy or trauma they can be rebuilt in childhood and even adulthood.

You can help pupils to develop their emotional intelligence by:
○ **developing their self-awareness** including helping them to recognise their feelings
○ **helping them to handle and express feelings** in appropriate ways

o **encouraging their self-motivation** by helping them to establish personal goals e.g. improving concentration, developing self-control and self-reliance.

o **developing empathy** by encouraging pupils to recognise the feelings, needs and rights of others. This gives them better social skills so they can interact more positively with others.

o **encouraging positive social interaction** by developing effective interpersonal skills through play and other co-operative group activities that improve relationships in the school, at home and in the community.

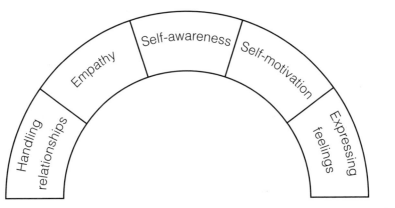

Emotional intelligence involves the above abilities.

Emotional intelligence

Supporting pupils in adjusting to a new setting

The process of adjusting to a new setting is known as a **transition**.

A transition involves the transfer of a child from one setting to another. For example:

o home to nursery, playgroup or school
o nursery or playgroup to school
o one year group to another e.g. reception to Year 1; Year 1 to Year 2
o Key Stage 1 to Key Stage 2
o Primary school to secondary school (Key Stage 2 to Key Stage 3)
o Key Stage 3 to Key Stage 4
o Secondary school to college or work
o Mainstream to, or from, special school.

Transitions involve change, separation and loss, so all children need:

○ help in preparing for such transitions
○ help in accepting transitions and settling into new settings
○ reassurance from adults to maintain their feelings of stability, security and trust
○ adult assistance in adjusting to different social rules and expectations
○ help in adapting to different group situations.

Preparing pupils for new settings and situations

Children's responses to transitions often depend on the way they are prepared for the new setting or situation. Many children experience anxiety and stress when they first attend a new setting due to:

○ separation from their parent or previous care-giver
○ encountering an unfamiliar group of children who may have established friendships
○ time in the setting e.g. 8.00am to 6.00pm in a day nursery or 9.00am to 3.30pm in school
○ differences in culture and language of the setting to child's previous experiences
○ unfamiliar routines and rules
○ worry about doing the wrong thing
○ unfamiliar activities/routines such as PE, playtime and lunchtime
○ an unfamiliar physical environment, which may seem overwhelming and scary
○ difficulties in following more structured activities and adult directions
○ concentrating on activities for longer than previously used to.

The transition from primary to secondary may cause additional concerns due to:

○ lack of sufficient information about individual pupils on transfer
○ discontinuity of Year 6 and 7 (Key Stages 2 and 3) curriculum in spite of the National Curriculum
○ having several subject teachers instead of one class teacher
○ decrease in pupil performance after transfer.

Preparing pupils aged 3–11 years for transitions

○ Talk to the pupils and explain what is going to happen.
○ Listen to the pupils and reassure them that it will be fine.
○ Read relevant books, stories and poems about transitions, e.g. starting nursery or primary school; moving to secondary school.

o Watch appropriate videos/television programmes that demonstrate the positive features of the new school or situation.
o Provide opportunities for imaginative play to let pupils express their feelings and fears about the transition.
o Organise introductory visits for the pupils and their parents/carers so that the children can become familiar with the school and the adults who will care for and support them.
o Provide information appropriate to both pupils and parents, e.g. information pack/brochure plus activity pack for the pupil.
o Obtain relevant information about each pupil, e.g. correct name and address, contact details, medical information, dietary requirements.
o Plan activities for an induction programme (the pupil's first day/week in the new school).

Preparing pupils aged 11–16 for transitions

o Encourage pupils and parents to attend open days and evenings for school/college.
o Year 6 could be taught by different primary teachers to prepare them for the difference in teaching and learning style e.g. from topic-based to subject-based.
o Start a project towards the end of the summer term to be completed in the first few weeks of secondary school to give a sense of continuity.
o Year 7 teachers visit and teach Year 6 pupils in primary schools during summer term.
o Teaching assistants visit new school/year group and work alongside teachers particularly if going to have responsibility for pupil or pupils with special needs.
o Taster days for pupils to experience the layout and routine of the school/college e.g. moving to different classrooms for lessons with different subject teachers through fun activities in science, IT and sport.
o Discussions between different Key Stage staff about individual pupils' performance.
o Exchange of relevant documentation e.g. SATs test results, teacher assessments, any special educational needs information including Individual Education Plans, Behaviour Support Plans, statements, etc.
o Pupil's record of achievement including their interests and hobbies not just school work.
o Encourage pupils with behaviour problems to look at this as a new start.
o School brochure, including information on homework and bullying, as these are often key areas of concern.
o Relevant information from parents.
o Provide opportunities for work experience to help pupils with transition from learning environment to world of work.

o Provide opportunities for careers advice and information on further education/training.

Exercise
1. Describe the procedures in your school for preparing pupils for transitions.
2. How well do you think these procedures meet pupils' social and emotional needs? Think about possible improvements.

Activities and strategies for settling in pupils new to the school

The first days (or even weeks) that pupils spend in a new school require a sensitive approach from adults to enable the pupils to cope with separation from their parents and/or adjustment to new routines and staff.

Remember the following points:

1 Follow a clear, structured daily routine to provide stability and security for the pupils.

2 Provide opportunities for pupils to express their feelings and concerns over separating from parents or starting in new school/year group/Key Stage.

3 Work with the teacher to identify pupils' individual needs during the transition period.

4 Provide activities and experiences appropriate to these needs.

5 Show an active interest in the pupils' activities.

6 Give particular praise and encouragement for effort not just achievement.

7 Work with the teacher and pupils to establish clear boundaries and rules.

8 Reassure younger pupils about their parents' eventual return.

9 Prepare parents for possible temporary effects of the transition e.g. children may demonstrate their feelings of anxiety by being clingy, hostile, aggressive or by regressing to previous developmental level.

10 Settling in can often be more stressful for the parents than their children; encouraging them to be relaxed, calm and confident will help their children who can sense their parents' anxiety.

 **KEY TASK**

1. Outline possible strategies for preparing a pupil or group of pupils for one of the following:
   - first day/week in a new school
   - first day/week in a new year group or Key Stage
   - meeting a visitor or unfamiliar adult in the school.
2. Consider these points:
   - the pupil's level of social interaction (e.g. age and ability to communicate)
   - the pupil's potential behaviour based on your existing knowledge of the pupil (e.g. are they likely to be co-operative or disruptive?)
   - the pupil's possible emotional responses and how to deal with them.

N.V.Q. Links: Level 2/3: 3–11.1

Supporting pupils in maintaining standards of health and hygiene

As a teaching assistant you will support the teacher in the promotion and delivery of PSHE in line with the school policy and any curriculum requirements. Your role includes helping pupils to:

○ develop and maintain basic hygiene skills (washing hands, blowing noses, etc.)
○ respect for their own and others' health and hygiene needs (playing/working safely)
○ keep healthy and make healthy choices (exercise and healthy eating habits)
○ access medical and health care when needed (what to do in the event of illness or accident). See Health and safety section in Chapter 10: Professional Practice.

You will need to follow any health and safety regulations and guidelines when dealing with the hygiene, health or medical needs of pupils.

You must be aware of the possible emotional responses and other signs in pupils which may highlight problems such as bullying (see page 47), drug misuse or child abuse (see Chapter 10) and immediately report these concerns to the pupil's teacher. Remember to follow the school and legal requirements for confidentiality of personal information at all times.

KEY TASK

1. Plan an activity which will help the pupil or pupils you work with maintain the health and hygiene standards of the school. For example:
   - hand washing routine
   - playtime safety
   - preparing/cooking healthy food
   - role play on what to if another pupil is ill or has an accident.
2. Discuss your plan with the teacher and, if possible, implement your activity.

NVQ Links: Level 2: 2–1.2; Level 2/3: 3–11.2, 3–10.1

Further reading...

Cooper, A. (2000) *Positive Action: A Resource Book for PSHE KS3 + KS4*. Birmingham Health Education.

Frederickson, N. (1991) *Social competence*. University College London.

Goddard, G. and Barbera, J. (2002) *PSHE and Citizenship 7–11 years*. Scholastic.

Goleman, D. (1996) *Emotional intelligence*. Bloomsbury.

Lindenfield, G. (2000) *Self esteem: simple steps to developing self-reliance and perseverance*. HarperCollins.

Masheder, M. (1989) *Let's Co-operate*. Peace Education Project.

Masheder, M. (1989) *Let's play together*. Green Print.

Mosley, J. (1996) *Quality Circle Time in the Primary Classroom: Your Essential Guide to Enhancing Self-esteem, Self-discipline and Positive Relationships*. LDA.

Nicholls, G. and Gardner, J. (1998) *Pupils in Transition*. RoutledgeFalmer.

Oliver, I. (2000) *Ideas for PSHE KS1*. Scholastic.

Parsons, R. (2001) *KS4 PSHE*. Coordination Group Publications.

Thinking and Learning 4

Key points:

- Some theories on intellectual development: Piaget, Vygotsky and Bruner
- How children think and learn
- Learning patterns and learning styles
- The importance of play and active learning
- The inter-related components of intellectual development
- The sequence of intellectual development
- Meeting pupils' intellectual needs

Some theories on intellectual development

Research into how children think and learn has made adults more aware of the need:

○ to observe and assess children's development very carefully
○ to listen to children and the way they express ideas
○ to take account of children's interests and experiences when planning learning opportunities.

General principles of Jean Piaget's cognitive theories

1 Children are *actively* involved in structuring their own cognitive development through exploration of their environment. Children need real objects and 'concrete experiences' to discover things for themselves.

2 The adult's role is to provide children with appropriate experiences in a suitable environment to facilitate the children's instinctive ability to think and learn.

3 Cognitive development occurs in four set stages, which are universal – they apply to all forms of learning and across all cultures. These four stages are: **sensori-motor**; **pre-operations**; **concrete operations**; and **formal operations** (See Diagram A).

Diagram A:

---

1. Sensori-motor (0–2 years)
- babies and very young children learn through their senses, physical activity and interaction with their immediate environment
- they understand their world in terms of actions.

---

2. Pre-operations (2–7 years)
- young children learn through their experiences with real objects in their immediate environment
- they use symbols (e.g. words and images) to make sense of their world.

---

3. Concrete operations (7–11 years)
- children continue to learn through their experiences with real objects
- they access information (using language) to make sense of their immediate and wider environment.

---

4. Formal operations (11–adult)
- children and adults learn to make use of abstract thinking (e.g. algebra, physics)

Piaget's stages of cognitive
development

4 Children will only learn when they are 'ready' for different experiences as determined by their current stage of cognitive development.

5 Children's use of language demonstrates their cognitive achievements, but does not control them. Piaget did not see language and communication as central to children's cognitive development because this development begins at birth before children can comprehend or use words. He does see the importance of language at later stages.

6 Children are **egocentric**. They are unable to see or understand another person's viewpoint. This also means they are unable to convey information accurately or effectively to others.

7 Piaget believed that children interact with their environment to actively construct their knowledge and understanding of the world. They do this by relating new information to existing information.

Piaget called this interaction:

○ **assimilation**: the need for further information;
○ **accommodation**: the need for organised information;
○ **adaptation**: the need for revised/up-dated information. (See Diagram B.)

All new information has to be built on existing information; there needs to be some connection between them. *Similar* information can be stored as it relates to existing information.

Diagram B:

Using Piaget's ideas of assimilation, accommodation and adaptation to understand how the brain processes information:

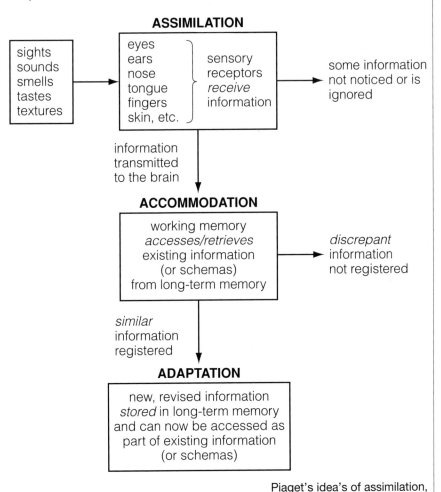

Piaget's idea's of assimilation, accommodation and adaptation

8 Piaget described internal mental processes as **schemas** and the ways in which they are used when thinking as **operations**. Mental processes or schemas do not remain static; they continually develop as we acquire new information and extend our understanding of the world.

EXERCISE:
Make a list of the main points of Piaget's theories of cognitive development.
Which points do you think accurately describe children's thinking and learning?
Give examples from your experiences of working with pupils.

The learning process: a social constructivist view

The social constructivist view of the learning process takes into account more recent research concerning how children think and learn within the context of home, school and the wider environment. Social constructivism integrates children's cognitive and social development within a useful framework. It moves away from the idea that the development of children's cognitive abilities occurs in stages at particular ages and that adults simply provide the means for this natural process. Rather adults assist children's cognitive development as part of the **social process** of childhood. Age is not the critical factor in cognitive development; assisted learning can and does occur at *any* age. The **key factor** is the learner's *existing* knowledge and/or experience in connection with the *current* problem or learning situation.

Like Piaget, L.S. Vygotsky was concerned with the active process of intellectual development. Vygotsky argued that cognitive development was not just a matter of the maturation of intellectual processes, but of 'active adaptation' to the environment. The interaction *between* the child and *other* people forms the basis of the developing intellectual processes *within* the child. This social interaction enables children to develop the intellectual skills necessary for thought and logical reasoning. Language is the key to this interaction. Through language and communication children learn to think about their world and to modify their actions accordingly.

Vygotsky (and later Bruner) viewed the adult as supporting children's cognitive development within an appropriate framework (See **scaffolding** below). Adults support children's learning by assisting the children's own efforts and thus enabling children to acquire the necessary skills, knowledge and understanding. As children develop competent skills through this **assisted learning**, the adults gradually decrease their support until the children are able to work independently. With adult assistance young children are able to complete tasks and to solve problems which they would not be able to do on their own. It is important that adults recognise when to provide support towards each child's next step of development and when this support is no longer required. Vygotsky used the idea of the **zone of proximal development** or area of next development to describe this framework of support for learning. The zone of proximal development can be represented in four stages (Tharp and Gallimore, 1991). For example, a pupil learning to read may progress in this way:

Stage 1: Assistance from others: Learns phonic, decoding and comprehension skills with assistance of parents, teachers, nursery nurses and/or teaching assistants.

Stage 2: Self-help: Sounds out difficult/unfamiliar words, reads aloud to self, lips move during silent reading, etc.

Stage 3: Auto-pilot: Reads competently using internal prompts.

Stage 4: Relapses to previous stages: When learning new words, reading complicated texts or learning to read in a different language may require further assistance.

Jerome Bruner (like Vygotsky) emphasises the importance of the adult in supporting children's thinking and learning. Bruner uses the term **scaffolding** to describe this adult support. Picture a builder using scaffolding to support a house while it is being built. Without the scaffold the house could not be built; but once the house is finished, the scaffolding can be removed. The adult supports the child's learning until they are ready to stand alone. Bruner also emphasises the adult's **skills** of recognising where and when this support is needed and when it should be removed. The structuring of children's learning should be flexible; the adult support or scaffold should not be rigid; it needs to change as the needs of the child change, that is as the child gains knowledge and understanding and/or acquires skills. Bruner believed that any subject can be taught to any child at any age as long as it is presented in an appropriate way. Learning does not occur in pre-determined **stages**, but is dependent on linking knowledge to children's existing knowledge in a holistic way.

Bruner's **sequence** of cognitive development is divided into three areas:

- O **Enactive:** understanding the world through action (relates to Piaget's sensori-motor stage)
- O **Iconic:** manipulation of images or 'icons' in child's thinking about the world (corresponds to Piaget's pre-operational stage)
- O **Symbolic:** use of language and symbols to make sense of the world (similar to Piaget's operational stage).

Bruner also views language as central to cognitive development and stresses how language is used to represent experiences and how past experience/knowledge is organised through language in ways which make information more accessible.

EXERCISE:
1. Summarise the main points of Vygotsky's and Bruner's theories concerning children's thinking and learning.
2. Think about how these ideas are related to your experiences of working with pupils.

How children think and learn

Learning pathways

Every learning experience can be viewed as a journey, travelling along different pathways to reach our destination or learning goal (Drummond,1994). At different points of a learning experience the learning may be:

- O very easy – speeding along a clear motorway
- O interesting, but uncertain in parts – taking the scenic route
- O very difficult and complicated – stuck in a traffic jam on Spaghetti junction
- O totally confusing – trying to find the correct exit from a big road traffic island
- O completely beyond us – entering a no-through road or going the wrong way down a one-way street.

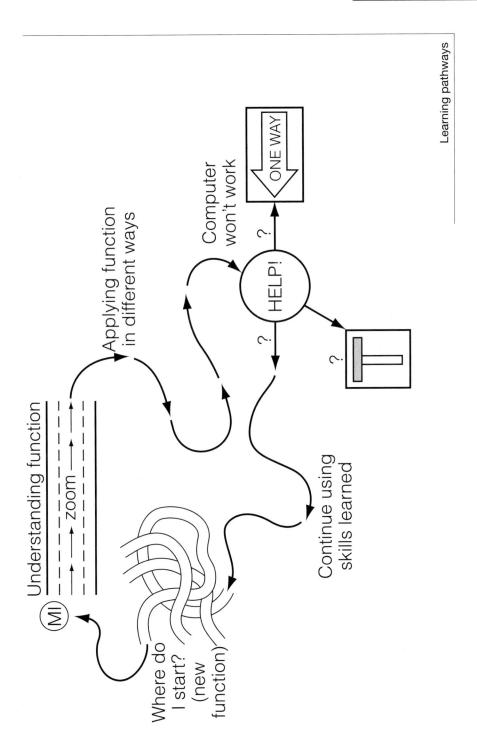

Learning pathways

MI

Understanding function

zoom

Applying function
in different ways

Where do
I start?
(new
function)

Computer
won't work

HELP!

?

?

?

ONE WAY

Continue using
skills learned

EXERCISE:
Think about your own experiences of learning:
- as an adult (e.g. learning to drive, cook, study; becoming a teaching assistant)
- as a child (e.g. learning to tie shoe laces, read, ride a bike, swim).

Draw diagrams to show your learning pathways or journeys. Your pictures might look something like the previous diagram.

Patterns of learning

The experience of learning is a never-ending cycle; learning new skills continues indefinitely. Once one skill is gained in a particular area, further skills can be learned. For example, once pupils have learned basic reading skills, they continue to develop their literacy skills even as adults by:

○ increasing their vocabulary
○ improving spelling
○ decoding unfamiliar words
○ reading and understanding more complex texts.

EXERCISE:
Think about the learning experiences of the pupils in your school. Select two pupils and draw diagrams of their learning experiences. Compare them with your own experiences of learning. Are there any similarities or differences?

As well as the circular nature of learning experiences, you may also have noticed the importance of *active participation* in all learning experiences. Watching someone else use a computer or read a book can only help so much – to develop the relevant skills, people need hands-on experience of using the computer or handling books.

Learning styles

Visual learners   gather information through observation and reading. Pupils with this learning style may find it difficult to concentrate on spoken instructions, but respond well to visual aids such as pictures, diagrams and charts. They tend to visualise ideas and remember the visual details of places and objects they have seen. According to research about 65 per cent of people have this learning style.

Auditory learners   process information by listening carefully and then repeating instructions either out loud or mentally in order to remember what they have learned. Research suggests that about 30 per cent of people use this style of learning. Pupils with this learning style tend to be the talkers as well as the listeners in group/class situations and benefit from being able to discuss ideas. Auditory learners can be easily distracted by noise and may concentrate better with background music to disguise potentially disruptive noises.

Kinesthetic learners   process information through touch and movement. All young children rely on this learning style to a large extent hence the importance of **active learning** (see below) especially in the early years. About 5 per cent of people continue to use this style even as adults. Pupils with this learning style benefit from physical interaction with their environment with plenty of emphasis on **learning by doing**.

People are not restricted to learning in only one way, pupils can learn to use different learning styles for different activities within the curriculum. However, research shows that working outside their preferred learning style for extensive periods can be stressful. Providing opportunities for pupils to use their preferred learning style wherever practical increases their chances of educational success. (Tobias, C. 1996.)

As well as relying on one particular style of learning, people also tend to use one of two styles of **processing information:**

o analytic
o global

Analytic learners process information by dividing it into pieces and organising it in a logical manner, for example, making lists, putting things in order, following clear instructions or rules and completing/handing in work on time. Analytic learners prefer order and a planned, predictable sequence of events or ideas.

Global learners process information by grouping large pieces of information together and focusing on the main ideas rather than details, for example, drawing spidergrams, using pictures or key words, and ignoring or bending rules including missing deadlines. Global learners prefer spontaneity and activities that allow them creative freedom.

EXERCISE:
1. Think about how the pupil or pupils you work with gather information. Do they prefer to:
- work as an individual or in a group?
- follow step-by-step instructions or have open-ended projects?
- read and talk about work?
- engage in practical activities and experiment for themselves?
2. Think about how the pupils you work with process information. Are they analytic or global learners?

The importance of play and active learning

Play is an essential part of the learning process as it enables pupils to:

- learn about and understand the physical world
- develop individual skills and personal resources
- communicate and co-operate with others
- develop empathy for others
- make sense of the world in relation to themselves
- do their own learning, in their own time and in their own way.

To pupils of *all* ages play involves:

- investigation – *What can this do? How does it work?*
- frustration – *I can't get it to work!*
- concentration – *trying hard to work it out.*
- satisfaction – *it works! Now what else can it do?*

How play helps children's thinking and learning

Creative play

Activities such as painting, drawing, model-making and music encourage:

o understanding of concepts, such as shape and colour
o development of visual discrimination and hand-eye co-ordination through pencil/brush control, using scissors
o exploration of the properties of materials e.g. textures
o problem-solving skills
o devising and using own ideas.

Imaginative play

Activities such as role play, dressing-up, dolls, puppets and drama encourage:

o language and communication skills which are essential to the thinking and learning process
o understanding of weighing and measuring through shop play
o understanding of volume/capacity and physical forces through sand and water play
o awareness of moral concepts such as sharing and helping others.

Physical play

Activities like outdoor play, ball games, gymnastics and athletics encourage:

o awareness of spatial relationships
o body awareness
o understanding of positional relationships (e.g. over and under)
o visual perception – differentiating between objects, judging distances, ball skills
o awareness of fairness and safety.

Manipulative play

Activities involving matching, grading and fitting; jigsaws and table-top games encourage:

o hand–eye co-ordination
o awareness of spatial relationships (how things fit together and relate to each other)
o visual perception and discrimination (e.g. shape recognition)
o understanding of sequencing
o understanding of number through games which involve counting
o understanding of turn-taking, following the rules of the game.

Research shows that play activities are effective in developing pupils' thinking and learning by providing opportunities for:

o well-motivated learning
o challenging and interesting learning experiences

Learning through play

o pupils to take responsibility for their own learning and to gain independence
o co-operative work between pupils
o developing problem-solving skills and improving concentration
o encouraging imagination and creativity.

As a teaching assistant, you can promote learning through play by:

1 Providing challenging and interesting play opportunities appropriate to pupils' needs, interests and abilities.

2 Providing varied resources and encouraging pupils to use them.

3 Participating in pupils' play, where appropriate, to stimulate language and extend learning.

4 Intervening *only* when appropriate to avoid stifling pupils' language or creativity.

5 Encouraging social interaction during play; some pupils may need coaxing to join in, others may need guidance on taking turns and sharing.

6 Linking play activities to real life situations (e.g. shop play links with real shopping trips)

7 Encouraging pupils' own imagination and creative ideas.

8 Being clear about your/the teacher's plans for play – what are the learning goals for the pupils? (See Chapter 5: Planning Learning Activities.)

EXERCISE:
Give an example of a play activity which you have used to assist a pupil's thinking and learning. Suggest other play activities which might extend this learning.

Active learning is an important part of all learning experiences. Not just for children but for adults as well. For example, at college/school you may find that learning situations take the form of workshops, group activities and discussions rather than formal lectures. It is essential that pupils become **actively** involved in the learning process. Learning needs to be practical not theoretical. Pupils need *concrete* learning experiences; that is, using real objects in a meaningful context. Children (and adults) learn by *doing*. Lectures would be a waste of time for children. Indeed, traditional lectures *are* a waste of time even for adults! This is because the average attention-span of an adult is 20 minutes! (This is why commercials are shown about every 20 minutes on television.) The average attention-span of a child is considerably less, more like 5–10 minutes or even as little as 2–3 minutes. In all learning situations it is important to provide information in small portions with plenty of discussion and activity breaks to maintain interest and concentration.

Active learning encourages pupils to be:

☆ Curious
☆ Handy at problem-solving
☆ Imaginative
☆ Creative.

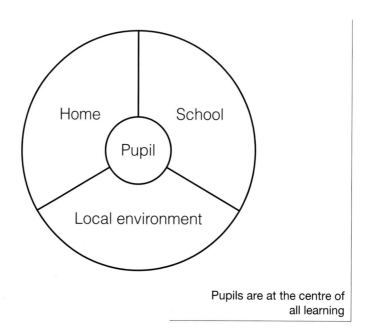

Pupils are at the centre of
all learning

What is intellectual development?

Intellectual or cognitive development involves the process of:

○ **gaining**
○ **storing**   ⎤
○ **recalling**   ⎦— **INFORMATION**
○ **using**

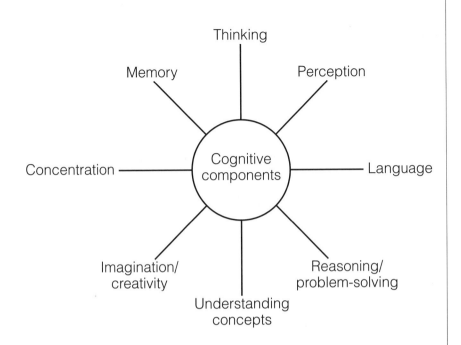

The inter-related cognitive components
of intellectual development

Thinking

Thinking can be defined as:

o *cognitive* – it occurs in the mind
o *a process* – it involves using or processing information
o *directed* – it works towards finding solutions.

We cannot see a person's thoughts because the thinking process is internal.
We can see the process and progress of a person's thinking through their
actions and **communications**.

Perception

Perception involves the ability to identify the differences between objects or
sounds. There are two types of perception:

o *auditory* – differentiating between sounds
o *visual* – differentiating between objects or the distance between objects.

Children use their senses to explore the objects and sounds in the world around them.

Language

Language provides the means to:

- make sense of the world around us
- process information in a more accessible form (before language, information is stored/recalled through images); language enables us to store more information and to make better connections between existing information and new information
- understand concepts
- interact with others to gain new experiences and information
- communicate more effectively with others (e.g. asking questions/ understanding the answers)
- verbalise and express our thoughts, opinions and ideas.

Language has such a key role to play in children's development that it is dealt with separately in Chapter 7.

Reasoning/problem-solving

Reasoning involves:

- using intellectual processes to make personal judgements
- making connections between existing information and new information
- problem-solving and the ability to think logically.

People use their existing knowledge and past experiences to solve problems. Children (and adults) often supplement their lack of knowledge or experience by experimenting – a process of *trial and error*. Making mistakes is part of the learning process. By using logic, people can make reasonable assumptions or predictions about what might happen in a particular situation or to a particular object. Logical thinking and problem-solving are essential to the ability to make mathematical calculations and scientific discoveries.

Understanding Concepts

Concepts are the ways in which people make sense of and organise the information in the world around them. Concepts can be divided into two categories: **concrete** and **abstract**.

Concrete concepts
Mathematical concepts include:

- sorting and counting – making comparisons, being able to discriminate between objects; matching objects, making sets
- number – understanding and using number; number/numeral recognition

and formation; number patterns; number operations (e.g. addition, subtraction, multiplication, division)

o sequencing – putting things in order; knowing and understanding number sequence
o weighing and measuring – making comparisons (e.g. heavy/light, long/short)
o volume and capacity – understanding that some objects hold more than others.

Scientific concepts include:

o object permanence – understanding that when an object is out of sight it still exists
o space – relating objects to each other and the gaps between them
o colour – distinguishing between colours; matching, naming and using colours; understanding colours in the environment (e.g. *red* means stop, *green* means go)
o shape – recognising different shapes and sizes is part of *classification*
o texture – exploring the tactile qualities of objects
o living and growing – understanding the processes of humans, animals, plants
o physical forces – understanding hot/cold, light/dark, floating/sinking; the changing properties of materials (e.g. water can be steam or ice as well as liquid)

Positional relationships include:

o inside and outside
o over and under
o same and different   — understanding the position of objects
o near and far
o high and low

Abstract concepts
Moral concepts include:

o right and wrong – understanding what is/is not acceptable behaviour
o fairness/justice – understanding that goodness is not always rewarded, but that we still need to do what is right
o helping others – recognising the needs and feelings of others
o sharing – understanding the importance of turn-taking, co-operating
o freedom – developing empathy for others and their beliefs even if we disagree with them.

Time   Understanding the sequence of events and the passage of time. Time waits for no one, not even children! This is a difficult concept for children to understand as they think the world revolves around them. Understanding time involves knowledge and awareness of:

○ today, tomorrow, yesterday
○ times of the day (morning, afternoon, evening)
○ days of the week, months and seasons
○ *before* and *after*
○ *next* – next week, next month, next year
○ telling the time (e.g. 8 o'clock, half past eight; 8:00, 8:30; 20.00, 20.30)

Higher number operations include:

○ understanding and using numbers *without* real objects (mental arithmetic, doing sums)
○ understanding and using more complex number operations such as algebra and physics.

Young children take longer to understand abstract concepts, but this depends on their individual learning experiences. For example, many children *do* understand the ideas concerning fairness and the rights of people (and animals) to live in freedom if these concepts are linked with *real* events.

Imagination and creativity

Imagination involves the ability to invent ideas or form images of things that are not actually there or do not exist. Creativity is the *use* of imagination in a wide variety of activities including:

○ play
○ art and design
○ music, dance and drama
○ books and stories.

Concentration

Concentration involves the ability to pay attention to the situation or task in hand. A person's concentration level or attention span is the length of time they are able to focus on a particular activity. Some children can concentrate for quite a long time, while some children (and adults!) find their attention starts to wander after just a few minutes. This may be due to a mismatch of activities to the individual's needs, interests and abilities, which can lead to boredom and a lack of concentration. A condition know as Attention Deficit Disorder (ADD) or Attention Deficit Hyperactive Disorder (ADHD) may also be responsible for poor concentration in certain people (see Chapter 2 for more information). Concentration is a key intellectual skill, which is necessary for the development of other cognitive processes such as conceptual understanding and language.

Memory

The other cognitive processes would be of no use to individuals without memory. Memory involves the ability to recall or retrieve information stored in the mind. Memory skills involve:

○ **recalling information** on past experiences, events, actions or feelings
○ **recognising information** and making connections with previous experiences
○ **predicting** – using past information to anticipate future events

Many cognitive processes involve all three memory skills, for example problem-solving activities in mathematics and science or the decoding and comprehension skills needed for reading.

EXERCISE:
From your experiences of working with pupils, list examples of activities that you think encourage and extend their cognitive/intellectual skills in each of the following:

1. Thinking
2. Perception
3. Language
4. Reasoning/problem-solving
5. Understanding concepts
6. Imagination and creativity
7. Concentration
8. Memory.

The sequence of intellectual development

You need to think in terms of a **sequence** of development rather than **stages** when looking at a pupil's intellectual capabilities. This is because intellectual development is affected by other factors besides the individual's chronological age. Factors affecting pupils' intellectual development include:

○ lack of play opportunities
○ unrewarding learning experiences
○ lack of opportunities to use language and communication skills
○ inappropriate learning experiences
○ introduction to formal learning situations at too early an age
○ physical skills (e.g. fine motor control is needed for hand-eye co-ordination)
○ cognitive difficulties.

The chart shown here only shows specific ages to indicate the **milestones** of *expected* intellectual development to help your knowledge and understanding of pupils' development. Remember all pupils are *individuals* and develop at their own rate. Please note that language abilities are not included in this chart although they are crucial to intellectual development. The sequence of language development is covered in detail in Chapter 7.

The Sequence of Intellectual Development: 3 to 16 years

Age 3–4 years
○ learns about basic concepts through play
○ experiments with colour, shape and texture
○ recalls a simple sequence of events
○ follows two- or three-step instructions including positional ones (e.g. 'Please put your ball in the box under the table')
○ enjoys imaginative and creative play
○ interested in more complex construction activities
○ concentrates on more complex activities as attention-span increases
○ plays co-operatively with other children; able to accept and share ideas in group activities
○ shows some awareness of right and wrong, and the needs of others
○ holds strong opinions about likes and dislikes
○ processes information using language.

Age 4–7 years
○ learns to read
○ is still very curious and asks lots of questions
○ continues to enjoy imaginative and creative play activities
○ continues to enjoy construction activities; spatial awareness increases
○ knows, matches and names colours and shapes
○ follows three-step instructions
○ develops interest in reading for themselves
○ enjoys jigsaw puzzles and games
○ concentrates for longer (e.g. television programmes, longer stories and can recall details)
○ shows awareness of right and wrong, and the needs of others
○ begins to see other people's points of view
○ stores and recalls more complex information using language.

Age 7–11 years
○ learns to read more complex texts
○ enjoys number work, but may still need real objects to help mathematical processes

o enjoys experimenting with materials and exploring the environment
o develops creative abilities as co-ordination improves e.g. more detailed drawings
o begins to know the difference between real and imaginary, but still enjoys imaginative play e.g. acting out ideas, pretending to be characters from television or films
o interested in more complex construction activities
o has longer attention-span; does not like to be disturbed during play activities
o follows increasingly more complex instructions
o enjoys board games and other games with rules; also computer games
o develops a competitive streak
o has increased awareness of right and wrong; and the needs of others
o sees other people's points of view
o seeks information from various sources (e.g. encyclopaedia, Internet)
o processes expanding knowledge and information through language.

Age 11–16 years
o reads more complex texts with improved comprehension
o develops understanding of abstract mathematical/scientific processes (e.g. algebra, physics)
o continues to enjoy experiments and exploration of the wider environment
o develops more creative abilities (e.g. very detailed drawings and stories)
o knows the difference between real and imaginary
o has increased concentration levels
o continues to follow more complex instructions
o continues to enjoy board games and computer games which require strategy skills
o has a competitive streak and may have particular interests which allow them to show off their intellectual abilities (e.g. chess, computer clubs)
o has well-defined understanding of right and wrong; can consider the needs of others
o sees other people's point of view
o continues to seek information from various sources (e.g. encyclopaedia, Internet)
o continues to process increasing knowledge and information through language.

Developing pupils' memory skills

A person's mind is like a computer, which stores information using a system of files to link different pieces of information together. Relating new information to existing information through this system makes it easier to access and use information. Information is stored in the short-term (or working) memory for about 10–20 seconds; from there the information is either forgotten or is passed on to the long-term memory where it is linked to existing stored information and 'filed' for future reference. (Look back at the diagram on how the brain processes information on page 77.)

Information is more likely to be stored and remembered if:

○ it is repeated several times
○ it is linked effectively to existing information (e.g. through personal experiences).

Young children have a limited number of experiences so their 'filing' system is quite basic. Gradually children create new files and have more complex filing systems to store the ever-increasing amount of information they receive through their own experiences, interaction with others and by developing knowledge and understanding of their environment. There is no limit to the amount of information that can be stored in the long-term memory. The difficulty lies in accessing this stored information.

Most people are unable to recall events or experiences before the age of three. From birth to about three years old memories are stored using our senses (sight, sound, smell and touch) rather than language. Once we develop language, we use words rather than our senses to recall information and lose the ability to remember our earlier sensory memories. It is as if these earlier memories were stored using a card-index file and once we have installed our 'computerised' filing system we no longer require the old card files or cannot find them. As children get older the process of remembering relies more and more on being able to use language to organise and retrieve information effectively.

Pupils may have poor memory skills because they are:

○ not paying attention or listening carefully in the first place
○ anxious about remembering; being nervous and feeling under pressure can have a negative effect on memory skills (e.g. when revising for SATs or GCSEs)
○ upset by unpleasant associations with previous similar experiences and so subconsciously do not want to remember the new information
○ not aware that the information is important and needs to be remembered

○ unable to connect the information to existing knowledge or experiences

○ not able to understand or process the information because it is too difficult or inappropriate.

Ways to help pupils develop memory skills

1 Encourage pupils to use their senses to remember new experiences, especially sight, sound *and* touch.

2 Make sure pupils are *looking* and *listening* attentively when giving new information.

3 Encourage pupils to repeat instructions or new information to check their understanding.

4 Explain how new information is connected to the pupils' existing experiences and knowledge (e.g. by linking activities with a common theme).

5 Use *action* to reinforce new ideas. Remember active learning.

6 Give new information in small pieces so pupils can learn bit-by-bit.

7 Try not to pressurise pupils into recalling information. They will remember more if they are relaxed.

8 Encourage pupils to feel confident about their memory skills.

9 Demonstrate your own memory skills and show them that remembering is not too difficult.

10 Provide lots of opportunities for pupils to practise and revise information. Use a variety of ways to reinforce learning (e.g. songs, rhymes, games, or play activities).

Developing pupils' attention-span and concentration

Being able to concentrate is an important part of the learning process. Pupils with short attention-spans find it more difficult to take in new information; they may also need extra time to complete activities. Pupils need to be able to focus on one activity at a time without being distracted by other things. This is an essential skill for learning, particularly within schools. Concentrating enables pupils to get the most out of learning opportunities.

Activities within the school may require different kinds of concentration:

○ **passive concentration** – such as listening to instructions, listening to stories, watching television, assemblies o **active concentration** – such as creative activities, construction, sand/water play, imaginative play, problem-solving activities including mathematics and science, literacy activities.

Some pupils have no difficulty paying attention to activities requiring **passive** concentration for quite long periods, for example watching a video or television programme or listening to a story tape. Other pupils may not be able to pay attention to such activities for long but are totally engrossed in activities requiring **active** concentration such as constructing a model or completing a complex jigsaw.

All pupils have times when they find it more difficult to concentrate because:

o they are simply not interested in the activity
o the activity is inappropriate (e.g. too difficult or too easy)
o they are distracted by inner thoughts (day dreaming!)
o they are distracted by outside influences: other pupils talking to them or around them; noises such as traffic or other groups/classes; weather conditions (*windy* days often make pupils more boisterous and inattentive, *snow* may make them too excited to concentrate, *rain* may make them restless if they are cooped up indoors all day)
o they are too tired or unwell
o they are emotionally distressed
o they have Attention Deficit Hyperactivity Disorder (ADHD) (See Chapter 2).

Ways to improve pupil concentration

1 **Minimise distractions** by providing a suitable learning environment where pupils can concentrate without being continually distracted or interrupted. For example, provide a quiet area for activities which require more concentration; quiet times when noisy activities are not permitted; carpets and screens to minimise noise levels.

2 **Be sensitive to individual needs and concentration levels.** Be flexible. Provide enough time for activities to be completed without pupils feeling under pressure. Too much time and pupils can become bored and disruptive.

3 **Keep activities short** to begin with, then gradually increase the time as the pupil's concentration improves. Divide complex activities into smaller tasks to make it easier for pupils to concentrate.

4 **Check the pupils understand the instructions** by asking them to repeat back instructions. Repeat instructions yourself as necessary.

5 **Use children's names** when asking them a question or giving an instruction. This attracts their attention and can help to maintain concentration.

6 **Use eye contact.** Make sure the pupils are looking at you when you talk to them. This encourages better understanding and minimises distractions.

7 **Use positive feedback and praise to encourage concentration.** Provide incentives or rewards for achieving targets, e.g. smiley faces or merit points for completing tasks.

8 **Use memory games** to encourage and extend concentration levels.

9 **Encourage observational and investigative skills** by asking pupils to look for specific items e.g. 'treasure' hunt, bug hunt, colour search, classroom orienteering activities.

10 **Identifying sounds;** encourage pupils to listen out for a specific sound e.g. bell ringing, car passing, person walking in corridor. They will need to concentrate and screen for that sound. Identify everyday sounds on a tape or musical instruments behind a screen.

11 **Reading or telling stories** is an enjoyable way to encourage listening skills. Choosing stories of particular interest to the pupils will encourage their concentration. Increase the length/complexity of the story as the pupils' attention-span increases.

12 **Singing songs and rhymes** also improves concentration. For example, following a number sequence in songs like *Five brown teddies, Ten green bottles, When I was One ...*

Developing pupils' imagination and creativity

Imagination involves the individual's ability to invent ideas or to form images. Children express their imagination through imitative play to begin with and then gradually through imaginary play. Imagination is important to the development of children's thinking and learning. As children explore their environment and find out what objects and materials can do, they use their imagination to increase their understanding of the world and their role within it. For example, through pretend or imaginative play children can become other people by dressing-up and behaving like them. Imaginative play assists the development of children's imagination through activities such as dressing-up, doll play, shop play, hospital play, or small scale toys.

Creativity is the use of the imagination in a wide variety of activities including play, art, design technology, music, dance, drama, stories and poetry. Children can express their creativity through creative activities such as painting, drawing, collage, play dough, clay, cooking, or design and model making. Creativity involves a process rather than an end product; it cannot be measured by the end result of an activity, but is based upon *how* the child worked and *why*. Creativity involves:

○ exploring and experimenting with a wide range of materials
○ thinking and learning about the properties of materials (e.g. colour, shape, size, texture)
○ developing physical skills to manipulate materials
○ developing problem-solving techniques
○ developing an understanding of the world and our personal contribution to it.

 KEY TASK

Observe a pupil or group of pupils during a creative activity. In your assessment focus on the pupils' intellectual skills especially:

• imaginative and creative skills
• concentration levels
• problem-solving skills
• use of language.

Suggest ways to extend the pupils' creative skills including appropriate resources.

N.V.Q. Links: Level 2: 2–3.1, 2–3.2; Level 3: 3–7.1, 3–7.2, 3–8.1, 3–8.2, 3–3.1, 3–3.2

 KEY TASK

Plan and implement a creative activity with a pupil or group of pupils.

Discuss the plan with the teacher and/or your assessor and negotiate when it would be convenient for you to implement your activity. Review and evaluate the activity afterwards.

N.V.Q. Links: Level 2: 2–3.1, 2–3.2; Level 3: 3–3.1, 3–3.2, 3–8.1, 3–8.2

Developing pupils' understanding in mathematics and science

Mathematics and science rely on the ability to understand abstract ideas. For young children this means developing a sound knowledge and understanding of concrete concepts first such as number, weighing/measuring, volume/capacity, shape, colour, space, textures, growth and physical forces. Experiences with real objects enable young children to develop problem-solving skills and to acquire understanding of these concepts. Some concepts require the understanding of other concepts beforehand, e.g. understanding *number* and *counting* comes before *addition*; understanding *addition* comes before *multiplication*.

Adults working with pupils need to ensure that they provide activities at the appropriate level for the pupils' intellectual development. There should be a balance between encouraging younger pupils to develop their own problem-solving skills through play with minimal adult intervention and complying with the objectives of the National Curriculum (e.g. daily maths lesson) or the early learning goals for mathematics and knowledge/understanding of the world.

Science

Pupils need lots of opportunities to develop these scientific skills:

○ observe
○ investigate
○ predict
○ hypothesise
○ record.

Primary pupils

1 **Life processes and living things.** Sing songs and rhymes about ourselves and the human body e.g. *'I've got a body, a very busy body …'* , *'Head and shoulders …'*. Do topics on babies. Use matching and drawing activities to learn names of major body organs (e.g. heart and lungs) and where these organs are in the human body. Study animals and plants by: visiting nature/garden centres, parks and farms; keeping pets; growing seeds like beans, mustard and cress; having a nature table (remember health and safety.) Use key features to identify and group animals and plants.

2 **Materials and their properties.** Sort different materials into groups, using words to describe their properties such as shiny, hard or smooth. Observe the changing states of materials e.g. frozen water is ice, water vapour is steam. Experiment with different objects to see which will

float or sink. Use questions to encourage predictions: will all heavy objects sink? Will all light objects float? What happens if change object's shape? (e.g. plasticine in a ball sinks, when reshaped as a bowl or boat it floats). Provide tactile experiences such as sand/water play, collage, touch table, 'feely' bag/box, play dough, clay, and cooking sessions.

3 **Physical processes**. Use toys to explore ideas about forces and energy e.g. pulling, pushing, pull-back, wind-up, battery, remote-controlled and electrical toys. Explore ideas about the weather by: observing and talking about different weather conditions; keeping a weather chart; making a windmill; making paper snowflakes; sharing weather stories and rhymes e.g. discussing temperature differences like hot and cold. Make a bulb light up using a simple circuit with a battery and a switch. Draw diagrams of simple electrical circuits.

Secondary pupils

1 **Life processes and living things.** Use models to draw and describe the main functions of human organs (e.g. the heart and lungs). Draw and describe the life cycle of humans and flowering plants, explaining their similarities and differences. Do experiments to explain how environmental conditions affect where different kinds of animals and plants can live (e.g. growing plants in the dark or without water).

2 **Materials and their properties.** Use the properties of metals (e.g. all metals conduct electricity) to sort metals from other solid materials. Do experiments to show how changes such as evaporation take place. Do experiments to demonstrate how a particular mixture (e.g. oil and water) can be separated and suggest ways to separate other mixtures.

3 **Physical processes.** Make changes to a circuit using a larger battery to increase the current. Draw/write about how abstract ideas can be used to describe familiar things, such as 'forces are balanced when an object is stationary'. Make and/or use simple models to explain the effects caused by the movement of the Earth (e.g. the length of a day or a year).

(Suggestions for developing pupils' mathematical skills are included in Chapter 9.)

KEY TASK

Plan and implement an activity for a pupil or group of pupils which involves developing their scientific skills.

Encourage the pupils to explore using their senses and to use appropriate scientific language. Review and evaluate the activity afterwards.

N.V.Q. Links: Level 2: 2–3.1, 2–3.2; Level 3: 3–3.1, 3–3.2, 3–8.1, 3–8.2

Further reading...

Bruce, T. and Meggitt, C. (2002) *Child care and education.* 3rd edition. Hodder & Stoughton.

Moon, B. and Shelton Mayes (1993) *Teaching and learning in the secondary school.* Routledge.

Morris, J. and Mort, J. (1991) *Bright ideas for the early years: learning through play.* Scholastic.

Neaum, S. and Tallack, J. (1997) *Good practice in implementing the pre-school curriculum.* Stanley Thornes.

Tobias, C. (1996) *The Way They Learn.* Focus on the Family Publishing.

Willig, C. J. (1990) *Children's concepts and the primary curriculum.* Paul Chapman.

Wood, D. (1997) *How children think and learn (Understanding Children's Worlds).* Blackwell.

Wyse, D. and Hawtin, A. (1999) *Children: a multi-professional perspective.* Arnold. [Covers child development/learning from birth to 18 years.]

5 Planning Learning Activities

{

Key points:

- Observing and reporting on pupil performance
- Why, where, what and how to observe pupils
- The basic principles of observation
- Observation methods
- Assessing and reporting on pupil performance
- Planning and evaluating learning activities
- The planning cycle
- The importance of evaluating learning activities
- The National Curriculum framework
- The Foundation Stage and early learning goals

}

Observing and reporting on pupil performance

The role of the teaching assistant in observing and reporting on pupil performance

Accurate observations and assessments form the foundation for all effective educational practice. To keep precise and useful records you need to know the pupil or pupils you work with well. Careful observations enable you and the teacher to make objective assessments concerning pupils and their individual:

o behaviour patterns
o learning styles
o levels of development
o range of skills
o learning achievements
o learning needs/goals.

The methods for record keeping depend on school policies and any legal requirements. (See section on record keeping in Chapter 1.) You may be able to help the class or form teacher to compile a portfolio of relevant information about each pupil. A portfolio could include:

o observations
o examples of the pupil's work

o photographs of the pupil during learning activities
o checklists of the pupil's progress.

Assessment of this information can help highlight and celebrate the pupil's strengths as well as identify any gaps in their learning. This information can form the basis for the ongoing planning of appropriate learning activities and be a useful starting point for future learning goals/objectives.

Observations and assessments should cover all relevant aspects of pupil development including: physical skills; language and communication skills; social and emotional behaviour during different learning activities. There are various methods for observing and recording pupils' learning and behaviour including: free description, structured description, pre-coded categories or checklists, and sampling. (See page 110 for examples of observation methods.) The teacher and your college tutor/assessor will give you guidelines for the methods most appropriate to your role as a teaching assistant in your particular school. Your observations and assessments must be in line with the school policy for record keeping and relevant to the learning activities of the pupils you work with. You must follow the school policy regarding **confidentiality** at all times. Before doing any key tasks for NVQ assessment involving observations of pupils you MUST negotiate with the teacher when it will be possible for you to carry out your observations and have written permission to do so.

Exercise
Find out what your school's policies are regarding:
• pupil observations
• confidentiality.
Keep this information in mind when doing your own observations of pupils.

Why do you need to observe pupils?

There are many reasons why it is important to observe pupil performance:

o to understand the wide range of skills in all areas of development
o to know and understand the sequence of children's development
o to use this knowledge to link theory with your own practice in school
o to assess children's development and existing skills/behaviour
o to plan activities appropriate to pupils' individual learning needs.

Thinking about observing

Portfolio building
- what to include?
- how to use your portfolio

Issues to think through

Why observe?
- developing quality practice

Pass it on?
- whom to pass it on to?
- what to pass on?
- when to pass it on?

What to observe?
- the importance of quality observation
- meeting the requirements of the course
- recognising a suitable opportunity to observe

Making assessments
- background information
- aims
- areas of development
- recommendations
- personal learning
- bibliography

Where to observe?
- working in a variety of settings

Methods of recording observations
- choosing a suitable method
- advantages and disadvantages of each method
- record keeping

How to observe?
- planning
- preparation
- aims
- front sheet
- observing
- evaluations
- presenting work
- getting work assessed

Source: *How to Make Observations and Assessments* by J. Harding and L. Meldon-Smith (1996) Hodder and Stoughton.

How to make observations and assessments

Regular observations are also helpful in identifying any potential problems pupils may have in their development, learning or behaviour. The observing adult can identify:

o the way in which the pupil learns
o how the pupil interacts with others (e.g. behaviour and social skills)
o any difficulties in performing the activity

A continuous record of a pupil's learning difficulties can help the adult to identify specific problems. Working with parents, colleagues and specialist advisors (if necessary) the teacher can then plan a suitable programme to enable the pupil to overcome these difficulties. Observations can provide a check that the pupil's learning is progressing in the expected ways.

Exercise
Write a short account explaining why it is important to observe and assess pupils' behaviour and development.

Where and what should you observe?

Try to observe the pupil in a place in the classroom/school where there is not too much interference or interruptions. Make sure that the situation is realistic and not artificial; you will usually be observing learning activities that are part of the pupil's school routine. You can observe pupils' learning and behaviour in a variety of situations.

For example, you might observe the following situations:

o a pupil talking with another pupil or adult
o an adult working with a small group of pupils
o a pupil or a small group of pupils playing indoors/outdoors
o a pupil during small or large group discussions (e.g. circle time)
o an adult reading/telling a story to a pupil or group of pupils
o a pupil or group of pupils participating in a creative activity (e.g. painting, drawing, design)
o a pupil involved in a literacy activity (e.g. writing, reading, comprehension exercises)
o a pupil doing a mathematics or science activity (e.g. number work, an experiment).

The basic principles of observation

Some important points have already been mentioned with regard to observing pupils' development and learning. You also need to consider the following:

1 **Confidentiality** must be kept at all times. You *must* have the teacher's permission before making formal observations of pupils.

2 **Be objective** – only record what you actually see and hear, not what you think or feel. For example, the statement '*The child cried*' is objective, but to say '*The child is sad*' is subjective, because you do not know what the child is feeling – the child could be crying for any number of reasons.

3 **Remember equal opportunities**. Consider children's cultural backgrounds e.g. pupils may be very competent at communicating in their community language, but may have more difficulty in expressing themselves in English; this does *not* mean they are behind in their language development.

4 **Be positive!** Focus on the pupil's strengths not just on any learning or behavioural difficulties they may have. Look at what the pupil *can* do in terms of learning and use this as the foundation for providing future learning activities.

5 **Use a holistic approach.** Remember to look at the 'whole' child. You need to look at *all* areas of a pupil's development in relation to the particular aspect of development or learning you are focusing on. For example, when observing a pupil's writing skills as well as looking at their intellectual development you will need to consider: their physical development (fine motor skills when using a pencil/pen); their language development and communication skills (vocabulary and structure of language used); their social and emotional development (interaction with others and behaviour during the activity).

6 **Consider the pupil's feelings.** Try not to make it obvious that you are observing; keep your distance where possible, but be close enough to hear the pupil's language. Where observation is obvious (e.g. tape recording) explain to the pupil simply what you are doing. Try not to interact with the pupil (unless it is a participant observation – see below), but if they do address you be polite and respond positively, keeping your answers short.

7 **Practise.** The best way to develop your skills at observing pupils' learning and behaviour is to have a go at doing observations, and keep on doing them.

How to observe pupils

When observing pupils you need to use an appropriate method of observation as directed by the teacher. When assisting the teacher in observing and reporting on a pupil's development ensure that you include all relevant aspects of development using:

☆ Social   ☆ Physical   ☆ Intellectual   ☆ Communication   ☆ Emotional.

You will probably observe a pupil or group of pupils on several occasions on different days of the week and at different times of the day. Use developmental charts for the pupil's age group to identify areas of development where the pupil is making progress, as well as those where the pupil is underachieving. For example, a pupil with limited speech may still be developing positive social relationships with other children by using non-verbal communication during play activities.

Types of observation

- **Naturalistic:** observation of pupil doing usual classroom activities (e.g. playing a game)
- **Structured:** observation of pupil during a particular activity set up to gain specific information about the pupil's learning or behaviour (e.g. a literacy activity to assess a pupil's comprehension skills)
- **Snapshot:** observation of pupil at a specific time (e.g. recording social interaction and behaviour during play time)
- **Longitudinal:** observations of pupil over a period of time (e.g. observing and recording pupil's language and literacy skills on a weekly basis for a year).

Accurate observation is the basis for sound educational practice

Methods of observation

o **Time sampling:** observation of pupil's behaviour at regular intervals during a set period of time, e.g. every ten minutes during a lesson. Time sampling can provide a clearer picture of behaviour changes throughout a lesson or day and help to identify when certain behaviour occurs during which activities.

o **Event sampling:** observations of particular events as they occur, e.g. pupil's emotional outbursts. A record is made of the number of times the target behaviour occurs, when it occurs and how long it lasts.

o **Participant:** observation where the observer is also involved in the pupil's activity.

o **Non-participant:** observation involves being as unobtrusive as possible while other members of staff assist pupil as necessary during the activity.

o **Target child:** observation concentrating on one particular pupil.

o **Trail or movement:** observations to monitor behaviour. On a plan of the classroom, lines are drawn indicating the movements of the pupil with brief notes about the length of time spent in each area, the pupil's behaviour and any social interaction.

Other useful methods for observing learning and/or behaviour include **checklists, coded observations** and **diaries.** Some observations of pupils may not be planned, for example you may take note of a pupil's unusual behaviour during an activity.

Assessing and reporting on pupil performance

Once you have recorded your observation of the pupil (or group of pupils), you need to **assess** this information in relation to:

o the aims of the observation
o what you observed about the pupil's learning and/or behaviour in *this* activity
o how this compares to the expected level of development/learning for a pupil of this age
o any factors that may have affected the pupil's ability to learn/behave, such as the immediate environment, significant events, illness, pupil's cultural background, special needs.

Observations require assessment of pupils' developmental progress, skills and/or behaviour. There are four stages in this assessment. Imagine a court case where evidence is being given by various people concerning the pupil's learning and development:

1 *The 'eye-witness'.* This is *your* statement of what actually happened; what you observed during the observation. Remember to concentrate

on the main focus of the observation (e.g. the pupil's writing skills during a literacy activity) , but include information on other related aspects of development (e.g. fine motor skills used for writing).

2 *The 'expert witness'.* Refer to at least two textbooks and see what education/psychology authors have to say about children's development. State the expected levels of development, as described by the experts, for children of the same age as the pupil you observed.

3 *The 'summing-up'.* With the information from your observation and the opinions of the experts, you can now make an assessment of the pupil's learning and development. Compare and contrast the similarities and differences between the abilities/skills demonstrated by the pupil during the observation with the levels of expected development, e.g. how this pupil's abilities compare to the intellectual development and literacy skills as expected for pupils of this particular age.

4 *The 'verdict'.* From this comparison, draw your own conclusions regarding the pupil's learning and development; state whether you think the pupil's abilities are ahead, equal to or behind the expected level of development as outlined by the experts. Remember to be tactful in your comments; also be positive! Your conclusions should focus on what the pupil **can** do. Do not forget to mention other factors that might affect the pupil's learning and development in general or in this particular activity. Include comments on how other aspects of the pupil's development affected the pupil's abilities in the focus area (e.g. poor concentration or limited motor skills); you should always look at the whole child.

When you have made your assessment, you need to record it accurately and legibly in an agreed format. This might be:

o A written descriptive account
o A structured profile (with specified headings for each section)
o A pre-coded system of recording.

Your assessment may include charts, diagrams and other representations of the data you collected from your observation (see pages 112 and 113).

Your college tutor or assessor should give you guidelines on how to present your observations. Otherwise you might find this suggested format useful:

Suggested format for presenting observations:

Date of observation:

Method:

Start time:

Finish time:

No. of pupils/staff:

Permission for observation:

Type of school and class: (*e.g. primary, secondary or special; Key Stage/year group*)

Immediate context/background information: *including the activity and its location*

Description of pupil: *including age in years and months*

Aims: *why are you doing this particular observation?*

Observation: *the observation may be a written report, a tape recording with written transcript, a pie chart or bar graph, tick chart*

Assessment: *including the following*

- *did you achieve your aims?*
- *your assessment of the pupil's learning, development and/or behaviour, looking at all aspects of the pupil's development but with particular emphasis on the focus area (e.g. writing skills)*
- *references to support your comments.*

Personal learning: *what you gained from doing this observation, e.g. what you have learned about this aspect of child development and using this particular method of observing pupils; was this the most appropriate method of observation for this type of learning activity?*

Recommendations:

- *on how to encourage/ extend the pupil's learning and development in the focus area e.g. make suggestions for activities and experiences to develop the pupil's writing skills.*
- *for any aspect of the pupil's development which you think requires further observation and assessment.*

References/bibliography: *list details of all the books used to complete your assessment.*

Examples of observation charts:

Tick Chart: *Group observations of children at snack/meal time*

Self-help skills	Children's names			
	Shafik	Sukhvinder	Ruth	Tom
goes to the toilet				
washes hands				
dries hands				
chooses own snack/meal				
uses fingers				
uses spoon				
uses fork				
uses knife				
holds cup with 2 hands				
holds cup with 1 hand				

KEY:

✔ = competent at skill.

↘ = attempts skill/needs adult direction.

✘ = no attempt/requires assistance.

Pie chart: *Time sample observation of child's play activities*

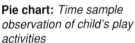
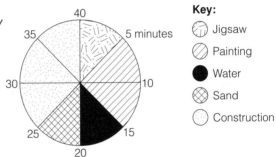

Key:

- Jigsaw
- Painting
- Water
- Sand
- Construction

Bar graph: *Time sample observation of child's social play*

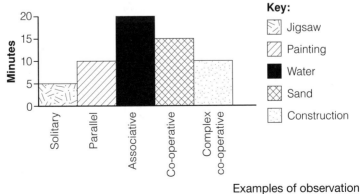

Key:

- Jigsaw
- Painting
- Water
- Sand
- Construction

Examples of observation charts

113

KEY TASK

1. Observe a pupil during a learning activity.
2. In your assessment, include information on:
   - The type of learning activity observed
   - The intended learning goals/objectives for the pupil
   - The actual development and learning skills demonstrated by the pupil
   - The pupil's behaviour during the activity
   - The pupil's language and communication skills
   - Suggestions for extending the pupil's learning in this area.

Use relevant chapters from this book (and education/psychology books) to help you with your assessment.

Remember to follow the school's guidelines for pupil observation.

NVQ Links: Level 2: 2–3.1; Level 3: 3–7.1, 3–7.2, 3–3.1, 3–8.1

Planning and evaluating learning activities

The role of the teaching assistant in planning and evaluating learning activities

As directed by the teacher, you will need to plan, implement and evaluate the learning activities of the pupil or pupils you work with in the school. When planning learning activities, your overall aims should be:

○ to support *all* the pupils you work with as directed by the teacher
○ to ensure each pupil has full access to the curriculum
○ to encourage participation by all pupils
○ to meet pupils' individual learning needs
○ to build on pupils' existing knowledge and skills
○ to help all pupils achieve their full learning potential.

Exercise
Describe how *you* plan, implement and evaluate learning activities for pupils in your school. Include examples of any planning and evaluation/record sheets you use.

The planning cycle

Following your observation and assessment of a pupil's learning, development and/or behaviour, your recommendations can provide the basis for planning appropriate activities to encourage and extend the pupil's abilities in specific areas.

Effective planning is based on pupils' individual needs, abilities and interests, hence the importance of accurate pupil observations and assessments. These needs have to be integrated into the curriculum requirements for your particular class; lessons and activities will be related to aspects of the National Curriculum at Key Stages 1–4 or to the early learning goals in the Foundation Stage (see pages 120–122).

Planning children's activities

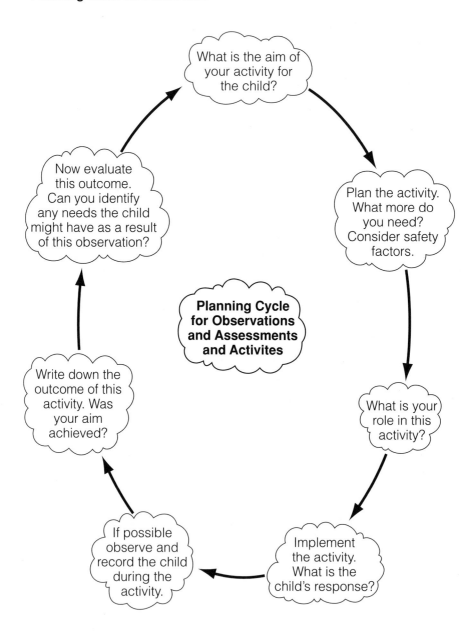

Source: *How to Make Observations and Assessments* by J.
Harding and L. Meldon-Smith (1996) Hodder and Stoughton.

Planning children's
activities

Exercise
Outline how observations fit into the planning cycle of providing
appropriate learning activities for the pupil or pupils you work with.

The importance of evaluating learning activities

After you have planned and/or implemented a learning activity, you will
need to evaluate it. Some evaluation also occurs during the activity,
providing continuous assessment of a pupil's performance. It is important to
evaluate the activity so that you can:

o discover if the activity has been successful, e.g. the aims and learning
   objectives or outcomes have been met
o consider the ways in which the activity might be modified/adapted to
   meet the needs of the pupil or pupils
o inform the teacher, SENCO or other professionals as to whether or not a
   particular activity has been successful.

You can evaluate learning activities by asking questions such as:

1   Did the pupil achieve the objectives/outcomes set? If not, why not?

2   If the pupil has achieved the objectives, what effect has it had? (e.g. on
    behaviour, learning, any special need).

3   Were the objectives too easy or too hard?

4   How did any staff involvement affect the pupil's achievement?

5   Was the lesson plan or overall curriculum plan successful? If not, why
    not?

Self-evaluation

Self-evaluation is needed to improve your own professional practice and to
develop your ability to reflect upon activities and modify plans to meet
the needs of the pupils. When evaluating your own practice you should
consider:

o Was your own contribution appropriate? Did you choose the right time,
   place and resources? Did you intervene enough or too much?
o Did you achieve your goals? (e.g. learning objectives/outcomes for the
   pupils and yourself). If not, why not? Were the goals too ambitious or
   unrealistic?
o What other strategies/methods could have been used? Suggest possible
   modifications.
o Who to ask for further advice? (e.g. class or subject teacher, SENCO).

The teacher and your college tutor/assessor should give you guidelines on how to present your activity plans. If not, you might find this suggested format useful:

Suggested format for activity plans:

- **Title:** *brief description of the activity*

- **Date:** *the date of the activity*

- **Plan duration:** *how long will the activity last?*

- **Aim and rationale:** *the main purpose of the activity including how it will encourage the pupil's or pupils' learning and development. The rationale should outline why you have selected this particular activity (e.g. identified particular pupil's need through observation; links to topics/themes within the setting). How does the activity link with any early learning goals or National Curriculum subjects?*

- **Staff and school:** *the roles and number of staff involved in the activity plus the type of school and Key Stage/year group of the pupil or pupils involved.*

- **Details of pupil(s):** *activity plans involving an individual pupil or small group of pupils should specify first name, age in years and months plus any relevant special needs; activity plans involving larger groups should specify the age range and ability levels.*

- **Objectives/learning outcomes for the pupil(s):** *these should indicate what the pupil(s) should gain from participating in the activity in each developmental area:*

  Social, Physical, Intellectual, Communication, Emotional.

- **Preparation:** *what do you need to prepare in advance? (e.g. selecting or making appropriate materials; checking availability of equipment) Think about the instructions and/or questions for the pupil or pupils; will these be spoken and/or written down e.g. on a worksheet/card or on the board? Do you need prompt cards for instructions or questions?*

- **Resources:** *what materials and equipment will you need? Where will you get them from? Are there any special requirements? Remember equal opportunities including special needs. How will you set out the necessary resources? (e.g. set out on the table ready or the pupils getting materials and equipment out for themselves).*

- **Organisation:** *where will you implement the activity? How will you organise the activity? How will you give out any instructions the pupils*

---

need? Will you work with pupils one at a time or as a group? Are there any particular safety requirements? How will you organise any tidying up after the activity? Will the pupils be encouraged to help tidy up?

- **Implementation:** *describe what happened when you implemented the activity with the pupil or pupils. Include any alterations to your original plan e.g. changes in resources.*

- **Equal opportunities:** *indicate any multicultural aspects to the activity and any additional considerations for pupils with special needs.*

- **Review and evaluation:** *review and evaluate the following:*

  - *the aims and objectives/learning outcomes*
  - *the effectiveness of your preparation, organisation and implementation*
  - *what you learned about pupils' learning and development*
  - *what you learned about curriculum planning*
  - *possible modifications for future similar activities.*

- **References and/or bibliography:** *the review and evaluation may include references appropriate to pupils' learning and development. Include a bibliography of any books used as references or for ideas when planning the activity.*

 KEY TASK

Using your suggestions from the observation on page 114, plan a learning activity to extend the pupil's skills in a specific area. After discussing your plan with the teacher, implement and then evaluate the activity.

NVQ Links: Level 2: 2–3.1, 2–3.2; Level 3: 3–8.1, 3–8.2, 3–3.1, 3–3.2

Being flexible in planning activities

Careful planning of appropriate activities for pupils is necessary to ensure they have opportunities to develop knowledge and skills within a meaningful context. Even though pupils are working within the National Curriculum framework or towards the 'early learning goals', your planning needs to be flexible enough to allow for pupils' individual interests and unplanned, spontaneous opportunities for language and learning. For example, an unexpected snowfall can provide a wonderful opportunity to talk about snow and for pupils to share their delight and fascination for this type of weather. Other activities may be provided within the setting that allow more spontaneous opportunities for pupils to express themselves without adult direction. This does not mean without adult supervision, as obviously this is always necessary to maintain pupil safety. *Without adult direction* means pupils are **free to choose** what and when to do particular activities. For example: computers, drawing, painting, design/construction, pretend/role play and sand can often be provided as activities that pupils can choose (or not) to do when they feel they want/need to or after they have completed adult-directed tasks. It is important that pupils have this freedom of choice to help represent their experiences, feelings and ideas. Adults may still be involved in these activities, but in more subtle ways such as encouraging pupils to make their own decisions, or talking with pupils while they are engaged in these types of activities.

Exercise
Describe how you have made use of an unplanned learning opportunity.

Adults also need to be sensitive to pupils' individual needs and interests. Remember to observe the pupils while they are involved in the activities and assess whether you need to change or extend the activities to meet their learning and developmental needs more fully. In addition, planning activities may be based on Individual Education Plans (IEPs) or Behaviour Support Plans – see Chapter 6: Supporting Learning Activities.

The National Curriculum framework

The National Curriculum applies to pupils of compulsory school age in schools in England and Wales. It sets out what pupils should study, what they should be taught and the standards that they should achieve. It is divided into four **Key Stages**:

Key Stage 1	5–7 year olds Year groups: 1–2
Key Stage 2	7–11 year olds Year groups: 3–6
Key Stage 3	11–14 year olds Year groups: 7–9
Key Stage 4	14–16 year olds Year groups: 10–11

The National Curriculum is divided into three **core subjects**:

o English
o Mathematics
o Science.

There are also nine **foundation subjects**:

o Design and technology
o Information and communication technology
o History
o Geography
o Modern foreign languages (not Key Stages 1 and 2)
o Art and design
o Music
o Physical education
o Citizenship.

For every Key Stage and subject area of the National Curriculum there are:

1 Programmes of study.

2 Attainment targets and level descriptions.

Programmes of study

Programmes of study provide detailed information on what pupils should be taught in each subject at each of the Key Stages. They provide the framework for planning schemes of work in schools. The National Literacy and Numeracy Strategies, as well as examples of schemes of work, demonstrate how the programmes of study and attainment targets can be converted into practical plans for effective teaching and learning.

Attainment targets and level descriptions

Each attainment target defines the *'knowledge, skills and understanding which pupils of different abilities and maturities are expected to have by the end of each Key Stage'* (Education Act 1996, section 353a). Except for citizenship, attainment targets contain nine level descriptions of increasing difficulty including a description for exceptional pupil performance. Each description explains the types and range of pupil performance at that particular level. These descriptions form the criteria for assessments of pupils' performance at the end of each Key Stage except Key Stage 4 (see below).

Pupils are assessed by national tests at the end of each Key Stage.

o Key Stage 1 assessments are taken at age 7

- Key Stage 2 assessments are taken at age 11
- Key Stage 3 assessments are taken at age 14
- Key Stage 4 is assessed by levels of achievement acquired at GCSE level.

When planning learning activities, schools also need to consider the **four general teaching requirements:**

1   Inclusion: providing effective learning opportunities for all pupils.

2   Use of language across the curriculum.

3   Use of information and communication technology across the curriculum.

4   Health and safety.

Please note that in Scotland there is no legally established National Curriculum, but the Scottish Executive Education Department provides guidelines for schools. In Northern Ireland the curriculum guidance is provided by the Northern Ireland Council for Curriculum, Examinations and Assessment.

The Foundation Stage

The National Curriculum only applies to pupils of statutory school age. For pupils in nursery and reception classes schools need to follow the **Curriculum guidance for the Foundation Stage** (DfES/QCA, May 2000). This sets out the **early learning goals** for children aged 3–5 years within six areas of learning:

- personal, social and emotional development
- communication, language and literacy
- mathematical development
- knowledge and understanding of the world
- physical development
- creative development.

The guidance also outlines '**stepping stones**' towards the early learning goals to help early years practitioners understand the knowledge, skills and attitudes young children should achieve throughout the foundation stage. The stepping stones show progression using yellow, blue and then green bands.

Exercise
1. What is the planning framework for the pupils you work with?
2. Provide examples of the planning you and the teacher use within this framework e.g. topic webs, overall plans, etc.

Further reading...

Harding, J. and Meldon-Smith, L. (2000) *How to make observations and assessments.* 2nd Edition. Hodder & Stoughton.

Hobart, C. and Frankel, J. (1994) *A practical guide to child observation.* Stanley Thornes.

Steiner, B. *et al* (1993) *Profiling, recording and observing – a resource pack for the early years.* Routledge.

Hobart, C. and Frankel, J. (1994) *A practical guide to activities for young children.* Stanley Thornes.

Morris, J. and Mort, J. (1997) *Bright ideas for the early years: learning through play.* Scholastic.

Qualifications and Curriculum Authority (2000) *Curriculum guidance for the foundation stage.* QCA.

6 Supporting Learning Activities

{
Key points:

The teaching assistant's role in supporting:
- Pupils during learning activities
- Pupils with general learning difficulties
- Pupils with specific learning difficulties
- Pupils with exceptional abilities
- Pupils with hearing impairment
- Pupils with visual impairment
- Pupils with physical impairment
- Pupils with structured learning programmes
- The use of ICT in the classroom
}

Supporting pupils during learning activities

Providing support for learning activities

To develop into healthy, considerate and intelligent adults, pupils require intellectual stimulation as well as physical care and emotional security. The pupils you work with will be constantly thinking and learning; gathering new information and formulating new ideas about themselves, other people and the world around them. During learning activities, pupils need:

o **to explore their environment** and/or investigate new information/ideas
o **to discover things for themselves** through a wide variety of experiences
o **to feel free to make mistakes** in a safe and secure environment using 'trial and error'
o **appropriate support from adults (and other pupils)** to encourage and extend their knowledge and skills
o **to develop autonomy** through increased responsibility and working independently
o **an appropriate learning framework** in which to make sense of new information/ideas.

The teaching assistant's role in supporting learning activities involves:

o providing learning activities as directed by the teacher

- ○ using appropriate materials and support strategies for each pupil's needs and abilities
- ○ modifying or adapting learning activities to meet intended learning goals/objectives
- ○ providing assistance at an appropriate level for each pupil
- ○ encouraging pupils to make choices about their own learning
- ○ promoting independent learning.

(For information on **scaffolding** and **assisted learning** see Chapter 4.)

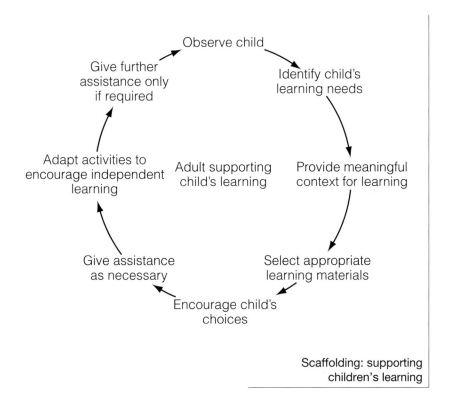

Scaffolding: supporting children's learning

Chapter 5 looked at the ways you **observe** and **plan** learning activities for pupils. This chapter concentrates on how you **support** pupils during these learning activities. As directed by the teacher you will provide support for pupils during learning activities based on observations and assessments of the pupils' learning needs.

 **KEY TASK**

Observe a pupil involved in a learning activity.

In your assessment you should:
- specify the learning objectives for the activity
- identify the intellectual skills demonstrated by the pupil during the activity (e.g. concentration, memory skills, imagination and creativity, mathematical or scientific skills, language and communication skills)
- Comment on the level of adult support provided during the activity
- Suggest ways to encourage and extend the pupil's learning in this area.

NVQ Links: Level 2: 2–3.1; Level 3: 3–3.1, 3–7.1, 3–7.2, 3–8.1

You will need to follow agreed plans for learning activities. When providing support for learning activities, you may be using several plans:

o **An overall curriculum plan** (usually linked to a topic or theme) demonstrating how the teacher intends to extend pupils' learning within the National Curriculum framework (or Foundation Stage) including the National Literacy and Numeracy Strategies.

o **Lesson or activity plans** with detailed information about the learning activities including specific learning objectives, resources/staff required and support strategies to be used.

o **A timetable for the school day**, outlining when and where the learning activities will take place and including routines that must be done at specific times (e.g. registration, break/playtime, lunchtime, tidying-up time, home time).

o **Structured learning programmes for individual pupils**, such as particular activities to encourage the development of pupils with special educational needs including Individual Education Plans (IEPs) and Behaviour Support Plans.

Despite careful planning, you may find that a learning activity is not appropriate for all the pupils you are working with. You need to monitor pupils' responses to learning activities and take appropriate action to modify or adapt activities to achieve **the intended learning objectives or** provide additional activities to extend their learning. You may need to provide an alternative version of the activity or you might be able to present the materials in different ways or offer a greater/lesser level of assistance.

You may need to modify or adapt activities for the following reasons:

○ the pupil lacks concentration
○ the pupil is bored or uninterested
○ the pupil finds the activity too difficult or too easy
○ the pupil is upset or unwell (if so, you may need to abandon/postpone the activity).

Pupil responses should also be considered when providing support for learning activities. Take notice of non-verbal responses and preferences demonstrated by the pupils; these are just as important as what the pupil says. You should be sensitive to pupil needs and desires.

You can use pupils' positive or negative responses to modify or extend activities to meet each pupil's needs more effectively. For example, if the learning objectives prove too easy or too difficult, you may have to set new goals. By breaking down learning activities into smaller tasks, you may help individual pupils to achieve success more quickly. In modifying plans you are continuing a cycle of planning and implementing activities. Remember to give the pupils positive encouragement and feedback to reinforce and sustain their interest and efforts in the learning process. (See Chapter 1, page 12. The importance of feedback and encouragement.)

You will need to be able to resolve any difficulties you may have in supporting the learning activities as planned. For example:

○ modifying or adapting an inappropriate activity (see above)
○ coping with insufficient materials or equipment breakdown (see Chapter 1)
○ dealing with unco-operative or disruptive pupils (see Chapter 2)

You must report any problems you are unable to resolve to the teacher.

After the activity use all the available relevant information to evaluate the effectiveness of your planning and implementation of the activity, for example responses/information from parents, colleagues and other professionals. You must provide feedback about the pupils' learning achievements to the teacher. Any suggested changes to future activity plans should be agreed with the teacher and other relevant staff.

When planning and implementing learning activities for pupils you should ensure that you make accurate and detailed records of what has been planned/implemented in order to:

o clarify the aims and learning objectives of activity plans
o avoid contradictory strategies/unnecessary duplication of work
o use the time available more effectively
o evaluate the success of plans/activities
o provide continuity and progression for future planning.

(See Chapter 5 for information on evaluating and recording learning activities.)

 KEY TASK

Plan and implement a learning activity for a pupil. You can use the assessment from the previous observation as the starting point for your planning. Include the following:
- the learning objectives/goals for the pupil
- a list of materials and/or equipment needed
- your intended strategies to support the pupil during the activity.

Review and evaluate the activity afterwards including any modifications to the activity or difficulties during the activity.

NVQ Links: Level 2: 2–3.1, 2–3.2; Level 3: 3–3.1, 3–3.2, 3–8.1, 3–8.2

Promoting independent learning

You need to arrange with the teacher the strategies and resources to be used to promote independent learning. This includes:

o encouraging and supporting pupils in making decisions about their own learning
o providing appropriate levels of assistance for individual pupils
o using technology to enable pupils to work more independently
o providing challenges to promote independent learning
o encouraging pupils to review their own learning strategies, achievements and future learning needs.

Some schools (especially in nursery and reception classes) take pupils' involvement in planning as the central basis for structuring their learning activities. The High/Scope philosophy encourages pupils to make decisions about their own choice of activities.

The 'plan-do-review' cycle of planning looks something like this:

'plan': in a small group with an adult, pupils discuss which activities they intend to do that session.

'do': the pupils participate in the activities of their choice and are encouraged to talk during this time with adults helping to extend the pupils' language and learning.

'review': at the end of the session the group come together again to look back on the session's activities.

The High/Scope system encourages language and learning by involving pupils in the planning, doing and reviewing of activities. The pupils still participate in some adult-directed activities such as story time, PE and other larger group activities as well as work to develop specific skills such as literacy and numeracy in small groups or as individuals.

Being flexible and allowing for pupils' choice in planning activities helps their learning and development by promoting:

○ discussion and effective communication skills
○ co-operative group work
○ opportunities for first-hand experiences and exploration
○ information skills (including referencing skills, finding and using different resources).

EXERCISE:
Give three examples of how you have encouraged pupils to work independently.

Supporting pupils with cognitive and learning difficulties

Some pupils may not develop their intellectual processes in line with the expected pattern of development for their age for a variety of reasons:

○ emotional and behavioural difficulties (see Chapter 2)
○ autistic spectrum disorders (see Chapter 7)
○ cognitive and learning difficulties.

Cognitive and learning difficulties can be divided into two main areas:

○ general learning difficulties
○ specific learning difficulties.

Defining general learning difficulties

The term 'slow learners' is sometimes used to describe pupils with below average cognitive abilities across all areas of learning; the term 'general learning difficulties' is preferable. The wide range of general learning difficulties is divided into three levels:

○ **Mild learning difficulties**: pupils whose learning needs can be met using resources within mainstream schools
○ **Moderate learning difficulties**: pupils whose learning needs can be met using additional resources in designated classes/special units within mainstream schools or in special schools
○ **Severe or profound learning difficulties**: pupils whose learning needs require the resources and staff usually available only in special schools.

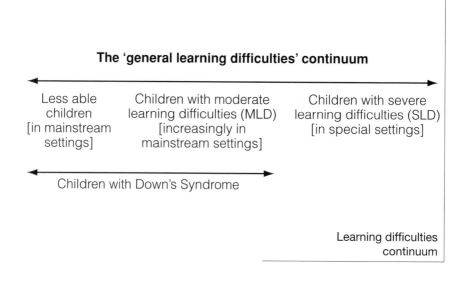

The 'general learning difficulties' continuum

Less able children [in mainstream settings] Children with moderate learning difficulties (MLD) [increasingly in mainstream settings] Children with severe learning difficulties (SLD) [in special settings]

Children with Down's Syndrome

Learning difficulties continuum

Identifying pupils with general learning difficulties

Pupils with general learning difficulties are usually identified by the adults working with them at an early stage. Here are some common signs to look out for:

○ delay in understanding new ideas/concepts
○ poor concentration/shorter than usual attention-span
○ inability to remember new skills without constant repetition and reinforcement
○ poor listening skills

o lack of imagination and creativity
o difficulty following instructions in large group situations
o difficulty comprehending abstract ideas
o limited vocabulary; often give one-word answers
o problems with memory skills
o poor co-ordination affecting hand-eye co-ordination, pencil control, etc.
o need lots of practical support and concrete materials
o delayed reading skills, especially comprehension
o delayed understanding of maths/science concepts.

Pupils with general learning difficulties (especially in mainstream schools) are often aware that their progress is behind that of their peers. This can be very damaging to their self-esteem. Some pupils may feel they are incapable of learning anything at all. Adults need to convince such pupils that they *can* and *will* learn as long as they keep trying and do not give up.

Supporting pupils with general learning difficulties

The following strategies may help to make learning a more positive experience:

o build on what the pupil already knows
o let the pupil work at his/her own pace
o provide activities that can be completed in the time available without the pupil feeling under pressure
o divide the learning into small steps in a logical sequence
o present the same concept or idea in various ways to reinforce learning and understanding
o use repetition frequently; short daily lessons are more memorable than one long weekly session
o demonstrate what to do as well as giving verbal instructions; use real examples and practical experiences/equipment wherever possible
o keep activities short; work towards increasing the pupil's concentration (see page 98)
o encourage active participation in discussion and group activities to extend language and communication skills
o provide more stimuli for learning activities rather than expecting the pupil to develop new ideas entirely by themselves
o help the pupil to develop skills in accessing information (e.g. use technology such as computers, Internet; also libraries, reference books; museums)
o *listen* to the pupil; take on board their points of view.

Praise and encouragement are essential to *all* pupils' learning. All pupils, regardless of ability, are motivated by achieving success. Make sure the learning activities you provide are appropriate by using your observations and assessments to plan activities (as directed by the teacher) which are relevant to each pupil's abilities and interests. Praise and encouragement are especially important to raise the self-esteem of pupils who find learning difficult.

Defining specific learning difficulties

Pupils with specific learning difficulties show problems in learning in one particular area of development; these pupils have difficulties in acquiring literacy skills and consequently other aspects of learning may be affected. The term **dyslexia** is often used when referring to pupils with such problems, but the phrase **specific learning difficulties** probably more accurately describes the scope of difficulties experienced by them. It is estimated that 4 per cent of pupils are affected by dyslexia.

Identifying pupils with specific learning difficulties

Recognising the signs of possible dyslexia in the under-fives:

- delay or difficulty in speech development
- persistent tendency to mix-up words and phrases
- persistent difficulty with tasks such as dressing
- unusual clumsiness and lack of co-ordination
- poor concentration
- family history of similar difficulties.

(Note: Many young children make similar mistakes; dyslexia is only indicated where the difficulties are severe and persistent, or grouped together.)

Recognising the possible signs of dyslexia in 5–9 year olds:

- particular difficulties in learning to read, write and spell
- persistent and continued reversing of letters and numerals (e.g. 'b' for 'd', 51 for 15)
- difficulty telling left from right
- difficulty learning the alphabet and multiplication tables
- difficulty remembering sequences (e.g. days of the week/months of the year)
- difficulty with tying shoelaces, ball-catching and other co-ordinated skills
- poor concentration
- frustration, possibly leading to behavioural problems
- difficulty following instructions – verbal and/or written.

Recognising the possible signs of dyslexia in 9–12 year olds:

o difficulties with reading including poor comprehension skills
o difficulties with writing and spelling including letters missing or in the wrong order
o problems with completing tasks in the required time
o being disorganised at school (and at home)
o difficulties with copying from chalkboard, whiteboard or textbook
o difficulties with following verbal and/or written instructions
o lack of self-confidence and frustration.

Recognising the possible signs of dyslexia in 12–16 year olds:

o reads inaccurately and/or lacks comprehension skills
o inconsistency with spelling
o difficulties with taking notes, planning and writing essays
o confuses telephone numbers and addresses
o difficulties with following verbal instructions
o severe problems when learning a foreign language
o frustration and low self-esteem.

(**Note:** Not all pupils with dyslexia will display *all* of these characteristics.)

Supporting pupils with specific learning difficulties

The following strategies may help when working with pupils with dyslexic tendencies:

o ensure the pupil is near you or at the front of the class/group
o check unobtrusively that copy-writing, note-taking, etc. is done efficiently
o use 'buddy' system (i.e. another pupil copies notes or other information for this one)
o give positive feedback and encouragement, without drawing undue attention to the pupil
o use computers to help the pupil (e.g. word processing with spell check facility)
o help the pupil to develop effective strategies and study skills which may differ from those used by other pupils.
o get specialist advice.

(Above information from The British Dyslexia Association.)

 **KEY TASK**

Describe how you could provide support for a pupil with either general or specific learning difficulties. Include information on how you would:

- encourage the pupil to participate in learning activities
- help the pupil to develop organisational, information processing and problem solving skills
- support the pupil in making decisions and taking responsibility for their learning
- modify learning activities to meet the pupil's individual learning needs
- report the pupil's progress to the teacher including achievements and any problems.

NVQ Links: Level 2: 2–3.1, 2–3.2; Level 3: 3–3.1, 3–3.2, 3–14.1, 3–14.2

Supporting pupils with exceptional abilities

Some pupils may have intellectual abilities that are well above the expected norm for their age group. Pupils with exceptional abilities ('gifted' pupils) may have:

- reached developmental milestones *much* earlier than the expected norm
- more energy than is usual for their age
- a never-ending curiosity
- sharp powers of observation
- advanced thinking and reasoning skills
- a preference for interaction with older pupils and adults.

Pupils with exceptional abilities need additional challenges and innovative ideas to stretch their cognitive capabilities. They need access to advanced resources with plenty of opportunities for independent, original and creative thought/action. Remember the pupils' social and emotional needs as well as their intellectual needs; if they are made to feel different or extraordinary they may find it difficult to mix with other pupils in the school.

Supporting pupils with sensory impairment

Adults in schools need to enable pupils with sensory impairment to participate in the full range of learning activities by:

o providing a stimulating language-rich learning environment that is visually attractive, tactile and interactive
o maximising the use of space in the school to allow freedom of movement for *all* pupils (including those who are visually impaired)
o ensuring accessibility of materials and equipment
o providing opportunities for all pupils to explore different materials and activities
o encouraging pupils to use the senses they have to their fullest extent
o providing sufficient time for pupils to explore their environment and materials; some pupils may need extra time to complete tasks
o encouraging independence (e.g. use computers, word processing, tape recorders)
o praising *all* pupils' *efforts* as well as achievements.

Defining hearing impairment

Hearing loss may range from a slight impairment to profound deafness. One in four pupils under the age of seven experience a hearing loss of some degree at some time. The loss may affect one or both ears at different levels. There are two types of hearing impairment:

1 **Conductive** – involving the interference of the transmission of sound from the outer to the inner ear. This may be due to congestion or damage to the inner ear. The loss may be temporary or permanent; it makes sounds seem like the volume has been turned down. Hearing aids can be useful to amplify speech sounds, but unfortunately background noise is also increased. The most common form of conductive hearing loss in younger pupils is '**glue ear**'. This temporary condition is caused by the collection of fluid behind the ear drum triggered by congestion during an ear, nose or throat infection. Sometimes 'glue ear' can cause language delay as it interferes with a young child's hearing at an important stage of speech development. Persistent or repetitive cases of glue ear may require a minor operation to drain the fluid and to insert a **grommet** (see diagram on page 136) or small tube into the ear drum to prevent further fluid build up.

2 **Sensori-neural** loss is a rarer condition that is more likely to result in permanent hearing impairment. The damage to the inner ear results in distorted sounds where some sounds are heard but not others. **High frequency loss** affects the pupil's ability to hear consonants; **low frequency loss** is a less common condition. Hearing aids are not as effective with this type of hearing impairment as the pupil will still be unable to hear the missing sounds. Pupils with sensori-neural loss therefore find it more difficult to develop speech and have a more significant language delay.

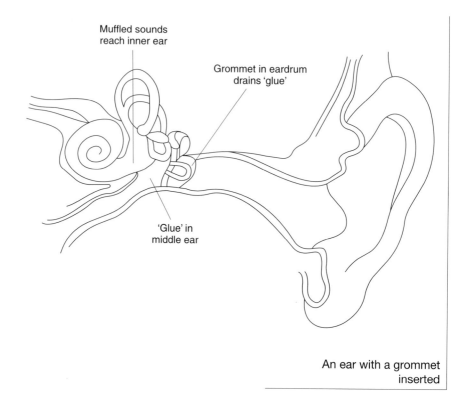

Muffled sounds
reach inner ear

Grommet in eardrum
drains 'glue'

'Glue' in
middle ear

An ear with a grommet
inserted

Identifying pupils with hearing impairment

Pupils with hearing impairment, especially those with conductive hearing loss, may be difficult to identify. However, even a slight hearing loss may affect a pupil's language development. Look out for these signs of possible hearing loss in pupils:

○ slow reactions
○ delay in following instructions
○ constantly checking what to do
○ apparently day-dreaming or inattentive
○ over-anxiety
○ watching faces closely
○ turning head to one side to listen
○ asking to repeat what was said
○ difficulty regulating voice
○ poor language development
○ spoken work more difficult to do than written work
○ may have emotional or aggressive outbursts due to frustration
○ problems with social interaction.

Pupils with hearing loss will use lip-reading and non-verbal clues, such as gesture and body language to work out what is being said. Some pupils will wear hearing aids to improve their hearing abilities. Some schools may encourage the use of signing systems such as British Sign Language or Makaton and have specially trained staff to facilitate the use of sign language throughout the school.

Supporting pupils with hearing impairment

The following suggestions may help when working with pupils with hearing impairment:

o reduce background noise (e.g. have carpets where possible)
o ensure the pupil is near to you
o use facial expressions and gestures
o use visual aids (e.g. real objects, pictures, books, photos, etc.)
o keep your mouth visible
o do not shout, speak clearly and naturally
o check the pupil is paying attention
o develop listening skills through music and games
o include the pupil in group activities in a sensitive manner.

Defining visual impairment

Some pupils may wear glasses to correct short or long sight, but these pupils are not considered to be visually impaired. A pupil with visual impairment has partial or total lack of vision in *both* eyes. Pupils with normal vision in only one eye (monocular vision) are not considered to be visually impaired, because one eye enables them to see quite well for most activities. Pupils with monocular vision will have difficulties with 3-D perception and judging distances. Remember pupils with a squint may be relying on the vision of the one 'good' eye. Some pupils may be 'colour blind' and have difficulty differentiating between certain colours, usually red and green. Again this is not a visual impairment, but may cause occasional difficulties in school e.g. when doing activities involving colour recognition, colour mixing, etc. There is also a safety implication – red for danger/ stop may be confused with green for go.

Identifying pupils with visual impairment

The majority of pupils with visual impairment will have been identified before they start school, but there may be a few pupils who have not, particularly in the younger age range.

Be aware of the following, a pupil who:

o blinks or rubs eyes a lot
o has itchy, watery or inflamed eyes
o frowns, squints or peers at work
o closes/covers one eye when looking at books
o bumps into people or furniture
o has difficulty with physical games/appears clumsy
o has difficulty forming letters and numbers
o omits words or sentences when reading
o says they cannot see the chalkboard or worksheet
o suffers from frequent headaches
o dislikes classroom/nursery lighting.

Supporting pupils with visual impairment

Vision is an essential component of learning in mainstream schools; visual impairment can affect language development in terms of written language and learning to read. It is essential to work with teachers, other colleagues and parents to provide the best care and education for pupils with visual impairment. Specialist advice and equipment may be necessary depending on the extent of the visual impairment.

Depending on the extent of visual impairment the following strategies may help:

o ensure the pupil is near to you
o make sure the pupil wears glasses if they are supposed to
o keep the room tidy and free from obstacles
o black writing on a matt white board is better than using a chalkboard
o make worksheets clear and bold
o allow time for writing when necessary
o keep writing to a minimum; use oral methods e.g. tape recorder
o use word-processing where possible
o enlarge worksheets and books
o use other senses e.g. touch and sound to reinforce learning
o use visual aids such as magnifier
o be aware of possible mobility problems during physical activities
o use talking books and story books with Braille on plastic inserts
o provide pre-Braille and Braille activities after consulting specialist advisor.

Braille alphabet and numerals							
a	b	c	d	e	f	g	h
i	j	k	l	m	n	o	p
q	r	s	t	u	v	w	x
y	z		1	2	3	4	
5	6	7	8		9	0	

Braille alphabet and numerals

Supporting pupils with physical impairment

Defining physical impairment

About 15 per cent of pupils have some kind of physical impairment: some pupils are severely disabled by physical difficulties due to damage to the neurological system, which controls motor functions (cerebral palsy and spina bifida); some pupils have relatively minor difficulties such as dyspraxia. Some pupils have multiple impairments, affecting several physical functions, such as hearing or visual impairment combined with motor disorders.

Cerebral palsy

There are different kinds of cerebral palsy; the two most common types are:

o *Spasticity:* stiffness which affects movement
o *Athetosis:* involuntary, jerky or writhing movements.

The degree of physical impairment ranges from minor to severe debilitation. Many pupils with cerebral palsy also have other problems such as visual impairment, language and communication difficulties and/or learning difficulties.

Spina bifida

This non-progressive disorder is caused by a defect in the development of the spinal column. A pupil with spina bifida may be mildly or severely impaired depending on which part of the spine is damaged. Most pupils with spina bifida also have hydrocephalus which is caused by blocked passages in the cranial cavity; a special valve is inserted to drain excess cerebro spinal fluid to relieve pressure on the brain. Visual impairment, incontinence and learning difficulties are also common.

Dyspraxia

Some pupils with no visible physical impairment may have great difficulty with performing activities such as dressing, PE, painting, drawing and handwriting. These pupils were previously labelled as 'clumsy' but the preferred term now is 'dyspraxia' (or 'developmental coordination disorder'). There appears to be no identifiable disease or medical condition. While their intellectual abilities are not affected by this disorder, pupils with dyspraxia may experience learning difficulties especially in secondary school where they cannot cope with the physical demands of note-taking and essay writing; SATs tests and GCSEs are particular problems as they require writing legibly at speed.

Providing support for pupils with physical impairment

You need to develop skills and strategies to enable pupils with physical impairment to participate in learning activities. When implementing learning activities planned by the teacher, remember that pupils with physical impairment may:

o not be able to make full use of materials and equipment
o not be able to participate fully in some activities with other pupils
o need the understanding and sensitive support of an adult or other pupils
o need specially adapted toys and other learning equipment.

Working with the teacher, you need to ensure that the classroom, learning activities and equipment are adapted where necessary to enable pupils with physical impairment to participate as fully as possible. If you are involved in planning how to adapt the classroom for a pupil with physical impairment, consider the space needed for a wheelchair, frame or other walking aids, and also where ramps will be required instead of steps. Provide sufficient space between tables and chairs to allow a pupil with mobility aids to move freely without obstacles. If you work in a mainstream school you will need to consider the needs of *all* the pupils.

Pupils should be encouraged to participate in a wide range of learning activities as appropriate to their needs including their level of development, physical abilities/limitations. Modified or specialised equipment and learning materials should be used to meet the pupils' needs allowing for maximum participation in learning activities. As directed by the teacher, you should provide appropriate challenges for the pupils, whilst maintaining their health and safety.

You can help support the pupils by:

o using learning activities that are self-correcting
o encouraging pupils to make choices (e.g. selecting materials for art or design activities)
o praising pupils for effort and small achievements
o having high but realistic expectations for their learning
o ensuring pupils are not ridiculed or bullied
o informing the teacher about the pupil's progress.

Supporting pupils with structured learning programmes

Your contribution to the planning of structured learning programmes will depend on your role and responsibilities within the school. Some teaching assistants are closely involved in a variety of planning sessions and meetings while others are simply required to implement the plans of teachers and/or specialists. Structured learning programmes may be either short-term (e.g. a week or half term) or long-term (e.g. a term or school year), and can cover a range of developmental/learning needs including social, physical, intellectual, communication or emotional. A plan for the school year or a whole term will obviously require more work than a plan for a week or two. The planning for structured learning programmes is based on detailed observations and assessments of the pupil's learning and development. These assessments will include information from parents and appropriate professionals as well as the observations and assessments made by you and the teacher.

KEY TASK

Observe a pupil with sensory or physical impairment over a period of time (e.g. a week, a month, half a term or whole term – whichever is appropriate to your role in school). Using your observations, assess the pupil's development and make suggestions for the pupil's future learning needs. See Chapter 5 and discuss with the pupil's teacher and/or your assessor which observation methods would be appropriate.

NVQ Links: Level 3: 3–3.1, 3–7.1, 3–7.2, 3–16.1

As part of your role in the planning process, you may be involved in making suggestions for the aims and learning objectives of a structured learning programme. You will work in conjunction with the teacher, the SENCO and possibly specialists such as educational psychologist, speech and language therapist, physiotherapist or occupational therapist. The learning objectives should indicate:

○ The pupil's level of development
○ The specific area of impairment or special need
○ The intended length of the programme
○ Where the programme is to be implemented, e.g. home, school or both.

Implementing a structured learning programme

As directed by the teacher, you will provide support for the pupil during learning activities as part of the structured learning programme. In addition to following the general information on supporting learning activities (at the beginning of this chapter) you also need to consider implementing learning activities in ways which maximise the benefit to the pupil. For example:

1 Implement at a time when the pupil is receptive.

2 Avoid unnecessary distractions for the pupil.

3 Keep disruptions to the usual classroom/school routines to a minimum.

4 Use appropriate resources including any specialised learning materials and/or equipment.

It is essential that you understand your own role (and that of colleagues) in planning and implementing the programme.

Providing information on the pupil's progress

Throughout the programme you will need to keep accurate and detailed records of the pupil's progress and responses to learning activities in order to feedback information to the teacher and other relevant people. You can record significant aspects of the pupil's participation levels and progress during the learning activity (if possible) or shortly afterwards so that you remember important points.

KEY TASK

Design a possible structured learning programme for a pupil with sensory or physical impairment based on your observations and assessments from the previous key task.

You could do an outline plan including the following:
1. A spidergram of learning activities and skills using headings appropriate to your school and the pupil's learning needs (e.g. National Curriculum subjects or early learning goals).
2. A list of the planning and preparation for the learning activities including resources and organisation.
3. The inclusion of the pupil's learning activities into the usual classroom routine including any necessary modifications.
4. Your role in supporting the pupil during the learning activities.
5. Any health and safety issues.
6. A timetable of the first week's learning activities from the plan.
7. A detailed description of the implementation of at least one learning activity. Remember to review and evaluate the activity afterwards.
8. A review and evaluation of the whole plan.

If you have never done an outline plan before ask your assessor for guidance or advice on another format which might be more appropriate to your role within the school.
NVQ Links: Level 3: 3–3.1, 3–3.2, 3–8.1, 3–8.2, 3–16.2, 3–16.1

Supporting the use of ICT in the classroom

Pupils need to be able to use Information and Communications Technology (ICT) to support their learning across all areas of the National Curriculum. Developing ICT skills helps prepare pupils for the world which is rapidly being transformed by technology. They need to learn the ICT skills necessary for work and everyday life, e.g. using the Internet and email or computer programs for business or home.

Pupils use ICT in the classroom to:

○ access information
○ develop their ideas
○ communicate with others
○ work together to solve problems.

At primary school pupils will learn how to control a computer including using a computer for word processing, developing pictures using 'paint' software, making tables or graphs, and accessing information via the Internet. Once pupils leave secondary school they will have used computers throughout their school career in various ways including using the Internet and email, digital cameras and scanners, recording equipment as well as computer software. The majority of pupils will have reached a standard equivalent to GCSE and many will have taken and passed a GCSE.

Preparing ICT equipment for use in the classroom

As a teaching assistant you may be involved in supporting the use of ICT in the classroom including the use of computers and concept keyboards for pupils with special needs. You should find out from the teacher which ICT

Learning in an ICT suite

equipment is needed and when it is required. You will need to ensure that this equipment is available and ready for use at the time required. You may need to book equipment in advance if it is shared between classes or check and set up equipment already in the classroom. You will also need to make sure that accessories and consumables (e.g. printer paper or spare bulbs) are the correct ones for the equipment being used. These should be stored safely but with easy access for when required. You should check that ICT equipment is in safe working order and is being used correctly by yourself and the pupils. After use make sure that the equipment is left safe and secure. Any faults with equipment should be promptly reported to the teacher and the person responsible for arranging maintenance or repair. You must make sure that any faulty equipment is made safe and secure until it can be removed and/or repaired.

Supporting pupils when using ICT equipment

As a teaching assistant you need to help pupils to develop their skills, competence and independence when using ICT equipment. Here is a brief outline of what you can expect from pupils using ICT within the National Curriculum.

Key Stage 1
By age 7, most pupils can:

○ use ICT to handle information in different ways including gathering, organising, storing and presenting information to others
○ use computer software in their everyday work (e.g. use a word processor to write and present their class work or use other computer packages which make use of graphics and sound)
○ use programmable toys, putting together computerised instructions in the right order.

Key Stage 2
By age 11, most pupils can:

○ use ICT to gather and present information including sharing ideas in different ways (e.g. using the Internet and email)
○ check the accuracy and reliability of information
○ write and test simple computer programs to control and monitor events (e.g. create programs to monitor temperature change or switch on a light bulb)
○ use simulation software and spreadsheets to test theories and explore data patterns.

Key Stage 3
By age 14, most pupils can:

- use information from various sources to develop ideas and enhance their work
- use ICT to present ideas in different ways to suit different audiences
- devise computerised instructions to perform different tasks (e.g. to control the movement of automatic doors or the temperature in greenhouses)
- use models to make predictions and test these predictions to check their accuracy (e.g. use spreadsheets to model the running of a school tuck shop or use simulation software to demonstrate scientific experiments)
- discuss the impact of ICT on their lives and society.

(Adapted from 'Learning Journey', DfEE, 2000.)

 KEY TASK

1. What are the procedures for preparing and using ICT equipment in your classroom?
2. Describe how you have used ICT to support a pupil's learning.

NVQ Links: Level 2/3: 3–17.1, 3–17.2

 Further reading...

British Dyslexia Association (October 1997) *Dyslexia: an introduction for parents and teachers and others with an interest in dyslexia.* BDA.

Crawford, R. (1997) *Managing information technology in secondary schools.* Routledge.

Dare, A. and O'Donovan, M. (1997) *Good practice in caring for children with special needs.* Stanley Thornes.

Dawkins, J. (1991) *Integrating visually impaired children.* RNIB.

Hobart, C. and Frankel, J. (1994) *A practical guide to activities for young children.* Stanley Thornes.

Penso, D.E. (1990) *Keyboard graphic and handwriting skills – helping people with motor disabilities.* Chapman and Hall.

Royal National Institute for the Deaf (1990) *The hearing impaired child in your class.* RNID.

Tingle, M. (1990) *The motor impaired child.* NFER-Nelson.

7

Developing Language and Communication Skills

> Key points:
>
> - What is language?
> - What is communication?
> - The inter-related modes of language
> - The sequence of language development
> - Helping pupils develop language and communication skills
> - Factors affecting language development
> - Supporting bilingual pupils
> - Supporting pupils with communication and interaction difficulties

Defining language and communication

What is language?

The word **language** is often used to describe the process of speaking and listening, but it is much more than verbal communication. All animals, including humans, can communicate through the use of **signals**. For example, a cat hisses and its tail bristles when it feels threatened. Humans also communicate using signals such as body language and gesture; what makes us different is the use of **symbols** (e.g. words) to indicate more complex needs and feelings. While animals are only able to deal with the here and now, humans can use language to store and later recall ideas, feelings and past experiences, and look forward to the future.

What is communication?

The human ability to utilise language depends on the use of **recognised systems of symbols** and a common understanding of what those symbols mean. For example, in this country the majority of people use the system of symbols known as 'English' and anyone who does not understand this system is at a disadvantage in terms of communicating effectively in an English-speaking society. Obviously there are many other systems of symbols as indicated by the many different languages and alphabet systems throughout the world.

At first, very young children are not able to use a complex system of symbols; it takes time to learn the system of their particular home or community language. While they are learning the system, they use other ways to **communicate** their needs and feelings to other people, for example: body language, gestures and facial expressions. However, these symbols can only be interpreted by others – we do not always know exactly what the child is trying to communicate to us, which can be very frustrating for both adult and child! When a baby cries it could mean the baby needs a nappy change, feeding, a sleep, a cuddle or entertainment. The adult's interpretation of the baby's cry will depend on how well they know the baby and their understanding of the baby's needs.

Communication means:

○ the passing of information
○ the receiving of information
○ the interpretation of information
○ the understanding of information.

Language is the **key factor** in all children's development as it provides access to all aspects of human interaction:

○ communicating with others
○ relating to others
○ exploring the environment
○ understanding concepts
○ formulating ideas
○ expressing feelings.

EXERCISE:
Describe the meaning of the terms *language* and *communication* in your own words.

Why do we communicate?

We communicate because we need to interact with others. Humans are social animals and desire the company of others. We use language as the most effective means of communicating with other people. Communication is a key factor in social interaction, which is an essential part of our daily lives. This applies to children as well as to adults. Young children use their communication skills (however limited these may be) to express their needs and desires in an **egocentric** way – they use language as a means of self-preservation. Children also use language to make sense of their environment and their everyday experiences; to organise their thoughts and feelings about themselves, other people and the world around them.

The inter-related modes of language

Children (and adults) use a variety of different ways to communicate. These **modes of language** are essential to being able to communicate effectively with others and to being fully involved in a wide range of social interactions. The different modes of language can be described as: non-verbal communication; thinking; listening; speaking; reading; writing. Each mode of language involves a variety of skills that are inter-related; some of the skills are required in more than one mode, such as reading and writing, which both involve the processing of oral language in a written form.

Adults working in schools should provide opportunities for pupils to develop the necessary skills needed to become competent at communicating. Remember that some pupils may be limited in their ability to use some aspects of language due to sensory impairment or other special needs.

EXERCISE:
Look at the modes of language diagram on page 150. Using the headings from the diagram, list examples of activities/experiences which would encourage each skill. Your list might look something like this:

MODES OF LANGUAGE	SKILLS	EXAMPLES
Non-verbal communication	Body language	*Drama or role play*
Thinking	Recalling images	*Drawing/painting past event*
Listening	Processing information	*Listening to instructions*
Speaking	Oral language	*Discussion or circle time*
Reading	Phonics	*Rhymes and word games*
Writing	Written language	*Writing story or essay*

Provide examples from your own experiences of working with pupils.

The sequence of language development

It is more accurate to think in terms of a **sequence** of language development rather than **stages** of development. This is because **stages** refers to development that occurs at *fixed ages;* while **sequence** indicates development that follows the same basic pattern *but not necessarily at fixed ages.* Language

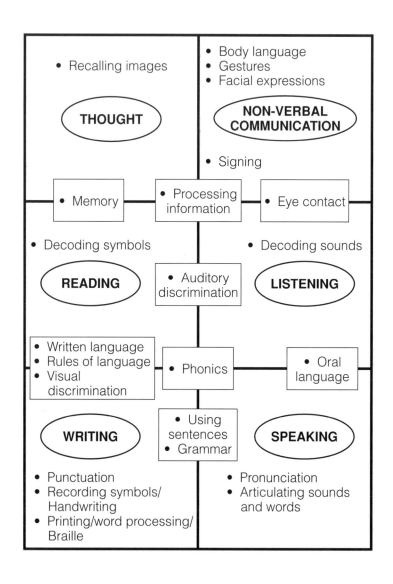

Inter-related components of
the modes of language

development in particular is affected by many other factors not just a pupil's chronological age. (See below for information on factors affecting pupils' language development and communication skills.) Another important factor to remember is that physical maturity plays a part in children's language development. Babies need to have physical control over their vocal chords, tongue, lips and jaw muscles to be able to articulate the sounds necessary to form their first words. In addition, children (and adults) have two areas of vocabulary usage:

1 **Passive vocabulary:** the language used by others that they can *understand.*

2 **Active vocabulary:** the words that they actually *use* themselves.

Children (and adults) can recognise and understand a larger number of words than they can speak (or write) themselves, whatever their level of development. The size of an individual's vocabulary (like all aspects of language development) depends on their language experiences especially access to books and reading. The chart shown here *does* indicate specific ages, but only to provide a framework for understanding pupils' language development. Remember all pupils are individuals and develop at their own rate.

The sequence of language development: 3–16 years

Age 3–4 years
- has vocabulary of between 900 and 1,000 words
- asks lots of questions
- uses language to ask for assistance
- talks constantly to people knows well
- gives very simple accounts of past events
- can say names of colours
- begins to vocalise ideas
- continues to enjoy books, stories, songs and rhymes
- listens to and can follow simple instructions
- can deliver verbal messages

Age 4–7 years
- may use vocabulary of about 1,500 to 4,000 words
- uses more complex sentence structures
- asks even more questions using what, when, who, where, how and especially **why!**

○ shows interest in more complex books and stories
○ develops early literacy skills
○ gives more detailed accounts of past events
○ vocalises ideas and feelings
○ can listen to and follow more detailed instructions
○ can deliver more complex verbal messages
○ continues to enjoy songs and rhymes
○ shows interest in simple poetry

Age 7–11 years
○ has extensive vocabulary of between 4,000 and 10,000 words
○ uses more complex sentence structures
○ develops more complex reading skills including improved comprehension
○ develops more complex writing skills including more accurate spelling, punctuation and joined-up writing
○ continues to enjoy books, stories and poetry
○ gives very detailed accounts of past events and can anticipate *future* events
○ vocalises ideas and feelings in more depth
○ listens to and follows more complex instructions
○ appreciates jokes due to more sophisticated language knowledge
○ uses literacy skills to communicate and access information (e.g. story and letter writing; use of dictionaries, encyclopaedia, computers, Internet, email).

Age 11–16 years
○ has an extensive and varied vocabulary of between 10,000 and 20,000 words
○ uses appropriate language styles for different occasions e.g. standard English for formal situations
○ has more complex reading skills, including detailed comprehension skills (e.g. can comment on structure and themes of a book or other piece of writing)
○ has more complex writing skills including accurate spelling and punctuation; neat and legible joined-up writing
○ can use different writing styles including word-processing on a computer
○ continues to enjoy more complex texts including fiction, poetry and factual books
○ gives very detailed accounts of past events using varied expression and vocabulary

○ can anticipate future events *and* give detailed reasons for possible outcomes

○ vocalises ideas and feelings in greater depth including justifying own views and opinions

○ listens to and follows complex sets of instructions

○ appreciates complex jokes and word play

○ continues to use literacy skills to communicate and access information (e.g. taking notes, writing essays and letters; using dictionaries/thesaurus, encyclopaedia; computers, Internet, email).

 KEY TASK

Observe a pupil communicating with another pupil or adult. Focus on the pupil's language and communication skills. In your assessment, comment on:

- any vocabulary used by the pupil
- the complexity of the pupil's sentence structure
- any non-verbal communication used (e.g. body language, gestures, facial expressions)
- the pupil's level of social interaction (e.g. did the pupil appear confident when speaking? Did they have a friendly and relaxed manner? Did they need coaxing to communicate?)
- suggestions for encouraging/extending the pupil's language and communication skills.

N.V.Q. Links: Level 2: 2–3.1, Level 3: 3–7.1, 3–7.2, 3–8.1, 3–18.3 (3–12.1, 3–12.2 bilingual pupils)

Helping pupils develop language and communication skills

Organisation for effective communication

The classroom needs to provide space and opportunities for effective communication to take place and enable pupils to use the different modes of language, while participating in all aspects of the curriculum. Suitable areas need to be created to facilitate the development of pupils' communication skills and learning abilities.

Examples for the **primary** classroom include:

○ **Writing tables:** enabling pupils to 'make their mark' using a variety of writing tools (crayons, pencils, pens, pastels, chalks) on different shapes, sizes and types of paper (e.g. plain, coloured, graph).

○ **Displays:** interest tables; displays of pupils' work and construction models; wall displays and posters to provide a stimulus for talk.

○ **Sand and/or water trays; science and mathematics equipment:** to encourage exploration and conversation.

○ **Pretend play areas:** home corner, shop, café, post office, space station to encourage language and communication skills through imaginative play.

○ **Book displays/story corner:** to promote pupils' interest in books and to develop their early literacy skills.

○ **Computers:** to extend the pupils' range of language and literacy skills (e.g. word processing, referencing skills).

The development of
communication and language
in the classroom

Examples for the **secondary** classroom include:

○ **Suitable writing tables and writing materials for the curriculum area:** pens for writing; pens, pencils and plain or graph paper for recording results in mathematics or science.

- ○ **Displays**: interest tables; wall displays including pupils' own work; posters to stimulate discussion.
- ○ **Varied and interesting science or mathematics equipment/materials**: to stimulate exploration and discussion during experiments.
- ○ **Books relevant to the curriculum area**: to promote interest in books, to develop literacy skills across the curriculum and to extend knowledge of the curriculum area.
- ○ **Computers**: to extend language and literacy skills (e.g. word processing, researching and referencing; to extend knowledge in other areas such as graphs, statistics, etc.).

EXERCISE:
1) Draw a diagram of the classroom where you mainly work with pupils.
2) Look at the resources available and indicate on your diagram how you could maximise the opportunities for language and learning within this classroom.

The role of the teaching assistant in developing pupils' language and communication

Adults working in schools play a vital role in extending, and encouraging the development of pupils' language use and communication skills by providing opportunities for pupils to talk and use language as a tool for exploring ideas and experiences. As a teaching assistant, you must be aware of, and provide for, appropriate language experiences to enable all the pupils you work with to develop effective communication skills.

You can encourage pupils' language and communication skills by:

1 **Talking** to pupils about anything and everything!

2 **Showing** pupils what you are talking about, e.g. use real objects/situations, pictures, books, and other visual or audio aids.

3 **Using straightforward sentences** with words appropriate to the pupils' level of understanding and development; avoid over-simplifying language; do not use 'baby talk' – all pupils need adult speech to learn language.

4 **Using repetition** to introduce/reinforce new vocabulary and ideas. Do not make pupils repeat things back over and over; this is boring and frustrating.

155

5 **Copying** the pupil's sounds/words, including any extensions or corrections, to positively reinforce and extend the pupil's vocabulary, sentence structures, etc. Never tell pupils off for making language errors; it will only make them reluctant to communicate in the future. Making mistakes is part of the language learning process.

6 **Being lively!** Use your tone of voice and facial expressions to convey your interest in what is being communicated.

7 **Remembering turn-taking** in language exchanges. Ask questions to stimulate pupil responses and to encourage speech.

8 **Looking at the pupils** when talking with them. Remember to be at their level, especially when communicating with individuals or small groups of pupils, e.g. sit on a low chair or even on the floor; do not tower over them.

9 **Letting pupils initiate conversations** and listen to what they have to say.

10 **Sharing books, stories and rhymes** with pupils of all ages. (See Chapter 8.)

Lively interaction is essential for the development of language and communication skills

KEY TASK

Plan, implement and evaluate a language activity such as:
- discussion during news or circle time
- playing a game with a pupil or small group of pupils
- sharing a rhyme or song
- doing a literacy activity.

Use the information gained from the observation on page 153 with your recommendations for encouraging/extending that pupil's language and communication skills as the starting point for this activity.

Discuss your plan with the teacher and/or your assessor and negotiate when it would be convenient for you to implement this activity. The activity must be appropriate to the age and level of development of the pupil.

Remember to review and evaluate the activity afterwards.

N.V.Q. Links: Level 2: 2–3.1, 2–3.2, 2–5.1; Level 3: 3–3.1, 3–3.2, 3–8.1, 3–8.2, 3–18.3

Helping pupils to understand the structure of language

As well as enabling pupils to use language, you can also help them to understand the *rules of language*. Once children start to combine words to make sentences, they progress through various stages during which the structure and organisation of language becomes gradually more systematic. This systematic structuring of language is called **grammar.**

Stage 1: Children use simple two/three word phrases or sentences. Grammatical indicators are not present at this stage: no plurals e.g. 'Many car' ; no possessive 's' e.g. 'Tom teddy'; no tense markers ('ed', 'ing') e.g. 'It rain'; no auxiliary verbs ('is', 'do') e.g. 'No like cake'. Children only use nouns, verbs, adjectives and adverbs such as 'now' or 'soon'.

Stage 2 : Children begin to use grammatical indicators previously missing. Note the irregular use of past-tense forms, e.g. 'comed' (came), 'goed' (went) and plurals e.g. 'sheep*s*'. Gradually children begin to use grammar in increasingly adult forms.

Children do not learn grammar through imitation alone; they need opportunities to discover the rules of language for themselves by experimenting and being creative with words in a variety of situations.

You can also help pupils with grammar by repeating back the correct form of language when the pupil makes a grammatical error. Some examples are:

○ **Possessive pronouns** – the child says: 'This Tom hat and that Teena hat'; the adult replies: 'Yes, that is *your* hat and this is *my* hat'.
○ **Possessive 's'** – the child says: 'Here Marly boots and teacher boots'; the adult replies: 'Yes, these are Marly*'s* boots and those are Ms Kamen*'s* boots'.
○ **Plurals** – the child says: 'We saw sheeps'; the adult replies: 'Yes, we saw *some sheep* at the farm'.
○ **Tense markers** – the child says: 'The cat goed out'; the adult replies: 'Yes, the cat *went* outside', or the child says: 'Mummy come!'; the adult replies: 'Yes, your mummy is com*ing* into the nursery now'.
○ **Auxiliary verbs** – the child says: 'We done play dough': the adult replies: 'Yes, we *did* make play dough this morning', or the child says: 'We is walking to the park'; the adult replies: 'Yes, we *are* walking to the park'.
○ **Negatives** – the child says: 'I not eat 'nana'; the adult replies: 'I see you *haven't* eaten your banana'.
○ **Questions** – the child asks: 'More?'; the adult asks: 'Would you like some more milk?'

Working with the teacher, the teaching assistant acts as a **facilitator** by providing appropriate learning activities to enable pupils to develop their language and communication skills in meaningful situations. You need to:

○ **provide appropriate opportunities for play** – especially activities that encourage language and communication (e.g. role/pretend play, creative play).
○ **provide opportunities for self-expression and self-evaluation** – through discussion, news time, 'circle' time, writing, music, art, design, drama and dance.
○ **be positive towards the pupil's attempts at language and communication** – by valuing pupils' home experiences/cultural backgrounds; considering pupils individual interests and abilities; being aware of pupils' special language needs.
○ **give positive feedback, praise and encouragement to *all* pupils** – by commenting positively on pupils' efforts at communicating in different ways.
○ **be aware of possible developmental/psychological difficulties** – through careful observation of pupils' language, learning and behaviour.

 **KEY TASK**

Observe a pupil involved in one of the activities listed below.

Focus on the language and communication skills used by the pupil.

In your assessment comment on:

- the verbal and/or non-verbal communication used by the pupil
- the complexity of any language used
- the level of social interaction
- the role of the adult in encouraging the pupil's language and communication
- suggestions for further activities to encourage/extend the pupil's language and communication skills.

N.V.Q. Links: Level 2: 2–3.1, Level 3: 3–7.1, 3–7.2, 3–18.3, 3–8.1

Activities to encourage or extend language and communication skills

All pupils need activities and materials that encourage language and help to develop communication skills. These activities can be divided into five basic categories:

1. Exploration

- ○ toys and other interesting objects to look at and play with, such as household objects (remember safety)
- ○ sounds to listen to including voices, music, songs, rhymes, musical instruments
- ○ construction toys including wooden bricks, plastic bricks
- ○ natural materials like water, sand, clay, cooking ingredients
- ○ creative materials, such as paint, paper, pencils, crayons, chalks, pastels
- ○ outings including visits to the park, museums, swimming.

2. Description

- ○ news or circle time
- ○ recording events, outings, visits, visitors
- ○ a variety of books and stories including cloth books, board books, activity books, pop-up books, picture books. (See Chapter 8.)

3. Conversation

○ talking about their day, experiences and interests with other pupils and adults
○ talking during imaginative play activities
○ talking about special events (e.g. birthdays, new baby)
○ talking while doing activities (not necessarily related to the task).

4. Discussion

○ problem solving during activities
○ follow-up to activities (e.g. after television programme or a story)
○ co-operative group work
○ games and puzzles
○ television programmes for their age group.

5. Instruction

○ preparation before an activity
○ explanation of what to do (verbal and/or written on a board)
○ instructions during an activity to keep pupils on task
○ extra support for individual pupils
○ introducing/extending knowledge on a specific skill
○ step-by-step instructions
○ worksheets/books/cards
○ delivering verbal/written messages, errands.

 KEY TASK

Plan, implement and evaluate an activity that encourages or extends a pupil's language and communication skills. You could use the assessment information from the previous observation as the starting point for your planning.

Try to include a variety of communication techniques such as:
• active listening
• leaving time for the pupil to respond/talk
• careful phrasing of adult questions and responses.

Consider how you could meet the language needs of bilingual pupils and pupils with communication/interaction difficulties with this activity (see pages 162 to 169).

NVQ Links: Level 2: 2–3.1, 2–3.2, 2–5.1; Level 3: 3–3.1, 3–3.2, 3–8.1, 3–8.2, 3–12.1, 3–12.2, 3–13.1, 3–13.2, 3–18.3

Factors affecting language development

To participate fully in all aspects of education (and society) pupils need to successfully develop a wide range of language and communication skills. Teaching assistants need to be aware of the wide variety of language experiences that pupils bring to the school – some pupils may not have reached the same level of language development as their peers or they may lack effective communication skills. Some pupils may even be ahead of what is usually expected for their age.

Environmental factors and social/cultural factors

It has been suggested that some children grow up within environmental and social circumstances (e.g. poverty; race and culture; parental background and/or low expectations), which may restrict their opportunities to explore the environment and to develop language and communication skills through positive and stimulating interactions with others.

Poverty

Research indicates that poverty and related problems such as poor housing can affect pupils' educational success (National Commission on Education, 1993). One of the reasons for this lack of success is due to problems involving language and communication – without appropriate language and communication skills, it is impossible to access and process the information that is essential to learning. No matter what level of importance parents place on language and learning, it may be very difficult to provide books and activities to stimulate children's interest in language and reading in some circumstances (e.g. no local library, travel costs to nearest library too high, financial worries/unemployment make providing stimulating language opportunities more difficult).

Race and culture

Some children starting school may not speak English at home. The national tests for 7 year olds indicate that these children perform less well then pupils whose first language is English (National Commission on Education, 1993). Social interaction depends on cultural patterns, for example, English-speaking children may be used to adults who modify their speech, adults who simplify their language to help their children's comprehension; while children from many non-English speaking backgrounds may be used to more adult patterns of speech and more direct language instructions from adults in their social interactions. Some pupils may find communicating within the school difficult because they find it hard to relate to other pupils or staff from different races and/or cultures. The lack of ethnic role models is a particular problem in schools where a very small number (around 2 per cent in 1997) of teachers are black or Asian British.

Parental background and/or expectations

In the past, researchers such as Bernstein suggested that 'working class' pupils were at a disadvantage in school because of their inability to use language in the same way as 'middle class' pupils. More recently it has been realised that it is the **social context of language** that is the important factor in children's language development – rather than any notions related to 'class'. It depends on *how individual families use language:* some families see language and learning as very important and pass this attitude onto their children; some families have other priorities (Foster-Cohen, 1999). Some parents may be unaware of the ways to assist their children's language development and communication skills. Some pupils may have various experiences of language and literacy which are not the same as the language experiences provided in schools.

Supporting bilingual pupils

Language diversity

We live in a multicultural society where a huge variety of languages are used to communicate. We are surrounded by different accents, dialects and other ways of communicating, such as sign language. All pupils should have an awareness and understanding of other people's languages, while still feeling proud of their own **community language** and being able to share this with others. Pupils in schools where only English is spoken still need an awareness of other languages to appreciate fully the multicultural society they live in.

Being **bilingual** is another factor that can affect a pupil's language development and communication skills. Bilingual means 'speaking two languages', which applies to some pupils (and staff) in schools in the United Kingdom. 'Multilingual' is used to describe someone who uses more than two languages. However, the term 'bilingual' is widely used for all children who speak two or more languages.

There are four important factors to consider when working with pupils who are bilingual. These are:

1 **Different and changing levels of competence involved in speaking several languages.** For example, *emerging bilinguals* are still learning their first language while adding words to their second language. Very young emerging bilinguals often do 'language mixing', which involves combining words from two or more languages when they talk.

2 **Different situations prompt the use of one language over another.**
Fluent young bilinguals are able to use whichever language is appropriate
to a particular situation. For example, a bilingual child might speak to
one grandparent using standard English, to another grandparent using
Mirpuri and Punjabi; while conversations with parents and siblings
might involve a mixture of Punjabi and English; and language at school
might involve the use of a local dialect, such as that used in the 'Black
Country' in the West Midlands.

3 **The range of literacy skills may be different in each language.** Pupils may
be aware of different writing systems being used by their families and in
the local community. They may be able to speak a particular language and
not be able to write in that language. Pupils may have seen writing that
went from right to left (as in the Arabic or Hebrew scripts) not just from
left to right as with English; or they may be used to vertical rather than
horizontal writing systems such as Mandarin Chinese or Japanese.
Developing literacy can be a confusing experience for the bilingual pupil
who could be learning to read and write in English in school while
learning the same skills in Punjabi at home or in a community school and
learning Arabic through studying the Koran at Saturday school.

4 **Changing circumstances can affect pupils' bilingualism.** For example,
moving to a different area where cultural attitudes may be different so
that more or less of the pupil's community language is used.
(Whitehead, 1996).

Pupils who are bilingual do not see their use of different languages as a
difficulty. Adults working in schools need to maintain this attitude and to
encourage young bilinguals to see their linguistic abilities as the asset it really
is in our multicultural society.

The value of pupils' community languages

You must respect the languages of *all* pupils in your school by providing an
environment that promotes language diversity through:

o welcoming signs in community languages
o learning essential greetings in these languages
o photographs and pictures reflecting multicultural images
o labels with different languages/writing styles
o books, stories and songs in other languages
o multicultural equipment (e.g. ethnic dolls and dressing-up clothes;
  cooking utensils)
o celebrating festivals
o preparing and sharing foods from different cultures.

EXERCISE:
Give examples of how your school promotes language diversity and encourages pupils to use their community languages.

While promoting language diversity we need to remember that we live in a society where English is the dominant language; developing language and literacy skills in English is essential to all pupils if they are to become effective communicators both in and outside the school. Most children starting school will speak English even if they have a different cultural background. However, there are some children who do start nursery or school with little or no English because they are new to this country or English is not used much at home. You can enable pupils to learn English as their second language by:

○ encouraging the pupils to use their community languages some of the time; this promotes security and social acceptance, which will make learning English easier
○ inviting parents/grandparents to read or tell stories in community languages or to be involved with small groups for cooking, sewing or art and design activities
○ using songs and rhymes to help introduce new vocabulary
○ using play opportunities to develop language skills in a meaningful context (e.g. focus on words used when playing in the home corner or sand pit)
○ using games to encourage language.

EXERCISE:
1. Find out about the languages used by the pupils in your school or local area.
• How many different languages are spoken? Which languages are spoken?
• Are there any pupils who are bilingual? Which languages do they use ? When do they use languages other than English?
2. Check out which resources are available locally to encourage pupils to develop their community language and/or English. (This might include things like story time for the under-fives at the local library or lessons in different Asian languages at the community centre.)
3. Design and make a leaflet using the information from your research.

Supporting pupils with communication and interaction difficulties

All pupils have *individual* language needs, but some pupils may have *additional* or **special needs** that affect their ability to communicate effectively with others. Remember not to stereotype pupils with special educational needs; you should always look at the individual *not* the disability. Being able to structure and use language is an enormous task for everyone; it takes the first seven to eight years of life to learn how to form all the different sounds correctly. Some sounds are more difficult to pronounce than others, for example: s, sh, scr, br, cr, gr and th. Most children have problems with these sounds at first, but eventually are able to pronounce them properly.

Lisping is a common problem for children learning to speak; it is caused by the child's inability to articulate a certain sound and so the child substitutes with another similar sound. Lisping usually stops without the need for adult intervention. Sometimes lisping may be a sign of a physical problem, such as hearing loss, cleft palate or faulty tongue action in which case specialist advice is needed.

Some children may experience a period of **stammering**, usually around three years old. This is called **dysfluency** and is part of the normal pattern of language development: the young child cannot articulate thoughts into words quickly enough hence the stammer. About 5 per cent of pupils stammer, but it can be difficult to identify them, because pupils who stammer are often reclusive and reluctant to talk. Most pupils conquer this communication difficulty especially with the assistance of well-prepared, sympathetic teachers and support staff as well as the help of speech and language therapists; only 1 per cent continue to stammer as adults.

Delayed and disordered language development

Some pupils may have difficulties with structuring language, for example problems with:

o **phonology** – the articulation of sounds, syllables and words (as mentioned above)
o **grammar** or **syntax** – words, phrases or sentence structure
o **semantics** – understanding language (**receptive** difficulties)
    – using language (**expressive** difficulties).

Delayed language development may be due to environmental factors such as those discussed earlier. Children with delayed language development go through the same stages of language development as other children, but at a slower rate. **Disordered** language development is more likely to be caused by:

○ **minimal brain damage** affecting areas relating to language
○ **physical disabilities** affecting articulation of sounds
○ **sensory impairment** affecting hearing or visual abilities
○ **cognitive difficulties** affecting the ability to process language.

Autistic spectrum disorders

The phrase 'autistic spectrum disorders' covers a wide range of communication difficulties from severe mental impairment to slight problems with social interaction. Autistic spectrum disorders are rare, but affect four times as many boys as girls. The causes are not known, but autistic tendencies are usually present from birth, although they may not be formally identified until the child attends nursery or school. Pupils with **Asperger's Syndrome** are at the more able end of the autistic spectrum; they are very intelligent, but have communication difficulties, which may be disguised as emotional and behavioural problems.

Pupils with autistic tendencies have difficulty in relating to other people; they do not understand the thoughts, feelings and needs of others. In addition, they are usually unable to express their own thoughts, feelings and needs effectively to others. This presents difficulties in acquiring communication skills and being able to understand the social world. Pupils with autistic tendencies appear indifferent to others or undemonstrative and do not like physical contact. A pupil with autistic tendencies may have problems with:

○ using verbal and/or non-verbal communication
○ being aware of other people, which affects the ability to communicate effectively
○ paying attention to other people (often more interested in objects) which affects listening and comprehension skills
○ socialising with other pupils.

Pupils with severe autistic tendencies may not develop language at all.

Cerebral palsy

Cerebral palsy is a condition caused by damage to the part of the brain that controls a person's movement; this damage may occur at or before birth. Cerebral palsy affects two children in every thousand and ranges from mild to severe disability. The effects on a child's language development depend on the severity of the condition. For example, the muscles necessary for speech may be affected causing communication difficulties. Speech therapy and communication aids (such as specially adapted computers) may be necessary. Due to their communication difficulties many people with cerebral palsy are mistakenly believed to have limited intellectual capabilities, but the reverse is more often the case.

Cleft lip and/or palate

A child with a cleft lip and/or palate has structural damage to their top lip, palate or both, due to the failed development of these areas of the mouth during the early weeks in the womb. The condition is clearly diagnosed at birth. A series of operations is essential to correct this impairment – this may result in significant language delay as correct speech cannot be articulated until the gaps in lips and/or palate have been successfully mended. Later speech and language therapy may be necessary.

Down's Syndrome

Children with Down's Syndrome have a genetic disorder that affects their physical appearance and overall development. The body's chromosomes are cell structures composed of genes; chromosomes are numbered and arranged in 23 pairs. Most children born with Down's Syndrome have an extra chromosome number 21.

Pupils with Down's Syndrome may have communication difficulties for the following reasons:

o small jaw, weak muscle tone and poorly developed nose may make articulation of sounds difficult
o language delayed compared to expected norm
o hearing loss.

Pupils who will not speak

Some pupils can be shy, withdrawn and uncommunicative for a variety of reasons, including:

o lack of confidence in group situations
o lack of social skills
o poor communication skills
o lack of experience in using English to communicate
o emotional trauma; physical or sexual abuse.

Check that there is no underlying cause for the pupil's reluctance or refusal to speak, such as hearing loss, or stressful event such as going into hospital or a death in the family. Most pupils who are uncommunicative lack confidence in themselves and their ability to relate to others, so it is important to develop their self-esteem and improve their social skills (see Chapter 3 for more information). Do not try to *make* a pupil speak when they are reluctant to do so; it only causes further anxiety. Give the pupil the *opportunity* to speak in a welcoming and non-threatening environment; sometimes they may contribute, sometimes they won't. Even if the pupil does not say anything, make sure they can still observe and listen to what is going on in the classroom.

Identifying pupils with communication difficulties

Here are some things to look out for when identifying a pupil's communication difficulties:

1 difficulty understanding in one-to-one situation

2 difficulty understanding in group/class situation

3 difficulty following instructions

4 difficulty in pronouncing sounds (e.g. 'wabbit' instead of 'rabbit')

5 reluctance or refusal to speak

6 giving one-word answers

7 repeating sentences

8 difficulty learning by rote (e.g. rhymes, songs, alphabet, times tables)

9 poor memory skills

10 inappropriate answers.

 KEY TASK

Observe a pupil who has difficulty communicating. Your assessment should give particular attention to:
- the vocabulary of the pupil
- the complexity of his/her sentence structure
- the pupil's level of participation and social interaction.

Suggest possible reasons for the pupil's communication difficulties and make recommendations on how to encourage/develop their communication skills.

NVQ Links: Level 2: 2–3.1, Level 3: 3–7.1, 3–7.2, 3–13.1, 3–13.2, 3–18.3

Strategies to help pupils with communication and interaction difficulties

Adults in schools can do a great deal to help pupils with communication and interaction difficulties. Many of the activities already suggested in this chapter will be suitable for *all* pupils, including those with special language needs. Some pupils, especially those with **disordered** language development, may need specialist help from a speech and language therapist.

Here are some things for you to consider when working with pupils with communication and interaction difficulties:

o keep information short and to the point; avoid complex instructions
o speak clearly and not too quickly
o be a good speech role model
o build up the pupil's confidence gradually (e.g. speaking one-to-one, then small group)
o develop concentration skills; play memory games
o encourage reluctant pupils to speak, but **don't insist** they talk
o use stories, cassettes and taped radio programmes to improve listening skills
o use rhythm to sound out names/phrases, music and songs.

You can also help pupils with communication difficulties by:

o using pictorial instructions and visual cues
o teaching social skills as well as language
o providing structured learning opportunities
o keeping to set routines
o preparing for new situations carefully
o using the pupil's favourite activities as rewards
o using music to communicate (e.g. singing instructions!)
o working with parents, colleagues and specialists to provide **consistent** care and education.

EXERCISE:
1) List three activities you have used to encourage language development. Explain how each activity encouraged the pupils' communication skills.
2) Outline how each activity could be adapted to ensure the participation of pupils with communication and interaction difficulties.

Specialist help for pupils with communication and interaction difficulties

Early assistance with communication difficulties can prevent more complex problems later on. The most important reasons for early intervention are:

1 Language and communication skills are part of intellectual development; language is an essential part of the learning process.

2 Language has a vital role in the understanding of concepts.

3 The main foundations of language are constructed between the ages of 18 months and $4^1/_2$ years during which time the majority of children have fully integrated language as part of the thinking and learning process. It is easier to assist with language development and communication skills during this critical three-year period than to sort out problems once children have reached school age.

4 Effective communication skills are essential to positive social interaction and emotional well-being. Communication difficulties can lead to isolation and frustration. Pupils who cannot communicate effectively may display emotional outbursts and/or aggressive, unwanted behaviour.

There are a number of agencies that offer specialist advice and support for pupils with communication and interaction difficulties, for example:

- health visitor
- speech and language therapist
- educational psychologist
- portage worker
- nursery provision for children with special needs
- hearing impaired unit
- advisory teacher
- special language unit
- special needs assistant
- charities (e.g. RNIB, RNID, AFASIC).

KEY TASK

Plan, implement and evaluate a language activity for a pupil with communication difficulties. Use your assessment of the pupil in the previous observation as the starting point for planning this activity.

Discuss your plan with the teacher and/or your assessor and negotiate when it would be convenient for you to implement your activity. The activity must be appropriate to the age and level of the pupil including the pupil's special language needs.

Remember to review and evaluate the activity.

N.V.Q. Links: Level 2: 2–3.1, 2–3.2, 2–5.1; Level 3: 3–3.1, 3–3.2, 3–8.1, 3–8.2, 3–13.1, 3–13.2, 3–18.3

Further reading...

Bruce, T. and Meggitt, C. (2002) *Child Care and Education.* 3rd edition. Hodder & Stoughton.

Burton, G. and Dimbleby, R. (1995) *Between ourselves: an introduction to interpersonal communication.* Revised edition. Arnold.

Dare, A. and O'Donovan, M. (1997) *Good practice in caring for children with special needs.* Stanley Thornes.

Gulliford, R. and Upton, G. (1992) *Special educational needs.* Routledge.

Harding, J. and Meldon-Smith, L. (2000) *How to make observations and assessments.* 2nd Edition. Hodder and Stoughton.

Hobart, C. and Frankel, J. (1994) *A practical guide to child observation.* Stanley Thornes.

Petrie, P. (1996) *Communicating with children and adults: interpersonal skills for those working with babies and children,* 2nd edition. Edward Arnold.

Whitehead, M. (1996) *The development of language and literacy.* Hodder & Stoughton.

8 Developing Literacy Skills

Key points:

- What is literacy?
- Why is literacy important?
- Learning to read and write
- The importance of books and stories
- National Curriculum targets for English
- The National Literacy Strategy
- The teaching assistant's role in developing literacy skills
- Using ICT to help pupils develop their literacy skills
- Helping pupils to access the curriculum

What is literacy?

Literacy means the ability to read and write. The word 'literacy' has only recently been applied as the definitive term for reading and writing in schools especially since the introduction of the National Literacy Strategy. It makes sense to use the term 'literacy' – the skills of reading and writing complement one another and are developed together. Reading and writing are forms of communication based on spoken language. Pupils need effective language and communication skills (see Chapter 7) before they can develop literacy skills.

Reading is the process of turning groups of written symbols into speech sounds. In English this means being able to read from left to right, from the top of the page to the bottom and being able to recognise letter symbols plus their combinations as words. Reading is not just one skill; it involves a variety of different abilities:

- visual discrimination
- auditory discrimination
- language and communication skills
- word identification skills
- conceptual understanding
- comprehension skills
- memory and concentration.

Writing is the system we use to present *'speech in a more permanent form'* (Moyle, 1976). There are two elements to writing:

1 **The mechanical skill of letter formation**: writing legibly using recognised word and sentence structures, including appropriate spaces between words and punctuation marks.

2 **The creative skill of 'original composition'**: deciding what to write and working out how to write it using appropriate vocabulary to express thoughts and ideas, which may be fact or fiction. (Taylor, 1973.)

Why is literacy important?

Developing literacy skills is an essential aspect of development and learning. Without literacy skills individuals are very restricted in their ability to:

o function effectively in school, college or at work
o access information and new ideas
o communicate their own ideas to others
o participate fully and safely in society.

Education depends on individuals being able to read and write. Nearly all jobs and careers require at least basic literacy (and numeracy) skills.

Our society also requires people to use literacy skills in everyday life:

o reading signs: street names, shop names, traffic and warnings
o reading newspapers, magazines, instructions, recipes, food ingredients
o dealing with correspondence: reading and replying to letters; household bills; bank statements; wage slips; benefits
o using computers, the Internet and email
o writing shopping lists, memos, notes.

At the centre of all learning are two key skills – literacy and numeracy. Literacy is probably the more important of the two as pupils need literacy to access other areas of the curriculum. For example, to tackle a maths problem they might need to read the question accurately before applying the appropriate numeracy skills; or they may need to record the results of a science experiment in a written form.

Learning to read

Being able to read does not happen suddenly. Reading is a complex process involving different skills, some of which (e.g. visual discrimination and communication skills) the individual has been developing since birth. Being able to use and understand spoken language forms the basis for developing reading skills. A pupil who has a wide variety of language will have developed many of the skills needed for learning to read.

Pupils who are pushed too hard by being forced to read and write before they are ready may actually be harmed in terms of their literacy development as they can be put off reading, writing and other related activities. The area of learning **communication, language and literacy** included in the early learning goals for the Foundation Stage provides guidelines to help early years staff (and parents) understand the importance of informal approaches to language and literacy.

Reading is essential for the development of literacy skills

There is no set age at which pupils are magically ready to read although most pupils learn to read between the ages of 4½ and 6 years old. The age at which a pupil learns to read depends on a number of factors:

○ physical maturity and co-ordination skills
○ social and emotional development
○ language experiences especially access to books
○ interest in stories and rhymes
○ concentration and memory skills
○ opportunities for play.

Reading skills checklist:

1 Can the pupil see and hear properly?

2 Are the pupil's co-ordination skills developing within the expected norm?

3 Can the pupil understand and follow simple verbal instructions?

4 Can the pupil co-operate with an adult and concentrate on an activity for short periods?

5 Does the pupil show interest in the details of pictures?

6 Does the pupil enjoy looking at books plus joining in with rhymes and stories?

7 Can the pupil retell parts of a story in the right order?

8 Can the pupil tell a story using pictures?

9 Can the pupil remember letter sounds and recognise them at the beginning of words?

10 Does the pupil show pleasure or excitement when able to read words in school?

If the answer is 'yes' to most of these questions, the pupil is probably ready to read; if the answer is 'no' to any of the questions, the pupil may need additional support or experiences in those areas before they are ready to read.

Reading methods

Whole word or 'look and say'

Pupils are taught to recognise a small set of key words (usually related to a reading scheme) by means of individual words printed on flashcards. Pupils recognise the different words by shape and other visual differences. Once pupils have developed a satisfactory sight vocabulary, they go onto the actual reading scheme. The whole word method is useful for learning difficult words, which do not follow the usual rules of English language. The drawback is that this method does not help pupils to work out new words for themselves.

Phonics

With this approach pupils learn the sounds that letters usually make. This method helps pupils establish a much larger reading vocabulary fairly quickly as they can 'sound out' new words for themselves. The disadvantage is that there are many irregular words in the English language; the same letters may make many different sounds, for example b*ough*, r*ough*, thr*ough*. However, pupils do better with this method than any other approach.

Apprenticeship approach

This method, also known as the 'story' or 'real books' approach, does not formally teach pupils to read. Instead the pupil sits with an adult and listens to the adult read; the pupil starts reading along with the adult until the pupil can read some or all of the book alone. This method does not help the pupil with the process of decoding symbols. There has been much criticism of this method, but it has proved effective in this country and New Zealand as part of the 'Reading Recovery' programme for older, less-able readers.

Most adults helping pupils to develop reading skills use a combination of the 'look and say' method to introduce early sight vocabulary and then move onto the more intensive phonics approach to establish the pupils' reading vocabulary. It is important to be flexible to meet the individual literacy needs of pupils. Adults in school should work with parents to develop their children's reading skills.

Exercise
1. Investigate the different approaches to developing pupils' reading skills. Think about:
   - how you learned to read
   - how your own children (if any) learned or are learning to read
   - approaches to teaching reading in your school.
2. Consider the similarities and differences between these approaches in developing pupils' reading skills.

Activities that help to develop early reading skills include:

- ○ **Talking:** pupils who are effective communicators often transfer these skills to reading
- ○ **Listening games** like 'guess the sound', sound lotto and using everyday objects or musical instruments to encourage auditory discrimination
- ○ **Sharing books, stories, poems and rhymes** (see below)
- ○ **Matching games** like snap, matching pairs, jigsaws to encourage visual discrimination.
- ○ **Memory games** like 'I went shopping …'
- ○ **Looking at other printed materials** e.g. newspapers, magazines, comics, signs
- ○ **Fun with letters:** 'I spy …' using letter sounds; going on a 'letter hunt' (looking around the classroom for things beginning with a particular letter); hang up an 'alphabet washing line'; sing alphabet songs and rhymes
- ○ **Television:** use education programmes to encourage and extend reading skills.

Learning to write

Pupils will experience written language through books and stories (see below) and learn that writing is made up of symbols or patterns organised on paper in a particular way. In English this means 26 letters in the alphabet written from left to right horizontally. Pupils also learn by watching adults and other children at home and in school that writing can be used for:

○ recording past events and experiences (e.g. news, outings, visitors, special events)
○ exchanging information (e.g. notes, memos, letters, postcards)
○ functional writing (e.g. shopping lists, recipes, menus, recording experiments or data)
○ sharing stories and ideas (e.g. story writing, poetry).

Writing is essential for the development of literacy skills

Pupils do not learn to write just through exposure to a writing environment. Writing is a skill that has to be taught. Learning to write involves learning specific conventions with regard to letter shapes, the sequence of letters in words, word order in sentences, the direction of writing, etc. It is usual to teach writing skills alongside reading. This helps pupils to make the connection between written letters and the sounds they make when read. Most of the activities used to develop pupils' reading skills will also help their writing skills. In addition, pupils need plenty of opportunities to develop the co-ordination skills necessary for writing:

○ hand-eye co-ordination
○ fine manipulative skills for pencil control
○ being able to sit still with the correct posture for writing.

Some pupils may have special needs that require writing using alternative means, such as Braille, voice-activated computer or word processor. (For more information see Chapter 6: Supporting Learning Activities.)

Developing writing skills is much more difficult then reading because of:

○ the considerable physical and cognitive demands (e.g. co-ordinating movements to write)
○ the need for legible writing (e.g. letters of consistent size and shape; gaps between words)
○ the need for punctuation and sentence structure
○ correct spelling requirements
○ the need for writing of the required length which makes sense.

Exercise
1. How did you learn to write?
2. Which activities for developing pupils' writing skills have you used and/or observed in school?

Activities that help to develop early writing skills

Provide lots of opportunities for younger pupils to develop the co-ordination skills needed for writing including drawing, painting, colouring in, tracing, threading beads, cutting and sticking, and sewing (remember safety). Learning to write takes lots of practise so provide plenty of opportunities for younger pupils to form letters in a variety of ways: in the air, in sand, using paints, with crayons, pencils, felt-tips, using plasticine, clay or play dough. Let pupils use their preferred hand when writing. Some pupils swap around for sometime until they establish which hand they feel most comfortable writing with. Give pupils lots of praise for their attempts at writing and put their efforts on display. Do not worry that it does not look neat in the early stages, it is having a go at writing that is important.

Encourage independent spelling techniques, such as word banks, key words on permanent display, topic words on the board or on paper at the pupils' tables, personal word books and dictionaries. Release younger pupils or those with co-ordination difficulties (such as dyspraxia) from their physical limitations in writing by allowing them to dictate their ideas while an adult acts as scribe, or use a tape recorder or word processor. Pupils should be given opportunities to write about their experiences as appropriate to their age and level of development. In addition to activities such as news and recording events, pupils need to be able to create their own stories and poems as a means of expressing their feelings and ideas.

 KEY TASK

Observe a pupil engaged in a writing activity.

In your assessment comment on:
- the pupil's manipulative skills
- the pupil's concentration
- the creativity of the finished piece of writing.

Suggest ways to encourage and extend the pupil's writing skills.

NVQ Links: Level 2: 2–5.1, 2–3.1; Level 3: 3–18.2, 3–7.1, 3–7.2, 3–3.1, 3–3.2, 3–8.1, (3–20.1)

The importance of books and stories in developing literacy skills

Why are books important?

Books and stories make the learning environment more attractive and interesting. They provide a lively stimulus in various ways ranging from the visual experience of sharing well-illustrated picture books to the vocal experience of sharing storytelling or the reading aloud of well-written texts. By sharing books with pupils, you show them a positive attitude towards books and that reading is an important skill, which is essential to everyday life. Sharing books and stories with pupils is the most positive and interesting way to encourage them to want to read for themselves. The time spent sharing books and stories is also a special time, creating a positive bond between adult and pupils.

These times can have an almost magical quality for pupils, especially if the adult:

○ develops interesting storytelling techniques including visual aids such as puppets
○ demonstrates clear and articulate 'reading-aloud' skills (e.g. voice and tone changes)
○ chooses appropriate and attractive books for the target audience
○ has a wide repertoire of rhymes and songs to include in story sessions.

Encourage pupils (and their parents) to use their local library; remember it's free! Check pupils are aware of the library as a valuable local resource for all kinds of information (e.g. the Internet) not just books. Many libraries have story sessions for the under-5's; some even have special story/activity sessions and homework clubs (which help develop referencing skills) for children aged 5+ as well as book-related activities during the school holidays.

Attractive books can be expensive, but many libraries and local authorities run special loan schemes for schools wishing to borrow books. Paperbacks (rather than hard cover versions) covered with plastic jackets are an economical way of investing in quality children's books. Running book clubs and having book fairs also encourages pupils' interest in books and stories. They can also be another useful source of books as schools receive a percentage of free books depending on the number of books bought by pupils, parents and staff.

How books help to develop literacy skills

Books and stories help to develop pupils' language and literacy skills by:

○ **encouraging listening skills and auditory discrimination** – being attentive during story time, distinguishing between sounds, being aware of rhyming words
○ **developing phonic skills** – knowing letter sounds, blends
○ **providing stimulus for discussion and literacy activities**
○ **introducing or extending pupil vocabulary**
○ **using repetition** to reinforce pupils' language and learning in a memorable way.

Selecting *appropriate* literature for pupils is essential. Pupils need books and stories that reflect their individual needs and interests. Here are some general points to consider when choosing books and stories:

○ attractive and colourful with well-drawn, appropriate illustrations
○ text appropriate for age and level of development e.g. one/two sentences per picture; several sentences and some pages without pictures; text only books
○ safe for pupils and well-made in a variety of good quality materials

Adult interaction can help in the
development of literacy skills

- O positive images reflecting our multicultural society, the roles of men and women and people with special needs in positive ways
- O home-made books about familiar objects and everyday life can be just as appealing as commercially produced books especially to younger pupils
- O photograph albums or books made using photographs of objects and people in the school
- O books are a source of information and not just for fun; make sure the information provided represents the wide range of pupil interests in your class (everything from animals to yo-yos); include illustrated factual books, dictionaries, encyclopaedia, atlases
- O less is more, a small selection of quality books carefully chosen is better than a large collection of poor quality, unsuitable ones. Quality books are expensive, but can be stretched to provide variety by rotating the books at frequent intervals (e.g. each class within a year group or Key Stage could have a selection of books that could be swapped every month or half-term). Remember to use any local resources as suggested earlier.

Positive images in books are important because pupils gain valuable information about themselves, other people and the world around them through books and stories. In the same way that television has a powerful influence on pupils' perception of the world, so do books. Pupils believe what they see, hear or read so it is vital that books and stories:

- o depict equality of opportunity in terms of gender, race, culture, special needs and age
- o develop pupils' confidence in their own backgrounds
- o promote awareness of other people's cultures
- o encourage positive self-esteem and self-image.

(Information on the language and literacy needs of bilingual pupils is included in Chapter 7: Developing Language and Communication Skills.)

Exercise

Give examples of books and stories you have used with pupils to promote positive images of race/culture, gender, special needs/disability or age.

Describe how you used each book and give examples of the pupils' responses.

Story telling/reading techniques

Story telling is not the same as *reading* stories from a book. Story telling involves recounting traditional tales in your own particular style or making up your own stories based on people or themes familiar to the pupils. When reading from a story book you can usually rely on pictures to provide the visual aids you need to maintain the pupils' interest and attention.

To make story telling more interesting and entertaining you can use:

- o Puppets and props or objects related to the story (e.g. hats to indicate different characters)
- o sound effects (e.g. musical instruments or encouraging the pupils to join in with appropriate sounds such as animal noises)
- o your own pictures, posters or photographs
- o pupils' drawings and paintings
- o pupils to act out key characters/situations.

Whether you read or tell a story follow these guidelines:

1 **Preparation**: you should know the story well to avoid stumbling over words or losing the thread. You should recognise where you need to change pace, pause or show excitement.

2 **Practise**: read or tell the story aloud to a friend, colleague or your own children. This way you will know how long the story takes to read/tell and the outcome of the story.

3 **Organisation**: sit the pupils comfortably on a soft surface, such as carpet or cushions in a semicircle. Make sure all the pupils in the group can see and hear you and have a clear view of the book and/or visual aids. 'Story steps' (almost like a mini-theatre) are an excellent way to set the stage for the unfolding of a story. If your classroom does not have built-in story steps, you could arrange chairs, cushions and mats to create a similar effect.

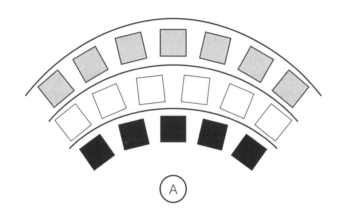

Key:

▨ Row of low chairs

☐ Row of cushions

◼ Row of mats/carpet squares

Ⓐ Low easy chair for adult storyteller

Story steps

4 **Introduction**: talk briefly about the story to gain the pupils' interest and create anticipation. Point out any links with related topics, themes or events within the school.

5 **Eye contact**: to maintain the pupils' interest and involvement in the story, frequent eye contact is essential.

6 **Expression**: vary your speed and tone of voice. Keep pace with the story. Use facial expressions to emphasise what the characters are saying/doing. If telling a story use gestures and body language as well to bring the characters to life. You can use different 'voices' for each

character, but only do this if you feel comfortable and if it does not spoil the flow of the story. As you become more confident, you will feel able to use different voices without losing your place or using the wrong 'voice'.

7 **Interruptions**: try to deal with these without losing the thread of the story, for example if pupils want to share their own similar experiences – if possible ask them to wait until after the story. Remember to ask them what they wanted to say when you have finished the story. Keep pupils you know to be potentially disruptive during story sessions close by you so that you can use a gentle touch or look to keep them under control rather than having to use verbal requests which interrupt the story.

8 **Conclusion**: usually one story (or one chapter with longer story books) at a time is enough; follow-up the story with discussion, related rhymes, poems and action songs to keep your audience interested and to further develop their language and communication skills. Encourage pupils to look at the book and/or visual aids afterwards.

 KEY TASK

Observe pupils during a story session. Focus on:
- how the adult communicates with the pupils
- the pupils' responses.

In your assessment consider the benefits of the story session to the pupils':
- language and communication skills
- literacy skills.

NVQ Links: Level 2: 2–5.1, 2–3.1; Level 3: 3–18.1, 3–18.2, 3–18.3, 3–7.1, 3–7.2, 3–8.1

Making books for pupils

Making books for pupils is another excellent way to develop their language and literacy skills. The great advantage of home-made books is that they can be personalised to make them more relevant and exciting stimuli to match *individual* language and literacy needs. For example, you could include pictures or photographs of the pupils' favourite things or interests. Nothing is guaranteed to get pupils' attention more than the knowledge that you have made a book especially for them.

When making books for pupils you can use a variety of materials, including pictures on thick card covered in clear sticky-backed plastic for younger pupils or a book/file with 10–20 plastic pockets with pages of pictures and activities for older pupils. When making books for pupils remember the following:

o ensure the book is safe for pupil use, sturdy and well-made
o the book is attractive and stimulating
o keep it simple – one picture and/or activity per page
o make sure the pictures/activities are appropriate for their age and level of development
o show awareness of equal opportunities, e.g. the pictures reflect positive images of race, culture, gender, special needs
o include text, pictures and activities that will encourage or extend the pupils' language and literacy skills
o use words that relate to the pictures/activities to maximise the opportunities for language. Use open questions. Remember the younger the pupils, the shorter the text. If possible, use a word processor for a more professional look. Also, remember to use the script preferred by your school.

Making books with pupils

Another exciting literacy activity for pupils is making their own books, which can be based on:

o a story that you have told rather than read to the pupils
o the pupils' version of a favourite story or traditional tale
o a group or class topic
o an account of a visit or event
o the pupils' daily routine
o the pupils' *own* stories, poems or rhymes.

Use large sheets of thick paper (minimum size A4) and if possible cover the finished pages of the book with clear sticky-backed plastic. (If this is too expensive, make sure at least the front and back are covered to keep them clean and more durable.) Depending on the age of the pupils you may need to help with the illustrations. You could draw outlines of the characters as suggested by the pupils which they can then complete using a variety of techniques: sponge painting; potato printing; rubbings; collage; filling in details with crayon or paint. Use the pupils' ideas for the text too. Use a word processor to give the book the look of a printed book. Pupils who are used to working with computers should be able to do the word-processing themselves.

KEY TASK

1. Plan a story session. Read or tell a story using the guidelines in this chapter.
2. Include a follow-up activity to extend the pupils' language and literacy skills e.g.
   - discussion about the story
   - rhymes and songs related to the story
   - drawings or paintings about the story
   - group or class book retelling the story.

NVQ Links: Level 2: 2–5.1, 2–3.1, 2–3.2; Level 3: 3–18.1, 3–18.2, 3–18.3, 3–3.1, 3–3.2, 3–8.1, 3–8.2

National Curriculum targets for English

Key Stage 1

To participate fully in school, pupils need to develop four basic skills: speaking, listening, reading and writing. As part of the National Curriculum for English, pupils learn how to express their ideas and experiences clearly and creatively using spoken and written forms of language. Pupils listen to and read stories, poems and rhymes from all over the world as well as using books to discover new information.

By age 7, most pupils can:

Speaking and listening

- listen carefully
- include details to interest listeners
- speak clearly
- tell stories and repeat rhymes/poems
- learn and use new words in discussions
- adapt speech for different people or situations.

Reading

- express opinions about events or ideas they have read
- read aloud and understand stories/factual books
- use different methods to work out the meaning of unfamiliar words.

Writing

- write stories with a beginning, a middle and an end

○ use writing for different purposes (e.g. lists or instructions)
○ use interesting and appropriate vocabulary
○ write in sentences, using capital letters at the beginning and full stops at the end
○ spell familiar words correctly
○ use spelling patterns to write unfamiliar words
○ shape letters correctly and write neatly and legibly.

Key Stage 2

To participate fully in learning at school pupils should continue to develop and extend the four key skills of speaking, listening, reading and writing. As part of the National Curriculum for English pupils learn to listen to and discuss the ideas of others in addition to presenting their own. Pupils read for pleasure and to discover new information as well as being able to discuss their opinions about what they have read. Pupils should now be able to put their thoughts into writing more easily due to increased understanding of language structure, spelling and punctuation.

By age 11, most pupils can:

Speaking and listening

○ listen to presentations and discussions
○ talk intelligently about what they have heard
○ develop ideas and stories
○ use language creatively to interest the listener
○ use some features of standard English when necessary.

Reading

○ understand important characters, events, ideas or themes
○ read between the lines
○ use references to a text to support their opinions about its content
○ find information using different methods (e.g. index or Internet).

Writing

○ write in an expressive and thoughtful way using different forms
○ organise ideas to capture the reader's attention
○ use wider vocabulary to be more adventurous with words
○ spell words accurately, most of the time
○ use punctuation to indicate where sentences start and finish
○ use punctuation to clarify meaning within sentences
○ write legibly and fluently using joined-up writing.

Key Stage 3

To participate fully in learning at secondary school pupils should continue to extend the effective use of the four key English skills by speaking clearly, listening closely, reading carefully and writing fluently. These skills will help pupils to express themselves creatively and increase their confidence about speaking in public and writing for others. Pupils should read classic and contemporary prose and poetry from around the world, examining how writers use language and considering the social/moral issues raised.

By age 14, most pupils can:

Speaking and listening

○ adapt their speech for a variety of situations
○ vary their expression and vocabulary to keep listeners interested
○ be active participants in discussions
○ be sensitive to the feelings and views of others
○ use standard English fluently in formal situations
○ undertake and maintain a role in drama.

Reading

○ find and comment on different layers of meaning in texts
○ discuss their feelings and opinions about literature
○ justify their views about literature and refer to different aspects (e.g. structure/themes)
○ summarise information gathered from various sources.

Writing

○ write in an interesting way to capture the reader's attention
○ use different writing styles and a varied vocabulary
○ structure written work clearly
○ use different sentence structures and organise ideas in paragraphs
○ spell and punctuate their writing accurately most of the time
○ write neatly and legibly
○ use word processing skills to improve presentation of written work.

(Adapted from Learning Journey, DfEE, 2000.)

The National Literacy Strategy

Key Stages 1 & 2

In September 1998, the National Literacy Strategy was introduced in schools to raise educational standards for all primary pupils. As part of the literacy strategy all pupils have a daily literacy hour, which includes work at word, sentence and text level.

The daily literacy hour

The literacy hour has moved the focus of teaching from individual work to more whole-class and group teaching, which means that pupils have more time for learning and working together. During the literacy hour pupils spend 45 minutes being taught as a whole-class or in smaller ability groups; about 15 minutes is spent on independent literacy tasks. The literacy hour provides opportunities for pupils to develop their literacy skills through: high quality oral work; the structured teaching of phonics, spelling and grammar; guided/shared reading and writing activities.

Key Stage 3

The Key Stage 3 National Literacy Strategy aims to improve the achievements of 11–14 year old pupils. Key Stage 3 is a crucial point in a pupil's education as evidence indicates that if pupils perform well in the SATs tests at age 14, they will achieve success in their GCSEs. Additional support is being provided to help 11 year olds have a better transition from primary school to secondary school. Many pupils receive support through 'booster' programmes in Year 6 while some pupils will attend literacy (and numeracy) summer schools in the holidays before entering Year 7. 'Catch-up' programmes have also been devised to provide additional support for pupils in Year 7. Half-termly Literacy Progress Units are available for pupils experiencing difficulty with reading and writing.

Lesson structure

The lesson structure will be similar to that experienced by pupils in primary school. A typical lesson will include:

○ A short starter activity for the whole class.
○ The main teaching activity, composed of the teacher's contribution and pupil tasks.
○ A summary session to consolidate the pupils' learning.

The teaching assistant's role in developing literacy skills

Helping pupils to develop their literacy skills

The teaching assistant plays a key role in supporting the teacher and pupils during literacy activities. You need to find out from the teacher how the literacy activities are to be organised and your specific role in supporting various learning activities including class discussions, group activities and tasks for individuals.

You need to know and understand:

1   what the pupils have to do

2   the learning goals/objectives for the pupils

3   the level of support pupils require

4   how to report any difficulties experienced by the pupils to the teacher.

When supporting **primary pupils** you will be helping them to:

- read and write confidently and fluently
- check their reading and correct their own mistakes
- know and understand the sound and spelling system
- use this spelling system to read and spell accurately
- develop fluent and legible handwriting
- be interested in words and their meanings
- develop and use an ever-increasing vocabulary
- know about and be able to write stories, poems and factual accounts
- understand how narratives are structured including setting, characters and plot
- plan, draft and revise their own writing
- be interested in books and read for pleasure
- assess and give reasons for their literary preferences
- develop their imagination, creativity and critical awareness.

When supporting **secondary pupils** you will be helping them to:

- read and appreciate a wide range of plays, poems and books, both fiction and non-fiction, including classic and contemporary writers and writers from different cultures
- learn to get more from reading and discover different layers of meaning
- understand there can be different interpretations of writing
- explore how writers compose characters and plots
- compare various styles and themes of writing from English literature and other cultures
- look at different ways of presenting writing
- use their experiences of fiction and non-fiction to create their own stories, poems, plays, articles and reviews
- develop different styles of writing for different purposes and readers
- extend their knowledge of grammar, spelling and punctuation

o learn how to proof-read their written work, assess its content and edit it as necessary

o write quickly and fluently with neat and legible presentation.

KEY TASK

Give a detailed account of how you have helped pupils with learning activities which develop their literacy skills. Include information on the following:

- the learning goals/objectives for the pupils
- the level of support required for individual pupils
- your role in supporting the pupils
- how you monitored pupil responses
- how you reported any difficulties experienced by the pupils to the teacher.

NVQ Links: Level 2: 2–5.1; Level 3: 3–18.1, 3–18.2, (3–20.1)

Using ICT to help pupils develop their literacy skills

Computers and other associated technology are now part of everyday life, so it is as important for all pupils to be **computer-literate** as it is for them to develop traditional literacy (and numeracy) skills. Computers can make learning more attractive and interesting by providing a different, more visual way of developing and using literacy skills. For this reason computers can be particularly helpful for pupils with language, literacy or learning difficulties, especially as computer programs often have in-built praise or reward systems to motivate the user. Word-processing can enable pupils to write more easily and clearly, freed from the physical constraints of pencil control, and can encourage correct spelling through the use of a spell-checker. Computers can also help referencing skills by encouraging pupils to access information in encyclopaedia on CD-ROM or via the Internet. (For more information see Chapter 6: Supporting Learning Activities.)

Helping pupils to access the curriculum

In addition to helping pupils to develop their reading and writing skills as part of the National Curriculum for English, you may be involved in providing literacy support to help pupils access other areas of the curriculum. To provide this type of support you will need to know and understand:

1   the literacy requirements for the learning activities

2   the level of support needed by the pupils to meet these requirements

3   your role in providing literacy support

4   how to recognise and respond to any difficulties experienced by the pupils.

Exercise

Describe how you have provided literacy support to help a pupil or group of pupils to access different subjects within the National Curriculum.

Further reading...

Clay, M. (1992) *Becoming literate.* Heinemann.

Berger, A. and Gross, J. (ed.) (1999) *Teaching the literacy hour in the inclusive classroom.* David Fulton Publishers.

Bentley, D. *et al* (1999) *The really practical guide to English.* Nelson Thornes.

Bielby, N. (1998) *How to teach reading – a balanced approach.* Scholastic.

Department for Education and Employment (2001) *National literacy strategy: developing early writing.* DfEE.

Qualifications and Curriculum Authority (2000) *Curriculum guidance for the foundation stage.* QCA.

Whitehead, M. (1996) *The development of language and literacy.* Hodder & Stoughton.

Developing Numeracy Skills

9

{
Key points:

- What is numeracy?
- Why is numeracy important?
- Learning numeracy skills
- Activities which help to develop early numeracy skills
- National Curriculum targets for mathematics
- The National Numeracy Strategy
- The teaching assistant's role in developing numeracy skills
- Helping pupils to access the curriculum
}

What is numeracy?

The term 'numeracy' was introduced in about 1982 to describe what was previously called arithmetic. Individuals who are competent at arithmetic have always been described as 'numerate'; now this competency is called 'numeracy'.

Numeracy skills involve confidence and competence with numbers and measures including:

- knowledge and understanding of the number system
- knowing by heart various number facts (e.g. multiplication tables)
- using a range of mathematical skills
- making mental calculations
- being able to solve number problems in a variety of contexts
- presenting information about counting and measuring using graphs, diagrams, charts and tables.

In primary schools, numeracy is the central part of mathematics, but pupils are also taught about geometry and the beginnings of algebra.

Why is numeracy important?

Being able to do number calculations confidently is an essential life skill and it is also very important as a first step in learning mathematics. We use maths in everyday tasks, including:

o Shopping: checking change; buying the right quantities; getting value for money
o Cooking: weighing ingredients
o Decorating: calculating the amount of wallpaper, paint, carpet or other materials needed for the required areas
o Sewing: measuring materials; using graph paper to plot designs
o Journeys and holidays: understanding transport timetables; planning the best route; calculating mileage or the journey time; working out how much petrol is needed for a car journey.

Learning numeracy skills

Pupils need to develop the following numeracy skills:

o understanding numbers and the number system
o making calculations
o problem-solving
o using shape, space and measures
o handling data.

Understanding numbers and the number system

Many children learn number names and how to count before they begin school. At home and/or in early years settings (e.g. day nursery or playgroup) they do counting activities and sing number songs and rhymes. During the primary school years pupils develop and extend their counting skills. Younger pupils begin with numbers 0 to 20, which are the most difficult to learn as each number name is different; numbers from 20 onwards have recognisable patterns, which makes learning numbers up to 100 or more much easier. Pupils begin by counting forwards, then backwards from 20; once they are confident with this they learn to count forwards and backwards in sets of 2, 5 and 10, which helps with sums and the early stages of multiplication.

Pupils should have learned to recognise and use:

o number symbols and words for whole numbers 1 (one) to 20 (twenty) by age 4–5 years o all the whole numbers to 100 (hundred) plus halves and quarters by age 6–7 years

o numbers to 10,000 including more fractions and decimal places by age 8–9 years

o all whole numbers, fractions, decimals plus percentages by age 10–11 years.

During the primary school years, pupils also develop knowledge and understanding of the mathematical language relevant to numbers: smaller, bigger; more/less than; even and odd numbers; factors and prime numbers, etc.

The teaching of numeracy is an essential part of the primary curriculum

Making calculations

From about 4–5 years old pupils begin to learn how to make mathematical calculations using real objects to add and subtract small whole numbers. Gradually they recognise number patterns which make doing calculations easier e.g. being able to add 4 + 8 means they can also add 400 + 800. Memorising number facts also helps with calculations e.g. learning multiplication tables by heart. By age 10–11 years pupils should have learned addition, subtraction, multiplication and division using whole numbers, fractions, decimals and negative numbers. As well as learning mental calculations pupils also learn the standard written methods for these four calculation operations.

Problem-solving

Pupils also need to develop problem-solving skills in order to work out the best approach to finding a mathematical solution. They need to learn which *questions* to ask as well as developing the appropriate skills to answer mathematical problems:

○ What is the problem?
○ Which maths skill needs to be used? (e.g. addition, subtraction, measuring)
○ Will a graph, chart or diagram help find the solution?

Using shape, space and measures

In addition to developing competency with numbers, pupils learn to recognise and name geometrical shapes; they also learn about the properties of shapes, such as a triangle has three sides; a square has four right angles. Pupils learn about directions, angles and plotting points on a graph. They also learn to measure mass, distance, area and volume using appropriate units e.g. kilograms, metres, centimetres or litres. Measuring also includes learning to tell the time in hours and minutes.

Handling data

Handling data is an essential skill in this technological age and using computers is an important aspect of mathematics today (see information on being **computer-literate** in Chapter 8). Pupils learn to gather, arrange and convert data into useful information, for example, working out the likelihood of rain so we know when to wear a raincoat or take an umbrella.

EXERCISE:
List examples of activities (for the pupils you work with) under these headings:
1. Understanding numbers and number systems
2. Making calculations
3. Problem-solving
4. Using shape, space and measures
5. Handling data.

Activities that help to develop early numeracy skills

o *Sorting and counting* involving stories, rhymes and songs like '*Goldilocks and the three bears*'; matching games e.g. lotto, snap; play activities such as dressing-up (e.g. pairs of socks, gloves, mittens) and organising sets of plates, cutlery, boxes, toys in the home corner or play shop; using toy vehicles for counting and matching activities.

o *Understanding and using number* through playing games like dominoes, 'snakes and ladders' and other simple board games; looking for shapes/sizes and making comparisons, price tags and quantities in shop play and real shopping trips; number songs and rhymes like '*One, two, three, four, five, Once I caught a fish alive ...*'

o *Sequencing* through activities involving comparing and ordering (e.g. in-set jigsaws, doll/toy sizes); putting events in order (e.g. stories, pattern of the day/week).

o *Weighing and measuring* activities such as shop play (using balance scales to compare toys and other items); real shopping (helping to weigh fruit and vegetables); sand play (heavy and light); cooking activities (weighing ingredients to show importance of standard measures). Encourage pupils to develop understanding of length by comparing everyday objects/toys and using mathematical language such as tall/taller/tallest, short/shorter/shortest, long/longer/longest, same height, same length. Encourage them to record information. Use non-standard measures (e.g. hand-spans to measure everyday objects); gradually introduce standard measures (e.g. metre, centimetres).

o *Volume and capacity* – using sand and water play including filling various containers to encourage understanding of full, empty, half-full, half-empty, nearly full, nearly empty, more/less than, the same amount. Use coloured water to make activities more interesting. Gradually introduce idea of standard measures (e.g. litre of juice, pint of milk).

 **KEY TASK**

Observe a pupil or group of pupils during a mathematics/
numeracy activity.

In your assessment comment on:
- the mathematical skills used
- the pupils' use of appropriate mathematical language
- pupil responses and concentration levels during the activity.

Suggest ways to extend these mathematical skills.

NVQ Links: Level 2: 2–5.2; Level 3: 3–7.1, 3–7.2, 3–19.1, 3–19.2

National curriculum targets for mathematics

Key Stage 1

By age 7, most pupils should:

Using and applying mathematics

○ recognise and describe number patterns
○ select an appropriate maths skill to tackle/solve a problem
○ use words, symbols and basic diagrams to record
○ give details about how they solved a problem.

Number

○ count, read and write whole numbers up to 100
○ count forwards or backwards in ones or tens starting from different
  numbers
○ recognise if numbers are even or odd
○ know an addition can be undone with a subtraction
○ know by heart addition and subtraction facts for whole numbers up to ten
  (e.g. $2 + 8 = 10$, $8 + 2 = 10$, $10 - 2 = 8$ and $10 - 8 = 2$, etc.)
○ know number pairs in tens that make 100 (e.g. $40 + 60 = 100$, $60 + 40 =
  100$)
○ know addition can be done in any order but it is easier to begin with
  larger numbers
○ understand multiplying is just adding more of the same number
○ be able to double or halve numbers
○ know by heart the multiplication tables for 2, 5 and 10.

Shape, space and measure

○ use the correct names for basic 2-D and 3-D shapes
○ know how many sides, corners or right angles a shape has
○ calculate how a shape would look in a mirror
○ identify movements such as whole turns, half turns and quarter turns or right angles
○ measure objects using appropriate units (e.g. centimetres, metres, kilograms or litres)
○ measure lines to the nearest centimetre using a ruler
○ tell the time: o'clock, half past and quarter past the hour.

Key Stage 2

By age 11, most pupils should:

Using and applying mathematics

○ tackle/solve a problem using different maths skills
○ use and apply maths to solve practical problems
○ try to use their own ideas in problem-solving activities
○ organise and present results clearly.

Number

○ be able to do mental calculations (e.g. multiply and divide decimals by 10 or 100 and whole numbers by 1000)
○ arrange a set of numbers to three decimal places
○ be able to do written calculations (e.g. work with decimals to add and subtract)
○ decrease fractions to basic forms (e.g. three-twelfths to one quarter)
○ calculate fractions of numbers or quantities
○ know that a percentage is the number rate per hundred
○ calculate simple percentages of whole numbers
○ solve number problems concerning ratio and proportion
○ know by heart all the multiplication tables
○ use multiplication tables for division as well as multiplication
○ use +, −, ÷, and × to solve problems stated in words involving numbers or measures
○ use written methods of multiplication and division for more difficult calculations (e.g. 848.75×8, $284 \div 8$ and 345×21).

Shape, space and measure

○ measure angles to the nearest degree using a protractor
○ work out the perimeter and area of shapes which can be divided into rectangles

○ read and plot coordinates in the four quadrants
○ correctly interpret numbers on different measuring instruments
○ tell the time in hours and minutes
○ solve problems relating to time using a 12-hour or 24-hour clock.

Handling data

○ tackle and solve a maths problem by gathering and using information in diagrams, graphs, tables and charts.

Key Stage 3

By age 14, most pupils should:

Using and applying mathematics

○ be able to plan how to tackle a problem by working out which maths skills and information they need to use
○ be able to solve difficult problems by dividing them into smaller tasks
○ explain mathematical problems using words, symbols and diagrams
○ connect their solutions to the original problem
○ present solutions with reasonable levels of accuracy
○ describe how they reached a solution
○ be able to start giving mathematical justifications for their solutions.

Number and algebra

○ perform some mental calculations involving decimals, fractions, percentages, factors, powers and square roots
○ divide and multiply whole numbers by 10, 100, 1000 and so on
○ estimate probable solutions to calculations
○ use standard written methods for addition, subtraction, multiplication and division involving whole numbers, decimals and fractions
○ employ effective methods to add, subtract, multiply and divide fractions
○ utilise the connections between fractions, decimals, percentages, ratio and proportion to tackle and solve problems
○ use a calculator including: the constant, the sign change key, pi, function keys for powers, roots and fractions; use brackets and the calculator memory
○ relate calculator display information to the context of a problem
○ know and use index notation and basic examples of index laws (e.g. $2^2 \times 2^3 = 2^5$)
○ organise and use equations and their graphs to solve word problems
○ simplify and convert algebraic equations

o know how to use symbols to indicate positive and negative numbers
o use algebra to describe the nth term of a simple sequence
o develop the use of methodical trial and improvement (e.g. to find approximate solutions to equations such as $3x - x = 100$).

Shape, space and measure

o use a ruler, protractor and compasses to create lines, angles and 2-D or 3-D shapes
o use the properties of straight-sided shapes, and intersecting or parallel lines to solve mathematical problems
o identify when two triangles are congruent (identical)
o know and use formulae to calculate: the circumference and area of a circle; the area of a straight-sided shape; the volume of a cuboid
o use 2-D diagrams to investigate 3-D shapes
o be able to rotate, reflect, translate and enlarge 2-D shapes and understand how such changes affect the sides, angles and position of shapes
o write instructions to create and change shapes on a computer.

Handling data

o design a survey or experiment
o collect the necessary data from various sources (e.g. from tables, lists and computer)
o select the appropriate type of graph to illustrate the data gathered
o summarise unprocessed data using range and averages
o reach conclusions using their interpretations of graphs and diagrams
o calculate probabilities and solve problems in circumstances where there are limited but equal possible outcomes (e.g. rolling a dice)
o estimate probabilities from data collected during experiments.

(Adapted from Learning Journey, DfEE, 2000)

The National Numeracy Strategy

Key Stage 1 & 2

The National Numeracy Strategy was introduced into all primary schools in England and Wales in September 1999 and supports the National Curriculum for mathematics. A key feature of the National Numeracy Strategy is the *Framework for Teaching Mathematics from Reception to Year 6*, which shows a systematic range of mathematics work to ensure that primary pupils develop essential numeracy skills. The Framework aims to assist primary, middle and special schools (with primary-age pupils) to know and

The daily maths lesson

understand how pupils should progress in the primary years and to establish high but realistic expectations for their pupils in relation to developing numeracy skills. Teachers and others working with older pupils who have severe or complex special educational needs may also find the contents of the Framework useful.

The structure of a typical daily maths lesson

Depending on the age of the pupils, a daily maths lesson is about 45–60 minutes. The main emphasis is on pupils discussing mathematics and using appropriate mathematical terminology. The lesson is typically separated into three key sections:

1 **Oral and mental starter**
   All pupils in the class are taught together for the first 10 minutes. They are encouraged to sharpen their maths skills by: counting (in ones, twos, tens, backwards and forwards, etc.) or remembering addition and/or subtraction number facts (including reciting multiplication tables for older pupils). The teacher may also ask questions or go over previous homework.

2 **Main teaching activity**
   The main teaching activity lasts for about 30–40 minutes. The teacher may **introduce** a new maths skill, provide opportunities to **practise**

previous work or **extend** their skills on more difficult problems. Pupils may work for short times in groups, pairs or individually.

3 **Plenary**

The lesson ends with a plenary (lasting about 10 minutes) when the whole class comes together for a summary of the main points of the lesson. The teacher discovers what the pupils have actually learned and repeats the key points or specific maths skills that the pupils need to remember. The teacher may also set maths homework.

Key Stage 3

To provide a smoother transition in terms of learning mathematics, the *Springboard 7* programme consolidates what pupils have already learned in Year 6 before proceeding with the curriculum requirements for Year 7. The *Framework for teaching mathematics: Year 7, 8 and 9* extends the *Framework for teaching mathematics from Reception to Year 6* and is aimed at teachers and trainee teachers; it will also be helpful for those who support mathematics in schools, such as teaching assistants who provide numeracy support for pupils in secondary schools.

The teaching assistant's role in developing numeracy skills

Helping pupils to develop their numeracy skills

The teaching assistant has a key role in providing support for the teacher and pupils during numeracy activities. You need to find out from the teacher how the numeracy activities are to be organised and your specific role in supporting various learning activities including whole class oral/mental maths activities, group work and tasks for individuals.

You need to know and understand:

o What the pupils have to do.
o The learning goals/objectives for the pupils.
o The level of support pupils require.
o How to report any difficulties experienced by the pupils to the teacher.

When supporting **primary pupils** you will be helping them to:

o know and understand numbers and the number system
o count, calculate, solve simple maths problems and make simple lists, tables and charts
o use and apply mathematics to tackle and solve practical mathematical problems

- communicate their reasoning about problems and explain their solutions using objects, pictures, diagrams, numbers, symbols and relevant mathematical language
- make mental calculations by imagining numbers and the relationships between them
- select, collect, organise and present appropriate data using graphs and diagrams.

The teaching of mathematics is a major component of the secondary curriculum

When supporting **secondary pupils** you will be helping them to:

- know and understand numbers and the number system including: positive and negative numbers; factors and prime numbers; equivalent fractions; how fractions, decimals and percentages relate to each other; ratio and proportion
- employ standard methods to perform mental and written calculations including addition, subtraction, multiplication and division using whole numbers, fractions, decimals and percentages
- use calculator functions to complete complex calculations and understand the answers calculators give in relation to the initial mathematical problem
- develop efficient problem-solving skills
- know and understand how to use letter symbols in algebra

o set up and use simple equations to solve problems
o select, collect and organise appropriate data using tables, surveys, questionnaires, and CD-ROMs; presenting results using graphs, pie charts and diagrams and relating these to the original problem
o solve increasingly demanding mathematical problems by breaking the problem down into smaller, manageable tasks and developing deductive reasoning.

(Adapted from Learning Journey, DfEE, 2000)

 KEY TASK

Describe how you have helped pupils during learning activities which develop their numeracy skills. Include information on the following:
- the learning goals/objectives for the pupils
- the level of support required for individual pupils
- your role in supporting the pupils
- how you monitored pupil responses
- how you reported any difficulties experienced by the pupils to the teacher.

NVQ Links: Level 2: 2–5.2; Level 3: 3–19.1, (3–20.2)

Helping pupils to develop their understanding and use of shape, space and measures

The teaching assistant can also provide support for the teacher and pupils during mathematics activities involving shape, space and measures. You need to find out from the teacher how these types of activities are to be organised and your specific role in supporting various learning activities including whole-class maths activities, group work and tasks for individuals.

You need to know and understand:

o what the pupils have to do
o the learning goals/objectives for the pupils
o the level of support pupils require
o how to report any difficulties experienced by the pupils to the teacher.

When supporting **primary pupils** you will be helping them to:

○ look at, handle and describe the common features of basic 2-D and 3-D shapes (triangles, rectangles, squares, hexagons, pentagons, cubes, cylinders and spheres)
○ describe positions, directions and movements and right angles
○ work and measure using units of time, length, weight and capacity
○ estimate and measure everyday items.

Shape, space and measuring
activities

When supporting **secondary pupils** you will be helping them to:

○ know and understand the properties of 2-D and 3-D shapes
○ recognise the properties of angles in certain situations
○ learn and use Pythagoras' Theorem
○ use coordinates to identify points and use what they know about shapes to find the coordinates of points on a grid
○ use instruments and scales for measuring including using appropriate units
○ convert one unit to another e.g. kilograms to pounds, kilometres to miles, litres to pints
○ use rulers, protractors and compasses to construct 2-D and 3-D shapes
○ use formulae to calculate the area and the volume of 2-D and 3-D shapes.

KEY TASK

Plan and implement a learning activity which involves helping a pupil or group of pupils to understand and use shape, space or measures. (You could use your previous observation of a mathematics activity if appropriate.)

Include information on the following:
- the learning goals/objectives for the pupils
- the materials and equipment required
- the preparation and organisation for the activity
- the level of support required for individual pupils
- your role in supporting the pupils.

Review and evaluate the activity afterwards including:
- how the pupils responded to the activity
- what the pupils actually learned
- suggestions for further activities to extend the pupils' learning in this area.

NVQ Links: Level 3: 3–19.2, 3–3.1, 3–3.2, 3–8.1, 3–8.2

Helping pupils to access the curriculum

In addition to helping pupils to develop their numeracy skills as part of the National Curriculum for mathematics, you may be involved in providing numeracy support to help pupils access other areas of the curriculum. To provide this type of support you will need to know and understand:

○ the numeracy demands of the learning activities
○ the pupils' existing mathematical knowledge and skills in relation to these requirements
○ appropriate strategies to enable pupils to manage the demands of the activities
○ your role in providing the appropriate level of support
○ how to recognise and respond to any difficulties experienced by the pupils.

EXERCISE:
Describe how you have provided numeracy support to help a pupil or group of pupils to access different subjects within the National Curriculum.

Further reading...

Briggs, M. and Pritchard, A. (2002) *Using ICT in primary mathematics teaching*. Learning Matters.

Qualifications and Curriculum Authority (2000) *Curriculum guidance for the foundation stage*. QCA.

Qualifications and Curriculum Authority (1999) *The National Numeracy Strategy*. QCA.

Tanner, H. *et al* (2002) *Developing numeracy in the secondary school: a practical guide for students and teachers*. David Fulton Publishers.

Thompson, I. (ed) (1999) *Issues in teaching numeracy in primary schools*. Open University Press.

Topping, K. and Bamford, J. (1998) *The paired maths handbook: parental involvement and peer tutoring in mathematics*. David Fulton Publishers.

Williams, S. and Goodman, S. (2000) *Helping young children with maths*. Hodder & Stoughton.

Wright, R.J. *et al* (2002) *Teaching number: advancing children's skills and strategies*. Paul Chapman Publishing.

{ Key points:

- The importance of teamwork
- Working as part of a team
- The roles of the teacher and the teaching assistant
- Working in partnership with the teacher
- Working with the special educational needs coordinator
- Understanding key school policies: equal opportunities; health and safety; child protection; confidentiality
- Liaising with parents
- Working with other professionals
- Reviewing and developing your professional practice. }

The importance of teamwork

Much of adult life involves working with other people usually in a group or team. Individuals within a team affect each other in various ways. Within the team there will be complex interactions involving different personalities, roles, and expectations as well as hidden agendas which influence the behaviour of individual members of the team. Teamwork is essential when working closely and regularly with other people over a long period of time. Teamwork is important because it helps all members of the team to:

☆ **T** ake effective action when planning and/or assigning agreed work tasks
☆ **E** fficiently implement the agreed work tasks
☆ **A** gree aims and values which set standards of practice
☆ **M** otivate and support each other
☆ **W** elcome feedback about their work
☆ **O** ffer additional support in times of stress
☆ **R** eflect on and evaluate their own working practices
☆ **K** now and use each person's strengths and skills.

Working as part of a team

As a teaching assistant you need to know and understand:

o The organisational structure of the school

○ Your role and responsibilities within the team (see Chapter 1)
○ The roles and responsibilities of other team members
○ How to contribute to effective team practice
○ How to participate in team meetings
○ Key school policies including: equal opportunities; health and safety; child protection; confidentiality
○ Your role and responsibilities in relation to these policies.

The organisational structure of the school

As a teaching assistant, you need to know and understand the different roles of the team members in your school and the process of decision making within the team. A teaching assistant in a primary, secondary or special school is part of a team, which will include some or all of the following:

○ other teaching assistants
○ class or subject teachers
○ deputy head teacher
○ head teacher
○ special educational needs coordinator (SENCO)
○ specialist teachers (e.g. to support pupils with sensory or physical impairment)
○ parent helpers and/or other volunteers
○ students on placement from college
○ pupils on work experience from secondary school.

You need to be very clear about the organisational structure of the school as information from different people can be confusing or even contradictory. In particular, you need to know who is your line manager; that is, the person who manages your work in school. Your line manager may not necessarily be the class teacher; depending on the size of the school and the responsibilities of senior staff, your line manager could be the head teacher, deputy head, head of department or key stage co-ordinator. If your work mostly involves supporting pupils with special educational needs then the SENCO may well be your line manager. Whoever your line manager is, you must always follow the directions of the teacher in whose class you are working with pupils. When the class teacher and your line manager are not the same person, their roles and responsibilities need to be understood both by them and by you.

The roles of the teacher and teaching assistant

Teaching assistants and teachers need to be aware of their different roles. The teacher's role is to plan lessons and to direct pupils' learning. The teaching assistant's role is to provide *support* for the teacher by supporting pupils during the teaching of the curriculum. The teaching assistant works with the teacher to support pupils' learning within the whole class, or works on their own to support the learning of an individual pupil or small group of pupils. The teaching assistant *always* works under the direction of the class or subject teacher. (For more detailed information on the teaching assistant's role and responsibilities see Chapter 1.)

It is only in recent years that teacher training has included the management of other adults (e.g. teaching assistants, nursery nurses and parent helpers) in the classroom. Some teachers may not be used to working with other adults in their classrooms and so only allow teaching assistants to do routine tasks when they could be providing the teachers with much higher levels of support. Senior staff within schools should provide clear guidelines on how teaching assistants can provide support in the classroom. Effective teamwork helps to establish clear roles and responsibilities as well as organising the classroom to ensure that teaching assistants have the necessary space to carry out their responsibilities.

Working in partnership with the teacher

Advanced planning (with clear objectives) and the detailed preparation of work are central to the effective delivery of the curriculum and to providing appropriate support for pupils' learning. Teachers need to involve teaching assistants in the planning and preparation of their work by having regular planning meetings about once a term or every half term. In addition, each day the teacher and the teaching assistant should discuss:

○ the teacher's lesson plans
○ the learning objectives for the pupils
○ the teaching assistant's contribution to the lesson
○ the type and level of support for the pupils.

These regular planning meetings and discussions will help to avoid confusion as both the teacher and the teaching assistant will then be clear about the exact tasks to be performed and the level of support to be provided. Short discussions after lessons are also helpful as teaching assistants can provide feedback to the teacher about the progress of pupils during group or individual activities. This feedback can make a valuable contribution to the teacher's assessment of pupils and help with the future planning of learning activities (see Chapter 5).

Teaching assistants also need to be familiar with the ways individual teachers deal with pupils who demonstrate difficult behaviour to avoid giving conflicting messages to pupils. While all staff in a school should work within the framework of the school's behaviour management policy, individual teachers may have different approaches to responding to difficult behaviour based on their own teaching style and the individual needs of their pupils (see Chapter 2).

Working with the special educational needs co-ordinator

Many teaching assistants are responsible for supporting pupils with special educational needs. As part of this responsibility the teaching assistant should:

- be aware of each pupil's special educational needs
- how these needs affect the pupil
- the special provision and learning support required
- their role in helping the pupil to access the curriculum.

This role will involve working with the teacher responsible for pupils with special educational needs – the special educational needs co-ordinator (SENCO). Regular meetings, usually once a week, help the teaching assistant and the SENCO to provide effective support for the learning and participation of pupils with special educational needs. Teaching assistants may also be involved in contributing to and reviewing individual educational plans (IEPs) or behaviour support plans because they spend more time working with individual pupils with special educational needs than the class teacher.

The process of decision making within the team

The head teacher, the senior management team and the school governors are ultimately responsible for decision making and what happens in school on a day-to-day basis. However, as a member of the team providing support for pupils within the school, you share collective responsibility for decisions made by this team. For example, if the team decides to implement a new type of learning activity, its success or failure is the collective responsibility of the whole team, not just the person who suggested the activity. When decisions are agreed by the team you must ensure that your work plans and practices are consistent with these decisions.

Regular team meetings are a
crucial part of good
professional practice

Exercise
1. Give examples of how the team makes decisions concerning the planning and allocation of agreed work tasks.
2. What is *your* role in the decision making process?

How to contribute to effective team practice

Effective communication is essential for developing effective team practice. Look back at the list of inter-personal skills needed for effective communication with children and adults in Chapter 1. Effective lines of communication are also important to ensure that all members of the team receive the necessary up-to-date information to enable them to make a full contribution to the life of the school. As a teaching assistant you may feel rather isolated if you work only part time, work in only one class or support an individual pupil with special educational needs. Make sure you check school notice boards, newsletters and/or staff bulletins for important information. You can also use informal opportunities such as break or lunch times to share information, experiences and ideas with the SENCO, teachers or other teaching assistants. Regular lines of communication are particularly important if more than one teaching assistant works with the same pupil or pupils. You might find a communications book or file may be useful as well as regular meetings with other teaching assistants. If you are a new (or student) teaching assistant you may benefit from the knowledge and understanding of existing teaching assistants; if you are an experienced teaching assistant you can make a valuable contribution to the induction or on-going training of new teaching assistants, possibly acting as a mentor.

How to participate in team meetings

As a teaching assistant you will also be involved in regular team meetings with the teacher (or teachers) in whose class you work and/or the SENCO. These meetings will enable you to make relevant contributions to provide more effective support for both the teacher and pupils. You may discuss specific plans the teacher has made relating to the pupils' learning, the progress made by pupils including their achievements and any difficulties plus the appropriate resources and support approaches.

You may also be invited to more general staff meetings. Where there are logistical problems in all teaching assistants being able to attend all staff meetings, you may be welcome to attend any meeting but be specifically invited to attend meetings where issues are to be discussed that are directly relevant to your work in schools.

You need to prepare for meetings carefully especially if you have been asked to provide information, for example, on the progress of a pupil with whom you work. Even if you are not required to make a specific contribution you still need to look at the meeting agenda and any relevant reports in advance so that you can participate in discussions during the meeting. At team meetings, participate in ways which are consistent with your role as a teaching assistant. Ensure your contributions are relevant and helpful to the work of the team. Express your opinions in a clear, concise manner and demonstrate respect for the contributions made by other team members. Make notes during the meeting to remind yourself of any action you need to take as a result of the issues discussed and decisions made by the team.

 **KEY TASK**

1. Participate in a team meeting relevant to your role in school; for example, a planning meeting to discuss a week's or half term's learning activities for the pupils. (When doing this task, for reasons of confidentiality, avoid meetings where problems concerning specific pupils are referred to in detail.)
2. Make notes on the key points discussed at the meeting. With the team leader's permission include a copy of the agenda.
3. Then consider the following points:
   - What preparation did you need to make before the meeting?
   - What was your contribution to the meeting?
   - What action did you need to take as a result of the meeting? (e.g. were you set specific tasks and if so, what were they?)

NVQ Links: Level 2: 2–4.1, 2–3.1, 2–3.2; Level 3: 3–21.1, 3–21.2, 3–3.1, 3–3.2, 3–8.1, 3–8.2 (3–14.1, 3–14.2, 3–16.1, 3–16.2 special needs)

Making an effective contribution to your team

In order to make a more effective contribution to your team you need to:

o develop and maintain confidence in your own abilities
o maintain or improve your self-esteem
o practice assertiveness techniques
o take care of your emotional well-being.

Self-esteem is developed from childhood; some children and adults have feelings of low self-esteem which have negative effects on their confidence in their own abilities. You may need to develop your own feelings of self worth to improve your self-esteem (see Chapter 3: PSHE and the suggestions for further reading at the end of this chapter).

Assertive people gain control over their lives by expressing personal feelings and exerting their rights in such a way that other people listen. Assertive individuals also show respect for other people's feelings. Practising assertiveness techniques involves:

1 being aware of your own feelings

2 putting your feelings into words

3 connecting how you feel with the actions of others

4 being aware of the other person's feelings

5 arranging a specific time and place for a discussion

6 making a statement showing you are aware of their feelings

7 listening actively to their feedback.

(Houghton and McColgan, 1995.)

Working with children or young people is a rewarding but often challenging or even stressful occupation. You need to take responsibility for your own emotional well-being and take the necessary action to tackle or reduce stress in your life. For example:

o develop assertiveness techniques
o take regular exercise including relaxation
o have a healthy diet
o manage time effectively.

Time management

Effective time management involves being clear about what you need to do and that you are able to do it. Unrealistic work goals lead to: work tasks piling up; unnecessary stress; feeling overwhelmed; time being wasted in unnecessary disagreements due to tempers flaring.

Essential steps to effective time management

1 Decide to use time more effectively.

2 Check what you need to do, then prioritise: urgent/essential down to unimportant.

3 Make 'to do' lists in order of priority.

4 Estimate the time needed for tasks realistically.

5 Say 'No' or delegate if you cannot do a task in the time specified.

6 Forward plan using a good diary.

7 Organise how you intend to do each task.

8 Do it!

9 Monitor or revise plans if necessary.

10 Value other people's time by being punctual for meetings and appointments.

Efficient organisation of the learning environment can also contribute to more effective time management. For example:

○ a chalk or white board may be used to indicate where people are
○ check that cupboards, desk drawers, filing cabinets, etc. are clearly labelled
○ remember 'A place for everything and everything in its place'
○ keep everything you need for specific tasks in one place
○ store items you use regularly in accessible places
○ throw away rubbish
○ find out if there is a quiet room/area for undisturbed work or discussions.

Exercise

How do you plan your time to include work duties, study requirements and home/family commitments? Make a list of the ways you could manage your time more effectively.

Responding to difficulties and conflict situations within the team

As a teaching assistant, you need to be able to recognise and respond to issues that affect the team's ability to work effectively. This includes dealing appropriately with difficulties and conflict situations, which affect your working relationships with colleagues. This may mean taking direct action and/or reporting your concerns to someone who has the authority to deal with these difficulties if you cannot resolve them or they are outside your role/beyond your capabilities. Conflicts are a part of everyone's working lives. Most conflicts are usually minor and quickly resolved especially when people work together effectively as a team. If communication and working relationships break down, then conflict situations can arise which seriously damage the atmosphere of the school. Conflicts can occur between: colleagues; staff and senior management; staff and parents; the school and the local education authority.

Most conflicts at work arise due to:

○ concerns about workloads
○ disputes over pay and conditions
○ disagreements about management issues
○ clashes between personalities.

Conflicts can also arise due to prejudice or discrimination; evidence of such attitudes or behaviour must be challenged as they are not only undesirable but unlawful. However, it is essential to follow school policy and procedures together with any relevant legal requirements when dealing with these issues.

Many difficulties and conflicts within schools can be resolved through open and honest discussion. Sometimes another person can act as a mediator to help those involved to reach a satisfactory agreement or compromise. Where serious difficulties or conflict situations cannot be resolved, then the school will have a grievance procedure to deal with it. This usually involves talking to your line manager about the problem in the first instance, they will then refer the matter to the senior management team/head teacher. If the problem concerns your line manager, then you may need to talk to the head teacher directly. You may also be asked to put your concerns in writing. If the matter cannot be resolved at this stage then, depending on the nature of the conflict, the school governors, the local education authority and relevant trade unions may be involved. Check with your line manager or the staff handbook for the exact procedures in your school.

 KEY TASK

1. Describe how you have responded (or would respond) to a conflict situation in school. (Be tactful and remember confidentiality!)
2. Outline the grievance procedure for staff in the school where you work.

NVQ Links: Level 2: 2–4.1, 2–3.2; Level 3: 3–21.1, 3–8.2

Understanding key school policies

All schools have policies and procedures relating to different aspects within the school e.g. school admissions; behaviour management; staff recruitment and training; grievance and disciplinary procedures; record keeping. Most school policies and procedures are based on legislation e.g. the National Curriculum requirements or the laws relating to health and safety, special educational needs, equal opportunities and child protection. Some of these policies and procedures have already been discussed in previous chapters; here we consider the following key school policies:

o Equal opportunities
o Health and safety
o Child protection
o Confidentiality.

Equal opportunities

All adults who work in schools must be aware of the relevant legislation relating to equal opportunities and anti-discriminatory practice. The Sex Discrimination Act (1975) and the Race Relations Act (1976) made it unlawful to discriminate on the grounds of sex, race, colour, ethnic or national origin. These Acts, with subsequent amendments, established statutory requirements:

○ to prevent discrimination
○ to promote equality of opportunity
○ to provide redress against discrimination.

Amendments in recent years and the new Disability Discrimination Act (1995) have developed and extended anti-discrimination legislation. The Race Relations Amendment Act (2000) introduced new statutory duties for the public sector including actively promoting race equality. Under a new European Union directive the grounds for discrimination will go beyond the three main areas of gender, race and disability (which are discussed in this chapter) to include age, religious belief and sexual orientation. Individual rights are also protected by the Data Protection Act (1998), Human Rights Act (1998) and Freedom of Information Act (2000).

Gender issues

Research shows that by the age of 5 years gender identity is clearly established. Children think girls are more polite, easily hurt and open about showing their feelings; while boys are more capable, stronger and aggressive. The origins of these perceived differences between boys and girls can be difficult to work out because social conditioning begins from birth, especially the expectations for female and male behaviour. These expectations are reinforced throughout childhood by parents, siblings, other family members, as well as by other adults and children in the following ways: the clothes and toys given to children; comments on children's behaviour; expectations for children's play and learning. Stereotyped gender expectations are also reinforced through advertising, television programmes, magazines, comics and books. Gender stereotyping is especially damaging to the self-image and identity of girls because it can lessen their confidence and lower their self-esteem. Boys too can be limited by gender stereotypes by being forced to behave in tough or less caring ways in order to conform and be accepted by others.

As a teaching assistant, you should:

○ challenge gender stereotypes in the media, literature and everyday life

- give all pupils the opportunities to play with a wide variety of toys and games
- provide role play opportunities (including dressing-up clothes), especially for younger pupils, which allow them to explore different roles
- deal explicitly with gender issues in PSHE including peer pressure
- ensure that neither gender thinks they are superior to the other
- expect the same standards of behaviour from all pupils regardless of gender.

Race and culture

Children are influenced by images, ideas and attributes that create prejudice and lead to discrimination or disadvantage. Research shows that by the age of 5 years, many white children believe black people are inferior; while many black children believe that they are viewed with less respect than white people. Children are not born with these attitudes; they *learn* them. Unfortunately, racism does exist in both urban and rural communities. All schools, even those with few or no ethnic minority pupils, must take action to challenge and prevent racism. Education has a central role in eliminating racism and valuing cultural diversity. Adults in schools have an essential part to play in promoting pupils' positive attitudes towards themselves, other people and cultures. Being proud of one's own identity is not the same as thinking you are superior to others.

Adults working with pupils must not have stereotyped views about their potential or have low expectations of pupils from particular ethnic or cultural groups. Many ethnic minority families have a strong commitment to education and their children's academic progress. Different child-rearing practices are evident in different cultures, but differences are also apparent in different families within the same culture.

As a teaching assistant, you need to:

- recognise and eliminate racial discrimination
- maximise each pupil's motivation and potential
- encourage pupils to feel a positive sense of identity
- ensure the school environment reflects pupils and their cultures in positive ways.

Special needs and disability

Pupils with special needs can also be affected by stereotypical images. For example: seeing stereotyped images of disability in the media (or the total absence of people with special needs, especially in magazines); being labelled by their special need rather than viewed as an individual; having restricted or limited choices; being viewed as 'handicapped'; being seen as disabled and therefore having to fit into the 'able' world.

As a teaching assistant, you should:

○ recognise the pupil as an individual not by their condition or impairment (e.g. 'pupil with autistic tendencies' not 'autistic child')
○ provide positive role models of people with disabilities
○ recognise the potential of all pupils
○ have high but realistic expectations for all pupils
○ encourage the 'able' world to adapt to pupils with special needs not the other way round.

Ways to promote equal opportunities

1 Books and stories about real-life situations with people the pupils can identify with.

2 Posters, pictures, photographs, displays, jigsaws, puzzles, toys and other learning materials, which reflect positive images of race, culture, gender and disability.

3 Activities that encourage pupils to look at their physical appearance in a positive light, such as games looking in mirrors; self-portraits (ensuring paints provided for all skin tones); drawing round each other to create life-size portraits.

4 Activities that encourage pupils to focus on their skills and abilities in positive ways, e.g. 'I can ...' tree with positive statements about what each pupil *can* do.

5 Activities that encourage pupils to express their likes and dislikes, plus confidence in their own name and who they are e.g. circle games such as *The name game* where each pupil takes it in turn to say 'My name is ... and I like to ... because ...' or *Circle jump* where each pupil takes a turn at jumping into the circle, making an action which they feel expresses them and saying 'Hello, I'm ...'; then the rest of the pupils copy the action and reply 'Hello ...[repeating the pupil's name]'.

6 Sharing experiences about themselves and their families through topics like *All about me* and by inviting family members such as parents/grandparents to come into the setting to talk about themselves and their backgrounds.

7 Providing opportunities for imaginative/role play which encourages pupils to explore different roles in positive ways (e.g. dressing-up clothes, cooking utensils, dolls and puppets that reflect different cultures).

8 Visiting local shops, businesses and community groups that reflect the cultural diversity of the school and the local community.

9 Inviting visitors into the school to talk positively about their roles and lives, e.g. (female) police officer or fire fighter, (male) nurse, people

with disabilities or from ethnic minorities. (Note: Avoid tokenism; include these visitors as part of on-going class topics or themes.)

10 Celebrating cultural diversity by celebrating the major festivals of the faiths in the local community; comparing similarities and differences between religions, e.g. the festivals of light include Diwali (Hindu), Channuka (Jewish), Christmas (Christian); sharing food such as different types of bread (naan, chapati, soda); looking at clothes and why different culture dress differently (e.g. tradition, religion, climate).

11 Valuing language diversity by displaying welcome signs and other information in community languages.

12 Provide positive examples of:

o Black/Asian people and women from all ethnic groups in prominent roles in society e.g. politicians, doctors, lawyers, business, teachers.

o Black/Asian people's past contributions to politics, medicine, science, education, etc. Look at important historical figures like Martin Luther King, Mahatma Gandhi, Mary Seacole.

o People with disabilities participating fully in modern society such as Stephen Hawking, David Blunkett, Marlee Matlin and Christopher Reeve as well as famous people from the past like Louis Braille, Helen Keller and Franklin D. Roosevelt.

 KEY TASK

1. Compile a resource pack that promotes equal opportunities. Include information and resources from the local community as well as materials you have made yourself. You might include the following:
   o posters and wall charts
   o photographs and pictures
   o booklets and leaflets
   o suggested activities
   o copies of worksheets, work cards, etc.
   o book list of relevant children's books and stories
   o list of useful organisations and addresses.
2. Plan, implement and evaluate at least one activity suggested in your resource pack.

NVQ Links: Level 2: 2–2.1, 2–2.2; Level 3: 3–2.1, 3–2.2

Health and safety

Health and safety legislation places overall responsibility for health and safety with the employer. However, as an employee working within a school you also have responsibilities with regard to maintaining health and safety:

'Employees have responsibilities too. The Health and Safety at Work Act 1974 and the Management of Health and Safety at Work Regulations 1999 apply to them as well.

Employees must:

o take reasonable care of their own and others' health and safety
o co-operate with their employers
o carry out activities in accordance with training and instructions
o inform the employer of any serious risks.' (TeacherNet/DfES, 2002)

All schools must have a health and safety policy with clear procedures to implement it. As a teaching assistant working in a school you will need to follow the legal and organisational requirements for maintaining the health, safety and security of yourself and others at all times. You should also be able to recognise any risks within the school environment and take the appropriate action to minimise them (e.g. reporting potential health and safety hazards to the relevant person). You will also need to use safe working practices in all that you do which includes ensuring that someone in authority (e.g. the teacher and/or your line manager) knows where you are at all times in case of an emergency.

Some health and safety issues have already been outlined in Chapters 1 and 3, here we look at the teaching assistant's role and responsibilities when:

o dealing with medical emergencies
o supporting pupils with medical needs
o helping to supervise pupils on educational visits.

Dealing with medical emergencies

In the event of a medical or health emergency, you must immediately summon assistance from the class teacher or the designated First-Aider and take appropriate action in line with your role and responsibilities within the school. If you are a *designated* First-Aider than you can administer first aid; if not, you can comfort the person with the health emergency by your physical presence and talking to them until the arrival of a designated First-Aider, doctor, paramedic or ambulance staff. You will then help to establish and maintain the privacy and safety of the area where the emergency occurred and provide support for any other people involved. Afterwards, you will need to follow the school's procedures for recording accidents and emergencies. This will normally involve recording the incident in a special book. Serious accidents are usually recorded on an official form. Accuracy in recording accidents and emergencies is essential because the information may be needed for further action by senior staff or other professionals.

First-aid in schools

You must know and understand the first-aid arrangements that apply in your school including the location of first-aid equipment/facilities and the designated First-Aider(s). First-aid notices should be clearly displayed in staff rooms; make sure you read this information. First-aid information is usually included in induction programmes to ensure that new staff and pupils know about the school's first-aid arrangements. Detailed information on the school's first-aid policy and procedures will also be in the staff handbook.

All school staff working with pupils must use their best efforts to maintain the safety and welfare of pupils at the school; their actions should be as those of a responsible parent, especially in emergencies. Staff in schools have no legal obligation to give first-aid, but any member of staff can volunteer to take on first-aid responsibilities. If so, the employer must arrange appropriate training and guidance for them; a designated First-Aider must complete a training course approved by the Health and Safety Executive.

First-aid equipment must be clearly labelled and easily accessible. All first-aid containers must be marked with a white cross on a green background. There should be at least one fully stocked first-aid container for each building within a school with extra first-aid containers available on split-sites/levels, distant sports fields/playgrounds and any other high risk areas (e.g. kitchens and science laboratories) and for educational visits.

All school staff must follow basic hygiene procedures and take the usual precautions for avoiding infection. Staff should use protective disposable gloves and be careful when dealing with spillages of blood or other body fluids including the disposal of dressings etc. (for further information see *Guidance on first aid for schools: a good practice guide, 1998,* DfEE.)

Supporting pupils with medical needs

Schools have to ensure that their health and safety procedures cover the needs of *all* pupils. All schools will have pupils with medical needs at some time. Some medical needs are short term, such as a pupil finishing a course of antibiotics or recovering from an accident/surgery. Some pupils may have long-term medical needs due to a medical condition. The medical conditions in pupils that usually cause concern in schools are asthma, diabetes, epilepsy and severe allergic reaction (anaphylaxis). The school will need additional procedures to maintain the health and safety of pupils with medical needs; this may include an individual health care plan (see below). Schools have a responsibility to ensure that all relevant staff are aware of pupils with medical needs and are trained to provide additional support if necessary.

The head teacher and other school staff must treat medical information in a sensitive and **confidential** manner. The head should agree with the pupil (if appropriate) and their parents, which staff members should have access to records and other information about the pupil's medical needs in order to provide a good support system. However, where medical information is not given to staff they should not usually be held responsible if they provide incorrect medical assistance in an emergency but otherwise acted in good faith.

Medication in schools

Parents are responsible for their own children's medication. Pupils under the age of 16 should not be given medication without their parent's written consent. The head teacher usually decides whether the school can assist a pupil who needs medication during school hours. The school will have a form for the parent to sign if their child requires medication while at school.

Most pupils with long-term medical conditions do not require medication during the school day. If they do, pupils can usually administer it themselves depending on their age/ability, medical condition and type of medication. School policies should encourage self-administration where appropriate and provide suitable facilities for pupils to do so in safety and privacy.

School staff have no legal duty to administer medication or to supervise a pupil taking it. This is a voluntary role similar to that of being a First-Aider. However, some support staff may have specific duties to provide medical assistance included as part of their employment contract. The head teacher, parents and relevant health professionals should support staff members who give assistance to support pupils with medical needs or who volunteer to administer medication by providing information, training, and reassurance about their legal liability. Arrangements should be made for when the member of staff responsible for providing assistance is absent or not available.

Staff providing support for pupils with medical needs must know and understand:

- the nature of the pupil's medical condition
- when and where the pupil may need additional support
- the likelihood of an emergency arising (especially if it is potentially life threatening)
- what action to take if an emergency occurs.

The health and safety of pupils and staff must be considered at all times. Safety procedures must be in place regarding the safe storage, handling, and disposal of medicines. Some medication (e.g. reliever inhaler for asthma or adrenalin device for severe anaphylaxis) must be quickly available in an emergency and should not be locked away. Relevant staff members and the pupil concerned must know where this medication is stored.

Health care plans for pupils with medical needs

Some pupils with long-term medical needs may require a health care plan to provide school staff with the necessary information to support the pupil and to ensure the pupil's safety. A written health care plan should be drawn up in consultation with the pupil (if appropriate), their parents and the relevant health professionals. The plan should include:

- details of the pupil's medical condition
- any special requirements (e.g. dietary needs)
- medication and its possible side effects
- what to do and who to contact in an emergency
- how staff can support the pupil in school.

(Supporting pupils with medical needs: a good practice guide, 1996, DfEE/DH.)

 KEY TASK

1. Find out the school policies and procedures for:
   - Health and safety
   - Dealing with medical or health emergencies
   - First-aid arrangements
   - Medication in school
   - Supporting pupils with medical needs.
2. Explain what your role and responsibilities are in the event of a medical or health emergency in the school.

NVQ Links: Level 2: 2–1.1, 2–2.1; Level 2/3: 3–10.1, 3–10.2, 3–11.2, 3–11.3; Level 3: 3–5.1, 3–5.2

Helping to supervise pupils on educational visits

The health and safety of pupils on educational visits is part of the school's overall health and safety policy. The most senior member of staff on the educational visit will usually have overall responsibility and act as the group leader. Any other teachers present will also have responsibility for pupils on educational visits at all times. Teaching assistants on educational visits should be clear about their exact roles and responsibilities during any visit.

Teaching assistants helping to supervise pupils on educational visits must:

o follow the instructions of the group leader and teacher supervisors
o not have sole charge of pupils (unless previously agreed as part of the risk assessment for the visit)
o help to maintain the health and safety of everyone on the visit
o help with the control and discipline of pupils to avoid potential dangers/accidents
o never be alone with a pupil wherever possible (this is for the protection of both the adult and the pupil)
o report any concerns about the health or safety of pupils to the group leader or teacher supervisors immediately.

(*Health and safety of pupils on educational visits: a good practice guide,* 1998, DfEE.)

Teaching assistants should be aware of pupils who might require closer supervision during educational visits (e.g. pupils with special educational needs or behavioural difficulties). Additional safety procedures to those used in school may be necessary to support pupils with medical needs during educational visits (e.g. arrangements for taking medication). Sometimes it might be appropriate to ask the parent or a care assistant to accompany the pupil to provide extra help and support during the visit.

Organising emergency procedures is a fundamental part of planning an educational visit. All participants, including staff, pupils and parents, should know who will take charge in an emergency during the educational visit and what their individual responsibilities are in the event of an emergency. The group leader would usually take charge in an emergency and must ensure that emergency procedures including back up cover have been arranged. (See section on dealing with a medical or health emergency.)

Child protection

Information on child protection issues can be found in the guidance document *Working Together to Safeguard Children,* prepared and issued jointly by the Department of Health, the Home Office and the Department for Education in 1999. This replaces *Working Together Under the Children Act 1989,* published in 1991. This new guidance is still informed by the requirements of the Children Act 1989, which provides a comprehensive framework for the care and protection of children. The guidance also echoes the principles covered by the United Nations Convention on the Rights of the Child, endorsed by the UK Government in 1991. It also takes on board the European Convention of Human Rights, especially Articles 6 and 8. In addition, under an amendment to The Education Act 2002, schools and local education authorities (LEAs) now have a legal duty to promote and safeguard the welfare of their pupils.

All schools have a pastoral responsibility towards their pupils. All schools should establish and maintain a safe environment for pupils and deal with circumstances where there are child welfare concerns. Through their child protection policies and procedures for safeguarding pupils, schools play an important role in the prevention of abuse and neglect. The school curriculum also has a preventive role by helping pupils to:

○ understand what is and is not acceptable behaviour towards them
○ stay safe from harm
○ speak up if they have worries and concerns
○ develop awareness and resilience
○ prepare for future responsibilities as adults, citizens and parents (see Chapter 3: PSHE).

Teachers and other school staff have contact with individual pupils on a day-to-day basis and so have an essential role to play in detecting indicators of possible abuse or neglect such as:

○ outward signs of physical abuse
○ uncharacteristic behaviour patterns
○ failure to develop in the expected ways.

Teachers and others working closely with pupils in schools are well-placed to identify the early signs of abuse, neglect or bullying. In addition, most pupils view their school as neutral territory where they may feel more able to talk with an adult they trust about what is happening to them. If you have concerns that a pupil at your school may be experiencing possible abuse, neglect or bullying than you **must** report these concerns promptly to the relevant person e.g. the class teacher or member of the senior management team; it will then be the school's responsibility to refer any concerns to the appropriate agency, usually the social services department.

As a teaching assistant, you need to be aware of:

- the signs of possible abuse, neglect and bullying
- to whom you should report any concerns or suspicions
- the school's child protection policy and procedures
- the school policy against bullying
- the school procedures for actively preventing all forms of bullying among pupils
- the school policy regarding the use of force to control or restrain pupils
- the school procedures to be followed if a staff member is accused of abuse.

Remember corporal punishment is against the law in all schools, including independent schools (see section on sanctions on page 37). However, teachers are permitted:

'... to use reasonable force to control or restrain pupils under certain circumstances. Other people may also do so, in the same way as teachers, provided they have been authorised by the head teacher to have control or charge of pupils.'

(*Working Together to Safeguard Children*, Department of Health, 1999; p.16.)

For information on bullying see Chapter 2. An excellent guide to child protection issues is *Child Protection, 2nd edition*, Lindon (2003).

 KEY TASK

Outline your school's policy and procedures regarding child protection.

NVQ Links: Level 2: 2–1.2; Level 2/3: 3–1.1, 3–1.2; Level 3: 3–6.1, 3–6.2, 3–9.3, 3–15.1

Confidentiality

You may find that the parents of the pupils you work with will talk to you about their problems or give you details about their family. Senior staff at your school may also tell you confidential information to help you understand the needs of particular pupils and so enable you to provide more effective support. Whether a parent or colleague gives you confidential information you must not gossip about it. However, you may decide to pass on information to colleagues on a '*need to know*' basis; for example, to enable other members of staff to support the pupil's learning more effectively or where the pupil might be in danger. If you think that a pupil is at risk then you **must** pass on confidential information to an appropriate person, such as the pupil's class or form teacher, the head teacher or the teacher responsible for child protection issues in your school. If you decide to pass on confidential information then you must tell the person who gave you the information that you are going to do this and explain that you have to put the needs of the pupil first. Remember that every family has a right to privacy and you should only pass on information in the genuine interests of the pupil or to safeguard their welfare.

Confidentiality is also important with regard to record keeping and the storage of information; only the appropriate people should have access to confidential records. Except where a pupil is potentially at risk, information should not be given to other agencies unless previously agreed. Where the passing of confidential information is acceptable then it should be given in the agreed format. Always follow the school policy and procedures regarding confidentiality and the sharing of information; check with the teacher (or your line manager) if you have any concerns about these matters.

 KEY TASK

What are the policy and procedures regarding confidentiality in your school?

Make a list of the key points.

NVQ Links: Level 2: 2–1.2, 2–4.1; Level 3: 3–21.1, 3–6.1, 3–7.2

Liaising with parents

Sharing information with parents

Parents usually know more about their children and their children's needs so it is important to listen to what parents have to say. You should therefore actively encourage positive relationships between parents (or designated carers) and the school. As a teaching assistant, you could provide a useful liaison between parents and their children's teacher because some parents may find you easier to talk to than the teacher. Some parents may find you more approachable especially if you live in the local community and your own children go/went to the same school.

Positive relationships between
parents and their child's school
should be encouraged

When communicating with parents use their preferred names and modes of address (e.g. the correct surname especially when a woman has changed her name following divorce or remarriage). Only give information to parents that is consistent with your role and responsibilities within the school – do not give recommendations concerning the pupil's future learning needs directly to parents if this is the responsibility of the teacher, senior colleague or other professional. Any information shared with parents must be agreed with the teacher and must comply with the confidentiality requirements of the school. When sharing information about a pupil with their parents ensure that it is relevant, accurate and up-to-date. Use language which the parent is likely to understand. Try to avoid 'jargon' or technical language especially if you are not clear about its meaning. Remember to pass on information from parents to the relevant member of staff. Requests for information that are beyond your role and responsibilities or any difficulties in communicating with parents should be referred to the appropriate person, such as the class/subject teacher, SENCO or head teacher. You may need guidance on how to handle sensitive situations regarding liaising with parents especially where a parent makes derogatory remarks about a particular teacher or school policy.

Teaching assistants who have additional communication skills may be very useful, for example being able to use sign language to communicate with a parent who has a hearing impairment or bilingual teaching assistants who can liase with parents whose community language is not English. Teaching assistants who share local community languages may help parents to feel more welcome in schools and help to avoid any misinterpretations concerning cultural differences.

Sharing information is an essential part of working with pupils and their parents. Adults working with pupils need essential information *from* parents including:

○ **Routine information** – medical history/conditions such as allergies; cultural or religious practices which may have implications for the care and education of the pupil, such as special diets, exclusion from R.E. and assemblies; who collects the pupil (if applicable) including the transport arrangements (such as taxi or minibus) for a pupil with special needs.
○ **Emergency information** – contact numbers for parents/carers, GP.
○ **Other information** – factors which may adversely affect the pupil's behaviour in school including family difficulties and crises such as divorce, serious illness or bereavement.

Always remember **confidentiality** with regard to information provided by parents.

Adults working with pupils will also need to *give* parents information on:

○ the main aims and objectives of the school
○ age range of pupils
○ class sizes and staff to pupil ratios
○ staff names, roles and qualifications
○ school hours and term dates/school holidays
○ admission and settling in procedures
○ record keeping and assessment
○ test/examination targets and results

- o an outline of approaches to learning (e.g. Foundation Stage or National Curriculum)
- o arrangements for pupils with special needs including the administration of medicines
- o school discipline and behaviour management
- o school procedures regarding food, drink, meal times
- o rules regarding uniform, dress code, jewellery
- o outdoor and/or swimming facilities.

This information is usually given to parents in the school's brochure, prospectus or information pack. Information can also be given to parents via letters, notice boards, newsletters, open days or parents' evenings.

Sharing the care and education of pupils with their parents

When liaising with parents about the care and education of their children you should consider the family's home background and the expressed wishes of the parents. You must also follow the school's policies and procedures with regard to the way you care and support pupils. You may need to give parents positive reassurance about their children's care and education. Any concerns or worries expressed by a pupil's parents should be passed immediately to the appropriate person in school. If a parent makes a request to see a teacher, then you should follow the relevant school policy and procedures.

 KEY TASK

1. Give examples of how your school shares information with the parents.
2. Get a copy of the school's brochure, prospectus or information pack.
3. What are your school's policy and procedures for parents wishing to discuss the care and education of their child with a teacher?

NVQ Links: Level 3: 3–23.1, 3–23.2

Working effectively with other professionals

The teaching assistant can make a valuable contribution to the school by providing effective support for colleagues and by liaising with parents. In addition, teaching assistants are involved in the network of relationships between staff at the school and other professionals from external agencies such as:

o **local education authority** – educational psychologist, special needs support teachers, special needs advisors, specialist teachers, education welfare officers
o **health services** – paediatricians, health visitors, physiotherapists, occupational therapists, speech and language therapists, play therapists, play workers, school nurses, clinical psychologists
o **social services department** – social workers; specialist social workers: sensory disabilities, physical disabilities, mental health or children and families
o **charities and voluntary organisations** – AFASIC, British Dyslexia Association, Council For Disabled Children, National Autistic Society, RNIB, RNID, SCOPE.

Exercise
Find out which external agencies and other professionals are connected with the care and support of the pupils at your school.

Pupils with special educational needs will often have support from external agencies. The teaching assistant is part of the educational support team, which also includes the teacher and the specialist:

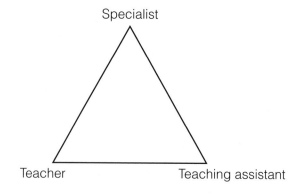

The education support team

Specialist

Teacher

Teaching assistant

The education support team

To provide the most effective care and support for the pupil, it is essential that the working relationships between the specialist, teacher and teaching assistant run smoothly and that there are no contradictions or missed opportunities due to lack of communication. With guidance from the teacher, teaching assistants can be involved with the work of the specialists in a number of ways:

o planning support for the pupil with the teacher
o assisting pupils to perform tasks set by a specialist
o reporting the pupil's progress on such tasks to the teacher.

Any interactions with other professionals should be conducted in such a way as to promote trust and confidence in your working relationships. Your contributions towards the planning and implementation of joint actions must be consistent with your role and responsibilities as a teaching assistant in your school. You should supply other professionals with the relevant information, advice and support as appropriate to your own role and expertise. If requested, you should be willing to share information, knowledge or skills with other professionals. You should use any opportunities to contact or observe the practice of professionals from external agencies to increase your knowledge and understanding of their skills/expertise in order to improve your own work in supporting pupil's learning and development.

 KEY TASK

Compile an information booklet which includes the following:

1. Links with other professionals from external agencies established by your school.
2. A diagram which illustrates how you and your colleagues work with other professionals to provide effective support for pupils (especially those with special educational needs) in your school.
3. Your role and responsibilities in working with other professionals to support pupils.
4. Where to obtain information about the roles of other professionals in the local area.

NVQ Links: Level 3: 3–22.1, 3–22.2, 3–16.1, 3–16.2

Reviewing and developing your professional practice

In this chapter we have seen how being an effective team member involves making an individual contribution through your participation in team meetings and working with your colleagues (and other professionals) to provide better care and support for the pupils in your school. Here we look at how having a reflective attitude will help you to review and develop your professional practice as a teaching assistant.

Reviewing your professional practice

You need to know and understand clearly the exact role and responsibilities of your work as a teaching assistant (see Chapter 1). Review your professional practice by making regular and realistic assessments of how well your working practices match your role and responsibilities (see section on self-evaluation in Chapter 5). Share your self-assessments with those responsible for managing and reviewing your work performance (e.g. during your regular discussions/meetings with the teacher and at your appraisal with your line manager). You should also ask other people for feedback about how well you fulfil the requirements and expectations of your role. You can also reflect on your own professional practice by making comparisons with appropriate models of good practice, for example the work of more experienced teaching assistants or other support staff in school.

Developing effective practice in a support role

To develop your effectiveness in a support role, you should be able to identify your own personal development objectives, which are:

☆ Specific
☆ Measurable
☆ Achievable
☆ Realistic
☆ Time-bound.

You should discuss and agree these objectives with those responsible for supporting your professional development. For example, you may consider that some of your work tasks require modification or improvement and discuss possible changes with the teacher. Or you may feel that you lack sufficient knowledge and skills to implement particular activities and need to discuss opportunities for you to undertake the relevant training. To achieve your personal development objectives you should make effective use of the people, resources and other development or training opportunities available to you.

A professional development portfolio highlighting your existing experience and qualifications can form the basis for assessing your training needs. This portfolio will also be a tangible record of your professional development and will help to boost your self-esteem.

Training opportunities

When assessing your personal development and training needs you need to consider:

o your existing experience and skills
o the needs of the pupils you support
o any problems with how you currently work
o any new or changing expectations for your role.

The areas of training and development identified by teaching assistants include:

o knowledge of curriculum subject content
o supporting literacy activities
o supporting numeracy activities
o behaviour management
o supporting specific special needs
o working with parents
o developing ICT skills.

Teaching assistants indicate that they prefer practical training opportunities and many of the courses available are skills or competency based. Research shows that some of the most effective training for teaching assistants takes place in schools as part of their INSET provision. However, it is not always possible to teach the necessary skills in schools especially those relating to specific special needs. Many LEAs provide training courses for teaching assistants employed directly by them or those recruited by individual schools.

Specific training and recognised qualifications for teaching assistants are also available:

o NVQ/SVQ Levels 2 & 3 for Teaching/Classroom Assistants
o CACHE Levels 2 & 3 Certificates for Teaching Assistants (CTA2 & CTA3)
o OCR Level 2 Certificate in Supporting Teaching and Learning
o CACHE Specialist Teacher Assistant award (STA)
o OCR Certificate for Literacy and Numeracy Support Assistants
o City & Guilds Learner Support 7321 course.

External training courses/qualifications can have a positive influence on improving the status of teaching assistants as well as enabling them to share examples of good practice with teaching assistants from other schools. Schools also benefit from having teaching assistants who are able to improve their expertise and increase their job satisfaction.

KEY TASK

1. Give examples of how you review and assess your own work performance.
2. Identify your own SMART personal development objectives.
3. Find out about the professional development and training opportunities for teaching assistants in your local area.

NVQ Links: Level 2: 2–4.2; Level 3: 3–4.1, 3–4.2, 3–21.2

Further reading...

Burton, G. and Dimbleby, R. (1995) *Between ourselves: an introduction to interpersonal communication.* Revised edition. Arnold.

Lewis, V. (1995) *53 Interesting ways to promote equal opportunities in education.* Technical and Educational Services Ltd.

Lindenfield, G. (2000) *Self Esteem: simple steps to developing self-reliance and perseverance.* Revised edition. HarperCollins.

Lindon, J. (2003) *Child Protection.* Second edition. London: Hodder & Stoughton.

Massey, I. (1991) *More than skin deep: developing anti-racist multicultural education in schools.* Hodder & Stoughton.

Mortimer, H. (2002) *Special needs handbook.* Scholastic.

Roet, B. (1998) *The confidence to be yourself.* Piatkus.

Sallis, E. and Sallis, K. (1990) *People in organisations.* Palgrave.

Sirjai-Blatchford, I. (1994) *The early years: laying the foundations for racial equality.* Trentham Books.

Woolfson, R. (1991) *Children with special needs – a guide for parents and carers.* Faber and Faber.

Yeo, A. and Lovell, T. (2002) *Sociology and Social Policy for the Early Years*, 2nd edition. Hodder & Stoughton.

Appendix: Record of Key Tasks

KEY TASK	**Date Completed**

Chapter 1: The Learning Environment

- ○ Listen to adults talking with children in a variety of situations.
- ○ Draw a plan of the classroom or areas you work in the most.
- ○ List the equipment you use in your school.
- ○ Outline the record keeping systems/procedures in your school.

Chapter 2: Behaviour Management

- ○ Negotiate and set goals and/or boundaries with a pupil or pupils.
- ○ Observe a pupil who regularly demonstrates unwanted behaviour.
- ○ Outline a step-by-step approach to encourage the pupil to behave in more acceptable ways.

Chapter 3: Personal, Social and Health Education

- ○ Plan and implement an activity which encourages pupils to relate positively towards others.
- ○ Observe a pupil demonstrating their self-help skills.
- ○ Devise a reward system which encourages pupils' self-reliance and promotes positive self-esteem.
- ○ Outline the policy for dealing with pupils' emotional outbursts.
- ○ Outline possible strategies for preparing a pupil or pupils for the first week in school, a new year group/Key Stage or visitor in school.
- ○ Plan an activity which will help the pupil or pupils you work with maintain the health and hygiene standards of the school.

KEY TASK

Chapter 4: Thinking and Learning

○ Observe a pupil or group of pupils during a creative activity.
○ Plan and implement a creative activity with a pupil or pupils.
○ Plan and implement an activity for a pupil or group of pupils which involves developing their scientific skills.

Chapter 5: Planning Learning Activities

○ Observe a pupil during a learning activity.
○ Plan and implement a learning activity to extend the pupil's skills.

Chapter 6: Supporting Learning Activities

○ Observe a pupil involved in a learning activity.
○ Plan and implement a learning activity for a pupil.
○ Describe how you could provide support for a pupil with either general or specific learning difficulties.
○ Observe a pupil with sensory or physical impairment.
○ Design a possible structured learning programme for a pupil with sensory or physical impairment based on your observations.
○ What are the procedures for preparing/using ICT equipment?

Chapter 7: Developing Language and Communication Skills

○ Observe a pupil communicating with another pupil or adult.
○ Plan, implement and evaluate a language activity.
○ Observe a pupil involved in a language activity.
○ Plan, implement and evaluate an activity which encourages or extends a pupil's language and communication skills.
○ Observe a pupil who has difficulty communicating.
○ Plan, implement and evaluate a language activity for a pupil with communication difficulties.

KEY TASK

**Date
Completed**

Chapter 8: Developing Literacy Skills

o Observe a pupil engaged in a writing activity.
o Observe pupils during a story session.
o Plan a story session.
o Give a detailed account of how you have helped
  pupils with learning activities which develop their
  literacy skills.

Chapter 9: Developing Numeracy Skills

o Observe a pupil or pupils during a
  mathematics/numeracy activity.
o Describe how you have helped pupils during learning
  activities which develop their numeracy skills.
o Plan and implement a learning activity which
  involves helping a pupil or pupils to understand and
  use shape, space or measures.

Chapter 10: Professional Practice

o Participate in a team meeting relevant to your role in
  school.
o Describe how you have responded to a conflict
  situation in school.
o Compile a resource pack which promotes equal
  opportunities.
o Find out the school policies and procedures for:
  health and safety; dealing with medical or health
  emergencies; first-aid arrangements; medication in
  school; supporting pupils with medical needs.
o Outline your school's policy/procedures regarding
  child protection.
o What are the policy/procedures regarding
  confidentiality in school?
o Give examples of how your school shares information
  with parents.
o Compile an information booklet which includes links
  with other professionals from external agencies.
o Give examples of how you review and assess your
  work performance.

Glossary

active learning: learning by doing; participation in activities in meaningful situations.

behaviour: a person's actions, reactions and treatment of others.

behaviour modification: using positive reinforcement to encourage acceptable behaviour.

carer: any person with responsibility for the care/education of a child during the parent's temporary or permanent absence.

cognitive: intellectual abilities involving processing information received through the senses.

community language: main language spoken in a child's home.

concepts: the way people make sense of and organise information.

conflict situation: verbal or physical disagreement (e.g. arguments, fighting, disputing rules).

curriculum: the course of study in a school.

egocentric: pre-occupied with own needs; unable to see another person's viewpoint.

emotional outburst: uncontrolled expression of intense emotion (e.g. rage or frustration).

facilitator: person who makes things easier by providing the appropriate environment and resources for learning.

holistic approach: looking at the 'whole' child (e.g. *all* aspects of the child's development).

inclusion or integration: the principle whereby all pupils with special educational needs should be educated in mainstream schools where reasonably practicable.

IQ or intelligence quotient: a person's mental age in comparison to their chronological age.

key factor: an essential aspect affecting learning and development.

language-rich environment: place where opportunities for language and communication are actively and positively promoted (e.g. through play, conversation, books and displays).

learning activity: an opportunity for development and learning which involves active participation and discussion.

milestones: significant skills which children develop in and around certain ages as part of the usual or expected pattern of development.

norm: the usual pattern or expected level of development/behaviour.

operations: the term used by Piaget to describe the way people use their cognitive abilities.

parent: person with parental responsibility (as defined in The Children Act 1989).

peers: pupils of similar age within the school.

personality: distinctive and individual characteristics which affect each person's view of themselves, their needs, feelings and relationships with others.

problem-solving: activities which involve finding solutions to a difficulty or question.

psychological: relating to the study of the mind and behaviour including language, cognitive, social and emotional development.

quality: standard of care and education provided (ideally high/excellent).

ratio: the number of adults in relation to pupils within the school (e.g. three adults working with a class of thirty pupils would be shown as a ratio of 1:10).

rationale: the main reason for implementing a particular learning activity; the principle behind an idea or opportunity.

regression: demonstrating behaviour characteristic of a previous level of development.

role model: significant person whose actions, speech or mannerisms are imitated by a child.

scaffolding: adult assistance given to support pupil's thinking and learning, as the pupil develops competence the adult decreases support until the pupil works independently.

schemas: term used mainly by Piaget to describe internal thought processes.

sequence: development following the same basic pattern but not necessarily at fixed ages.

social constructivism: the viewpoint that *all* learning takes place within a social and cultural context.

social constructivist: a person who believes in the above viewpoint.

social context: *any* situation or environment where social interaction occurs (e.g. home, early years setting, local community).

social interaction: *any* contact with other people including actions and reactions (e.g. play, verbal and non-verbal communication).

sociological: relating to social questions and human society; involving social development and interaction with others.

specialist: a person with specific training/additional qualifications in a particular area of development or learning (e.g. speech and language therapist, educational psychologist).

special educational needs: all pupils have *individual* needs, but some pupils may have *additional* needs due to physical disability, sensory impairment, learning difficulty or emotional/behavioural difficulty.

special educational needs co-ordinator (SENCO): the teacher responsible for co-ordinating the support for pupils with special educational needs in a school.

stage: development which occurs at a fixed age.

stereotype: simplistic characterisation or expectation of a person based on perceived differences or prejudices relating to their race, culture, gender, disability or age.

structured learning programmes: particular activities to encourage the development of individual pupils with special educational needs including Individual Education Plans and Behaviour Support Plans.

teaching assistant: an adult whose main role is to assist the teacher in supporting the development and learning of pupils in a primary, secondary or special school.

temperament: person's disposition or personality especially their emotional responses.

time-out: a short break or suspension of an activity which allows a cooling off period for all involved but which especially gives a pupil the chance to calm down.

zone of proximal development: Vygotsky's description for a child's next area of development where adult assistance is only required until the child has developed the skill and can do it independently.

Bibliography

ATL Report (June/July 2000) 'ATL guide to: children's attitudes'. London: ATL Association of Teachers and Lecturers.

ATL Special Educational Needs Working Group (April 1994) 'Achievement for all'. London: ATL Association of Teachers and Lecturers.

Ball, C. (1994) *Start Right: The importance of early learning.* London: RSA.

Bartholomew, L. and **Bruce**, T. (1993) *Getting to know you: a guide to record-keeping in early childhood education and care.* London: Hodder & Stoughton.

Berger, A. and **Gross**, J. (ed.) (1999) *Teaching the literacy hour in the inclusive classroom.* London: David Fulton Publishers.

Booth, T. and **Coulby**, D. (ed.) (1987) *Producing and reducing disaffection.* Milton Keynes: Open University Press.

Booth, T., **Potts**, P. and **Swann**, W. (ed.) (1987) *Preventing difficulties in learning.* Oxford: Blackwell/Open University Press.

Booth, T. and **Swann**, W. (ed.) (1987) *Including pupils with disabilities.* Milton Keynes: Open University Press.

Brennan W. K. (1987) *Changing special education now.* Milton Keynes: The Open University Press.

British Dyslexia Association (October 1997) 'Dyslexia: an introduction for parents and teachers and others with an interest in dyslexia'. London: BDA.

Bruce, T. and **Meggitt**, C. (2002) *Child care and education.* 3rd edition. London: Hodder & Stoughton.

Burton, G. and **Dimbleby**, R. (1995) *Between ourselves: an introduction to interpersonal communication.* Revised edition. London: Arnold.

Commission for Racial Equality (December 1989) ' From cradle to school: a practical guide to race equality and childcare'. London: CRE.

Crawford, R. (1997) *Managing information technology in secondary schools.* London: Routledge.

Cunningham, B. (1993) *Child development.* London: HarperCollins.

Davie, R. (1984) 'Social development and social behaviour' (see **Fontana**, D.)

DfEE (1998) *Guidance on first aid for schools: a good practice guide.* London: DfEE.

DfEE (1998) *Health and safety of pupils on educational visits: a good practice guide.* London: DfEE.

DfEE/Department of Health (1996) *Supporting pupils with medical needs: a good practice guide.* London: DfEE.

DfEE (2000) *Learning Journey [Ages 3–7; 7–11; 11–16].* London: DfEE.

DfEE (2001) *National literacy strategy: developing early writing.* London: DfEE.

Department for Education and Skills (1978a) *Special education needs.* (The Warnock Report). London: HMSO.

Department for Education and Skills (2001) *The Special Educational Needs Code of Practice 2001.* London: HMSO.

Department of Health (1991) *The Children Act 1989: Guidance and regulations, Volume 2: Family support, day care and educational provision and young children.* London: HMSO.

Department of Health, Home Office and **DfEE** (1999) *Working Together to Safeguard Children.* London: HMSO.

Dessent, T. (1987) *Making the ordinary school special.* London: The Falmer Press.

Donaldson, M. (1978) *Children's minds.* London: Fontana.

Drummond, M. *et al.* (1994) *Making assessment work.* NFER Nelson.

Fontana, D. (1984) 'Personality and personal development' in D. Fontana (ed.)

The education of the young child. Oxford: Blackwell.

Foster-Cohen, S. (1999) *Introduction to child language development.* Harlow: Longman.

Fox, G. (1998) *A handbook for learning support assistants.* London: David Fulton Publishers.

Frederickson, N. (1991) *Social competence.* London: University College London.

Gipps, C., **Gross**, H. and **Goldstein**, H. (1987) *Warnock's eighteen per cent:children with special needs in primary schools.* London: The Falmer Press.

Goleman, D. (1996) *Emotional intelligence.* London: Bloomsbury.

Green, C. and **Chee**, K. (1995) *Understanding ADD.* London: Vermilion.

Harding, J. and **Meldon-Smith**, L. (2001) *How to make observations and assessments.* 2nd edition. London: Hodder & Stoughton.

Houghton, D. and **McColgan**, M. (1995) *Working with children.* London: Collins Educational.

Hutchcroft, D. (1981) *Making language work.* London: McGraw-Hill.

Kamen, T. (2000) *Psychology for childhood studies.* London: Hodder & Stoughton.

Kay, J. (2002) *Teaching assistant's handbook.* London: Continuum.

Laing, A. and **Chazan**, M. (1984) 'Young children with special educational needs' (see **Fontana**, D.).

Laishley, J. (1987) *Working with young children.* London: Edward Arnold.

Leach, P. (1994) *Children first.* London: Penguin.

Lee, V. and **Das Gupta**, P. (eds.) (1995) *Children's cognitive and language development.* Oxford: Blackwell.

Lindenfield, G. (1995) *Self esteem.* London: Thorsons.

Lindon, J. (2003) *Child Protection, 2nd edition.* London: Hodder & Stoughton.

Light, P., **Sheldon**, S. and **Woodhead**, M. (eds.) (1991) *Learning to think.* London: Routledge.

Masheder, M. (1989) *Let's Co-operate.* London: Peace Education Project.

Masheder, M. (1989) *Let's play together.* London: Green Print.

Matterson, E. (1989) *Play with a purpose for the under-sevens.* London: Penguin.

Meadows, S. (1993) *Child as thinker: the development of cognition in childhood.* London: Routledge.

Mort, L. and **Morris**, J. (1989) *Bright ideas for early years: getting started.* London: Scholastic.

Moyle, D. (1976) *The teaching of reading.* London: Ward Lock Educational.

Modgil, C. and **Modgil**, S. (1984) 'The development of thinking and reasoning' (see **Fontana**, D.).

Mulvaney, A. (1995) *Talking with kids.* Sydney: Simon & Schuster.

Munn, P., **Johnstone**, M. and **Chalmers**, V. (1992) *Effective discipline in secondary schools and classrooms.* London: Paul Chapman Publishing Ltd.

National Commission on Education (1993) *Learning to succeed.* London: Heinemann.

Neaum, S. and **Tallack**, J. (1997) *Good practice in implementing the pre-school curriculum.* Cheltenham: Stanley Thornes.

Oliver, I. (2000) *Ideas for PSHE KS1.* Leamington Spa: Scholastic.

Petrie, P. (1989) *Communicating with children and adults.* London: Edward Arnold.

Prisk, T. (1987) 'Letting them get on with it: a study of unsupervised group talk in an infant school' in A. Pollard (ed.) *Children and their primary schools.* London: Falmer Press.

Qualifications and Curriculum Authority (2000) *Curriculum guidance for the foundation stage.* London: QCA.

Rogoff, B., **Gauvain**, M. and **Ellis**, S. (1991) 'Development viewed in its cultural context' (see **Light**, P.).

Rutter, M. (1991) *Maternal deprivation reassessed.* London: Penguin.

Sameroff, A. (1991) 'The social context of development' in M. Woodhead, R. Carr and P. Light (eds.) *Becoming a person.* London: Routledge.

Sears, N. 'Stammerers offered the time to talk' *The Times Educational Supplement* (7.11.97)

Taylor, J. (1973) *Reading and writing in the first school.* London: George Allen and Unwin.

Tharp, R. and **Gallimore**, R. (1991) 'A theory of teaching as assisted performance' (see **Light**, P.).

Tizard, B. (1991) 'Working mothers and the care of young children' (see **Woodhead**, M.).

Tobias, C. (1996) *The Way They Learn.* Focus on the Family Publishing.

Tough, J. (1976) *Listening to children talking.* London: Ward Lock Educational.

Tough, J. (1994) 'How young children develop and use language' (see **Fontana**, D.).

Train, A. (1996) *ADHD: How to deal with very difficult children.* London: Souvenir Press.

Whitehead, M. (1996) *The development of language and literacy.* London: Hodder & Stoughton.

Wood, D. (1991) 'Aspects of teaching and learning' (see **Light**, P.).

Wood, D. (1988) *How children think and learn.* Oxford: Blackwell.

Woodhead, M. (1991) 'Psychology and the cultural construction of children's needs' in M. Woodhead, P. Light and R. Carr (eds.) *Growing up in a changing society.* London: Routledge.

Woolfson, R. (1991) *Children with special needs: a guide for parents and carers.* London: Faber & Faber.

Woolfson, R. (1989) *Understanding your child: a parents' guide to child psychology.* London: Faber & Faber.

Yardley, A. (1994) 'Understanding and encouraging children's play' (see **Fontana**, D.).

Yeo, A. and **Lovell**, T. (2002) *Sociology and Social Policy for the Early Years, 2nd edition.* London: Hodder & Stoughton.

INDEX